**Vivian Ibrahim** is Croft A:
International Relations at the
Research Associate for the Lon
She holds a PhD in the History of the Modern Middle East from
the School of Oriental and African Studies (SOAS), University of
London and is co-editor of *Political Leaderships, Nations and Charisma*
(2012).

# The Copts of Egypt

## THE CHALLENGES OF MODERNISATION AND IDENTITY

### VIVIAN IBRAHIM

I.B. TAURIS

LONDON · NEW YORK

Paperback edition published in 2013 by I.B.Tauris & Co ltd
6 Salem Road, London W2 4BU
175 Fifth Avenue, New York NY 10010
www.ibtauris.com

Distributed in the United States and Canada
Exclusively by Palgrave Macmillan
175 Fifth Avenue, New York NY 10010

ISBN 978 1 78076 466 5

A full CIP record for this book is available from the British Library
A full CIP record for this book is available from the Library of Congress

Library of Congress catalog card: available

Printed and bound in Great Britain by CPI Antony Rowe, Chippenham
Camera-ready copy edited and supplied by the author

*To My Loving Parents and my Brother Nader*

# CONTENTS

# LIST OF ILLUSTRATIONS

# LIST OF TABLES

# NOTES ON TRANSLITERATION
# AND TRANSLATION

All transliterations have been carried out using a modified format of the *IJMES* translation guide. Diacritical markings have been omitted except the use of ' for *'ayn* and ' for hamza: for example, *'ulama'*.

All transliterated words have been italicised unless they feature in Webster's collegiate dictionary or the *IJMES* word list. Transliterated titles of organisations and concepts have been capitalised, for example: *Al-Ikhwan al-Muslimin*. The definite article *al-* is in lowercase unless it appears as the first word of the sentence or as a title, e.g. Al-Banna.

All names of people have been kept in their common Egyptian colloquial form: for example, Gamal not Jamal.

I have carried out all translations from Arabic to English unless otherwise stated.

# ACKNOWLEDGEMENTS

These short words are in no way a full reflection of the gratitude that I acknowledge—to those near and far—for their encouragement and support in making this book a reality.

A special thank you goes to Boutros Boutros-Ghali who reviewed and read the book; his time, observations and feedback were priceless and valuable. To Nelida Fuccaro, my former supervisor, who tirelessly read and rigorously commented on the PhD and this manuscript – I am forever indebted to you. A special thank you is extended to my former history department at the School of Oriental and African Studies (SOAS), University of London. To Kirsten Schulze (LSE), Youssef Choueiri (Manchester), Anthony Gorman and Marilyn Booth (Edinburgh) for reading drafts, feedback and incredibly useful help. A warm thank you to the Association for the Study of Ethnicity and Nationalism (ASEN) at the London School of Economics- my five years working there exposed me to a multitude of ideas and perspectives. I am also grateful to the network of 'Christians in the Middle East' based at St Andrews in Scotland and CRAASH at the University of Cambridge for giving me the opportunity to present my ideas. To Joanna Godfrey, Nicola Denny and Nadine El-Hadi at I.B.Tauris—my gratitude for your patience and help is endless.

I am deeply indebted to those who actively eased the research process in Cairo. A special thanks to Mr Rida al-Waziri, head of periodicals at *Dar al-Watha'iq al-Qawmi* and his team for their

endless assistance: Haga Nabawiya, Ustaz Fathi, 'Abd al-Aleem
Ismail the poet, Ahmad Zaqazouq, Hani, Tamer and Mahmoud.
Particular thanks go to Ustaz Maged and Madam Esther for their
advice and help with Coptic periodicals. I would also like to thank
those who generously helped finance part of this research: the
Royal Historical Society, the Central Research Fund (Senate
House), SOAS research fund and the LSE. Thanks to my
wonderful new colleagues at the University of Mississippi for their
generous Southern hospitality, funding and assistance with this
second edition.

   This book would not have been possible without my friends
who have shared with me smiles, endless cups of coffee, numerous
rants and their critical eyes.

   I dedicate this book to my family. The love and support of my
father Islam Ibrahim, my mother Ahlam El-Akkad, and my brother
Nader Ibrahim mean everything to me.

# PREFACE

When the first edition of this book was being sent to print in late 2010, I could never have predicted the events that were about to take place in the Middle East. The Arab Spring, which began with Tunisia in December 2010, saw millions of people in Libya, Syria, Yemen, Bahrain and Egypt, take to the streets against their oppressive and authoritarian dictators. This was not a spontaneous 'awakening', each of these countries had been plagued by decades of deep-seated social, political and economic grievances.

On New Years Day 2011, just twenty-five days before the start of Egypt's uprising, Al-Qaddisayn church in Alexandria was bombed killing twenty-one Copts. Attacks against churches and Copts had been—and unfortunately continue to be—frequent. Al-Qaddisayn was particularly significant however; it served as a rallying point for many activists who would go on to protest and topple Mubarak only weeks later. The bombing had represented not only intolerance in Egypt but also the failure of the state security services. In a symbolic act of solidarity, friends, activists, Muslims and Christians sought to protect churches against further possible reprisals. Posters and banners of an intertwined cross and crescent, reminiscent of Egypt's 1919 revolution, were held up on Christmas Eve (6th January), representing the inseparability of Muslims and Christians in the nation.

Enthused by the fall of President Ben Ali of Tunisia, a wave of popular protests broke out in Egypt on 25th January lasting for eighteen days. While mainly confined to the northern urban areas of the country, differing classes gathered to demand 'bread, freedom and social justice'. Again, symbolism was to play an important role, as Tahrir Square in the heart of Cairo became a focal point and *hayat al-midan* (the life of the square) the embodiment of an Egyptian utopia. During Friday prayers on 4th February 2011, Copts—brandishing their tattooed wrists with a cross—protected Muslims while they performed their prayers. Two days later, Muslim crowds encircled Copts at Sunday Mass in Tahrir, ensuring that they too had a safe space for worship.

The optimism and ideal of *hayat al-midan* was short lived however. Post-uprising, frequent sectarian attacks continued against Copts including the burning of a church in Sol and an attack on a church in Imbaba, which left fifteen dead. In October 2011, following yet another attack in Upper Egypt, Coptic demonstrators gathered at the state television building in Maspiro, Cairo. Armed with the same spirit of mobilisation that had reigned during the uprising, and rather than seeking the traditional intervention of the church as an intermediary, demonstrators demanded justice. The outcome was brutal; twenty-eight Copts were massacred by thugs of the armed forces, the main institution to survive and indeed thrive post-uprising.

The massacre at Maspiro had multiple consequences. On a national level this was a public assault on the Copts as a religious group protesting against on-going sectarianism. The murders had taken place by the very same institution, which had claimed to serve and 'protect the nation'. On a communal level, both the uprising and Maspiro scarred the Coptic community. Pope Shenouda (1971-2012), the spiritual leader and *de facto* political representative of the Copts, appeared to be weak in maintaining the religious and political rights of the Copts. During the uprising, Shenouda had played a cautious role calling on the Coptic community to refrain from participation. While some heeded his call, others took part, the Coptic 'community' was not exceptional - like the rest of the Egyptian population, participation and solidarity in the uprising was contingent on a number of factors, not least class and ideological belief. Pope Shenouda, unsurprisingly, stood by the existing power structures in Egypt; his actions were consistent with an elderly statesman aware of potential political consequences.

At Christmas Mass, less than three months after Maspiro in January 2012, Pope Shenouda blessed the very armed forces that attacked protestors in October, calling them the 'protector of the Copts'. This led to fierce criticisms, especially by a faction of Coptic youths who claimed that Shenouda had abandoned the welfare of the community and that his words revealed a leader out of touch.

Pope Tawadros II, who took office in November 2012 following Shenouda's death, faces deep challenges in Egypt's changing environment. On a national level, he will have to negotiate a space with newly elected President Mohammad Morsi of the Muslim Brotherhood, in order to ensure Coptic civil and religious rights. From within, Tawadros inherits a deeply factionalised Coptic community which is both multi-dimensional in character and increasingly willing to challenge the scope and the authority of the patriarch. Tracing the historical roots to some of these challenges, the following pages of *The Copts of Egypt*, have even more relevance today.

Vivian Ibrahim

# INTRODUCTION

On 6th January 2010, six Coptic deacons were murdered as they emerged from Eastern Christmas Mass in the city of Naga Hammadi in the Upper Egyptian Governate of Qena. The incident was widely held to be in retaliation for an assault on a 12-year-old Muslim girl in November 2009, a sentiment publicly endorsed by Qena Governor and Copt, General Magdi Ayoub. Despite this, speculation continued in the days following from activists, analysts and academics, on the 'true' motives behind the incident. For Coptic organisations, both within Egypt and in the wide Coptic diaspora, the attack was evidence of systematic persecution: the Copts were a 'beleaguered minority'. The International Coptic Council (ICC), an umbrella body for over 100 Coptic organisations worldwide, issued a statement condemning the assault and released a series of recommendations aimed at safeguarding 'the rights of the Coptic minority'.[1]

In contrast, the government was quick to view the attack as a case of criminality and not within a framework of sectarianism. At an emergency Shura Council session, Mufid Shehab, Minister of Legal Affairs and Parliamentary Councils, claimed that: 'No religious dimension should be attached to this incident, only a criminal one'.[2] Despite this verbal facade however, a high visible police and military presence was kept in the areas surrounding the attacks in order to avoid sectarian clashes in the days following the attacks. While the government continued to claim in public that this was a 'civilian criminal' case, it sought to remedy the problem within the State Security apparatus.[3] The government publicly condemned the murders and quickly, in an ad-hoc manner, sought to apprehend suspects in order to draw a line under the incident.[4] Closely linked to the official state perspective, Rafiq Habib, a prominent Coptic writer, dismissed claims that this was another example of sectarianism in Egypt, adding that it was an anomalous event. Sessions in Parliament led by Chairman Safwat al-Sherif reiterated the age-old Egyptian slogan, 'religion for God and the nation for all', an expression of the division between religion and the state.[5] The attempt to downplay the incident and promote an image of national unity was also highlighted when Fouad Allam, the former head of Egyptian State Security, suggested the involvement of foreign bodies. These 'terrorists', he argued, aimed to penetrate the country as was the case in Lebanon and Iraq by undermining national security and promoting sectarianism in Egypt.[6]

These perspectives serve as a useful benchmark to assess how issues related to the Copts in Egypt are viewed both within and outside the country. For those cited, the events of Naga Hammadi fit into a broader framework of persecution, criminality, an anomalous event or terrorism. The government, its supporters and those who wish to coalesce in an attempt to avoid retribution by the state, advocate the latter three benchmarks; this most-commonly rears itself under the banner of national-unity. While for the vast majority of Coptic commentators and a substantial number of Non-Governmental Organisations, charities and activists, the incident was a clear-cut case of persecution. Examination of this amongst other incidents, are clearly bound within fixed benchmarks and definitions, placing persecution and national unity as the main opposing bulwarks. Contestability of these benchmarks, result in accusations by the state and those who place national unity above a public discussion of communal discord, as damaging to the integrity and cohesiveness of the Egyptian nation. In contrast, remonstration against the Copts, in any form, is met by a response of pitting the majority Muslim population and state against a minority Christian community.

This book challenges some of the long-established modes of analysis that have emerged both within the Arabic and Western discourse relating to the Copts. It is maintained that the existing approaches on the Copts fail to take into account the divergent opinions prevalent within the Coptic community, which, consequently, is depicted as monolithic and stagnant.[7] The lack of power accounted to individual Coptic actors is replaced by an assessment of Coptic history through the lens of a fixed internal hierarchy headed by the Coptic Pope. This view fails to address the impact that modernisation of the Egyptian state and of Church structures had on the relationship between various actors and existing structures. Similarly, the Coptic community is portrayed as passive and submissive in its response to inter-communal tensions that have arisen in Egypt. The outcome of this is a community defined exclusively in relation to its Muslim Egyptian counterparts. The vast majority of analysis which places the Copts within the framework of a 'minority under threat' or within the folds of 'national unity', reveal socio-political agendas which are peculiarly localised to Egypt. While such analyses offer some insight into understanding the Copts, they are intrinsically problematic.

To begin with, there are two inherent yet flawed assumptions in the discourse which views Copts as under threat. Firstly is the assumption that all Copts are distinguishable from their Muslim counterparts, thus serving to solidify the traditional *millat*/minority label applied to the Copts as a unified community. The second assumption being that this threat is omnipresent from organised hostile groups or random mob violence. Both Westerners and Egyptians have perpetuated these points of view throughout the modern period. For example, Kyriakos Mikhail, a Copt living in Britain presented a series of articles in 1911.[8] In the preface by Reverend Professor Sayce (1846–1933), an Egyptologist and linguist at Oxford University, he described the Copts as:

> The genuine Egyptians […] They alone trace an unadulterated descent from the race to whom the civilisation and culture of the ancient world was so largely due. Thanks to their religion, they have kept their blood pure from admixture with semi-barbarous Arabs and savage Kurds, or other foreign elements whom the licentiousness of Mohammedan family life has introduced into the country.[9]

Sayce's comments highlight an opinion that was prominent in the early twentieth century, maintaining that Copts were the purest form of Egyptians as the ancestors of the Pharaohs. As a result, he defined the Copts as a minority in relation to the Muslims who were of 'barbarous' origins.[10] Continuing in the same vein, Coptic writers, who published their works after the death of President Gamal 'Abd al-Nasser and Pan-Arab nationalism in the 1970s, have argued that since the Arab invasion of 641, Copts have been actively persecuted and have feared for their own safety.[11] The image of the Copt as the beleaguered minority under constant threat is perpetuated by the reconstruction of the historical persecutions faced by the Copts beginning with Emperor Diocletian (c.236–316). The massacre, which started in 302 AD but is counted from the beginning of Diocletian's reign in 284 AD, is maintained in the community's imagination through the adoption of a calendar which is dated to 'The Era of Martyrs' (AM or *Anno Martyrum*).[12] The impact of the Era of Martyrs cannot be underestimated when discussing Coptic attitudes towards their community given that between 144,000 and 800,000 people were martyred in Egypt from the third century onwards.[13]

The Egyptologist and cultural historian Saphinaz Amal Naguib, has argued that, following the massacre in the third century, the Coptic Church built around the community a shared history of persecution, which has surrounded a narrative arc of events dating back to the Era of Martyrs.[14] Thus, the Church acted as the protector of communal inclusion and cohesiveness of identity against external aggression; it cemented a barrier of exclusion in opposition to those who wished to perpetuate harm against the Copts. The creation of a new calendar, based on the Era of Martyrs, served to record Coptic history against obliteration by dominant persecuting forces ensuring that the Copts would not become 'history-less' nor would they be excluded from the narrative of the state. Instead their history would be placed alongside and run concurrently to an Egyptian national grand narrative. Thus, the Era of Martyrs narrative asserted that a 'multiplicity of histories' could co-exist within the same geographic region.[15]

The Era of Martyrs has also become a useful tool by which modern Copts can identify any form of persecution or discrimination as part of a historical process of eternal martyrdom. This is attained through the recreation of the image of the Coptic martyr throughout history. Commemoration is, even today, bolstered by the abundance of literature and icons dedicated to past and present martyrs, some of whom became saints. Therefore, while the commonality of suffering created a cohesiveness of identity as argued by Naguib, it should also be noted that the Era of Martyrs served to reinforce the ecclesiastical hierarchy by painting religious affinity and spirituality through persecution as one of the main unifying features of the community. Naguib has failed to recognise that the 'multiplicity of histories' that she discusses also assisted in the reinforcement of an official 'Church narrative', thus denying a voice to the various Coptic actors and the multiple Coptic histories that arose in conjunction with, in opposition to and separate from the Era of Martyrs narrative.

The persecuted minority discourse is best highlighted however, by the abundance of literature, in both Arabic and Western languages that has appeared since the 1970s. The historical context is significant, since it was with the ascendancy of President Anwar al-Sadat to power in October 1970 that a new approach towards politics and a wave of intolerance in Egypt developed. Sadat's move towards a liberalised free market, through his policy of *infitah* (Open Door), and his subsequent leniency towards the Muslim Brotherhood, which had been oppressed under Nasser, changed the social, political and economic landscape of Egypt.[16] With Sadat's announcement to alter the Egyptian Constitution in 1971 from Sharia Law being *a* source of legislation, to *the* principle source of legislation, a clear state trend towards alienating non-Muslims from public participation was asserted.[17] Clashes between Islamists and Copts in the 1970s, including the burning of a prominent Church in Khanka, thirty kilometres outside Cairo, in September 1972, has led to the increasing currency of theoretical frameworks which view communal tensions between Copts and the Muslim Egyptian community as either a clash of civilisations or as the inevitable outcome of the Copts status as a 'minority'.[18] This further bolsters the assumption that organised hostile groups and mob violence against the Copts are a constant threat. The implicit result of this is that the definition of a Copt is always in relation to a Muslim. No consideration or examination is made of the various Coptic factions and 'the Copt' is not compared to 'other Copts' from different social classes or of differing ideological persuasions. Instead, the cohesive minority approach has served to reinforce earlier representations of the battle against the forces of oppression and persecution as manifested by the Era of Martyrs discourse.

Conversely, the same period also saw a rise in a number of accounts, mainly written by Coptic commentators and social scientists, who used the context of the tensions of the 1970s to promote the idea of Egyptian national unity. This co-existence and co-operation, they argued, had been prevalent since the 1919 revolution. Milad Hanna's, *Na'am Aqbat, lakin Misriyun*, (Yes Copts, but Egyptian), published in 1980, was an attack on the violence of the late-1970s.[19] Hanna argued that Egyptian identity was made up of elements of at least seven pillars, which married, amongst others, Egypt's: 'Sunni face, Shia blood, Coptic heart, and Pharaonic bones' a reference to Egypt's historical lineage.[20] It was only through understanding the various components of Egyptian identity and looking at selected historical examples, such as the growth of Egyptian nationalism in the face of British occupation between 1882 and 1952, that one could argue that differences between Egypt's multiple communities were negligible.[21] Similarly, historian Tariq al-Bishri also used the period of the British occupation as the backdrop for his discussion concerning Coptic-Muslim relations; he argued that whilst historical relations were at times tense, the shared experience of colonial occupation meant integration and co-operation, especially during the 1919 Revolution, became inevitable.[22] Thus, this nationalist discourse has supported the idea that the Copts were, and still are, an integral component of the Egyptian state.[23] This approach is once again problematic as this narrative denies the Copts self-agency to promote a different version of events; instead, Copts, Muslims and other participants in 1919 are grouped together as a cohesive unit and labelled 'Egyptian'. The Copts are presented as a monolithic whole who adopted a one-dimensional unified approach to the question of national independence.

What the above discussions on the Copts, although vastly different in outlook, share is their failure to address a problem in their main term of reference: *The* Coptic community is referred to as an undifferentiated, undivided mass. Historian Paul Sedra, whilst correctly highlighting this, only addresses the cleavages through identifying Coptic history in relation to the Muslim Brotherhood and the Egyptian state in the 1970s.[24] While Sedra does not give the Copts the 'victim' label, he nonetheless inadvertently adopts the 'Era of Martyrs' approach of analysis by viewing the Copts as being eternally in resistance to persecuting forces. This fails to recognise that Coptic *intra*-communal cleavages or factionalism existed and that it is necessary to understand these in order to fully appreciate the ways in which the Coptic 'community' responded to wider national events.

Taking these considerations on board, this book addresses a number of developments within the Coptic community from the mid-nineteenth century onwards. It seeks to address a shortcoming in the extant literature, which has thus far neglected to take *intra*-Coptic divergences of opinion into account. As will be discussed in the following work, a more nuanced understanding of Coptic perceptions of the 'community' is necessary, and in achieving this understanding, a reassessment of the relationship between various segments of the 'community' and the Egyptian state, radicalised political groups, foreign actors and ultimately with itself will be made.

Most of the existing historical literature in the Arabic language uses limited primary documentation, interviews or memoirs.[25] Conversely, the literature produced in the West can be criticised for its near-complete dependence on the use of British archival materials.[26] This book utilises both Arabic and Western sources. The archives at *Dar al-Watha'iq al-Qawmi* (The Egyptian National Archives) and the United Kingdom National Archives (TNA), known as the Public Records Office, in Kew, have been used extensively, when access to the documents was possible. Other Western primary sources used include the Lambeth Palace Anglican Church Archives (LP); Newspapers in Western languages, particularly English and French, held at Colindale Newspaper Library and the British Library have also been used in order to contextualise and assess with contemporary sources the periods under consideration.[27] Given the sensitivity of Coptic-related issues in Egypt today, access to view documents at *Dar al-Watha'iq al-Qawmi* was limited.[28] Extraordinarily, the Egyptian Ministry of Interior applies less stringent restrictions on periodicals which are also housed at the same location. A more gradated image of the Coptic community has been attained through the consultation of magazines printed by Coptic philanthropic and benevolent societies[29], religious societies[30], individual communal leaders[31] and mainstream dailies.[32] Use of these sources makes this work unique as the vast majority of these Coptic periodicals have never been consulted in any other work hitherto published in either English or Arabic. Further to this, diaries and memoirs of prominent politicians, such as Sa'd Zaghlul, alongside published editions of archival material in Arabic from *Dar al-Watha'iq* have also complemented these materials.[33]

Two main themes run throughout the forthcoming chapters. First, the ways in which the notions of social, political and cultural identity were used by Copts, Egyptians and Westerners in the nineteenth and twentieth centuries: Coptic group identity, as defined by their *millat*, was based on a collective understanding of 'self' founded on commonality of religious beliefs. This book will question whether this definition of Coptic identity manifested itself as a collective Coptic response to various historical situations.[34] Similarly, the question of the evolution of an Egyptian national identity based on a processual collective self-understanding, which was particularly spearheaded by anti-colonial opposition between 1882 and 1952, will be analysed. Moreover, this book seeks to address the extent to which notions of inclusion and exclusion can be used as analytical tools to explain the evolution of social and political identities in Egypt.

This book is divided into two sections: Part One addresses the *inter*-communal relations between Copts and the Egyptian state against the backdrop of the development of Egyptian politics and society between 1805 and 1946. Chapter 1 provides a historical analysis of the modernisation policies implemented by the 'father of modern Egypt', Muhammad 'Ali (1769–1849) and the impact that the notion of equality, advocated and pursued in part by 'Ali, had on the Coptic community. Similarly, the roles played by Pope Kyrillos IV, also known as Abu Islah (1854–1861), and the European missionaries on the community in the nineteenth century, is discussed in light of the formation of the *Majlis al-Milli* or community council and a new Coptic landowning elite. Chapter 2 considers the formation of new national identities following the British occupation of Egypt, assessing the impact of colonial rule on the administration and development of the Coptic community up to 1919. In particular, Coptic-British relations are discussed between 1882 and 1914, including the role played by Copts in government and bureaucratic positions, considering whether a policy of 'divide and rule' was followed. The emergence of party politics and the articulation of a supposed 'united national identity' is assessed during the Coptic Question of 1908 to 1911. This raised pertinent questions concerning British policies over the issue of equality in the years preceding the First World War. Similarly, the role played by Coptic 'agitators' in party politics in the years leading up to 1919 are used as evidence of Coptic mobilisation. The case-studies of Akhnoukh Fanous and Qommus Sergius highlight some of the varied and often opposing opinions prevalent within the community concerning participation in Egyptian politics as well as in the wider national movement of 1919. Chapter 3 investigates the impact of interwar politics on the Coptic community. Following the 1936 Anglo-Egyptian Treaty, the Wafd which had been considered the traditional nationalist party of Egyptian politics, declined in prominence. With this in consideration, the chapter assesses the diminishing role of Copts in public employment and the question concerning the distribution of government public funds on the community. The case study of prominent Coptic politician, Makram Obeid (1870–1971), and the 'Black Book' scandal are examined in light of the twilight of the Wafd Party and the emergence of other nationalist political parties. Moreover, this chapter examines Coptic responses to the emergence of political Islam in Egypt following the Second World War. In particular, the two case studies of Salama Musa, a secular Coptic writer, and Qommus Sergius, a religious reformer, provide evidence of various political and intellectual responses to the Islamic threat.

Part Two of this book addresses *intra*-communal dimensions of the community including factionalism and internal developments. Chapter 4 concentrates on the emergence of Coptic benevolent and philanthropic societies from the late nineteenth century until 1945. These were led essentially, although not exclusively, by the new Coptic educated classes who had benefited from the process of modernisation implemented by the Church and by the Egyptian state. This chapter highlights the essential role played by politically active urban Coptic elites who provided palliative and social care for the community beginning in 1881. This included establishing educational facilities and funding social welfare, and thus presented a source of support as an alternative to the welfare provided by the Church and the state. In particular, this chapter assesses the role played by the lay *Majlis al-Milli*, and the various societies in their attempt to regulate the distribution of *awqaf* as a form of beneficence between 1883 and 1927, which they argued, was under the maladministration of the Church hierarchy. Both Chapters 5 and 6 are case studies which specifically address Coptic internal factionalism between 1944 and 1954. Chapter 5 investigates the different factions that participated in: first, the election of Pope Macarius in 1944 which was for the first time articulated as a modern political campaign. Second, the issue concerning the nature of and control over Coptic *waqf* following Macairus' victory is examined. The chapter demonstrates that the *waqf* debate, rather than modernise the community, propelled it into greater factionalism. Similarly, Chapter 6 examines the impact of the 1952 Free Officers revolution on the Coptic Church highlighting the radicalisation of the activities of Coptic youths following the revolution and the ways in which both lay and religious Coptic reformers were able to negotiate a place for themselves in post-revolutionary Egypt. It is argued that the policy of *Al-tathir* (cleansing/purification), initiated by the Revolutionary Command Council (RCC) against the old political orders beginning in 1952, was appropriated by a group of lay educated Coptic youths. *Jama'at al-Ummah al-Qibtiyyah* (JUQ), who were aggravated by the continuous *waqf* disputes and rumours of corruption within the Church, abducted Pope Yusab II with the aim of implementing a policy of reform and modernisation in 1954.

# PART I

# *INTER*-COMMUNAL RELATIONS: THE COPTS AND THE STATE (1805–1946)

# 1

# RELIGION AND STATE-BUILDING IN THE KHEDIVAL PERIOD (1798–1882)

## Muhammad 'Ali and the Khedival Period

The beginnings of the modern Egyptian state are usually accredited to the policies of Muhammad 'Ali (1769–1849), who along with his successors, brought about a period of great economic, political and social change to Egyptian society in the nineteenth century.[1] This process had an impact on the Copts in both social and political spheres.[2] Muhammad 'Ali became the ruler of Egypt in 1805 when he deposed his chief Mamluk rival with the support of the *'ulama'* of Cairo. Between 1809 and 1812 he succeeded in destroying the remnants of the power of the Mamluks, who had up until the French invasion of 1798 been the nominal rulers of Egypt.[3] Following the entrapment and massacre of the Mamluks at the citadel in 1811, Muhammad 'Ali followed a comprehensive program of political modernisation.[4] The policies by Muhammad 'Ali and his successors, contributed to blurring the social, political and legal boundaries between residents in Egypt. Exact records of the numbers in the various communities in Egypt are difficult to find given the fact that no births or deaths were registered until the latter half of the nineteenth century.[5] Nonetheless, a rough calculation was made in the late-1820s to ascertain the size of the population. This was based on the number of houses in Egypt and the assumption that the inhabitants of each house in the cities amounted to eight dwellers, with four in the provinces. British travel writer Edward Lane estimated 2,500,000 inhabitants in Egypt. Of these numbers, 1,750,000 were Muslim Egyptians, while there were 150,000 Copts, representing the largest ethnically 'Egyptian' Christian community in Egypt. Lane also calculated that the number of Turko-Circassians in Egypt was 10,000 whilst Syrian, Greek and Jewish communities amounted to 5,000 inhabitants each, and were mainly based in urban centres such as Cairo and Alexandria. Armenian Christians were said to number 2,000, and the remaining 70,000 were uncertain and variable.[6]

Born around 1769 to an Albanian family in the town of Kavala in the Ottoman Empire, now in modern-day northern Greece, Muhammad 'Ali's own ethnic origin is a highly contested question, particularly in post-revolutionary Egypt; he has widely been considered to be the founder of the modern Egyptian state.[7] Muhammad 'Ali was clearly a member of the Ottoman elite. He arrived in Egypt under the direction of the Ottoman Sultan in 1801 with 6,000 Albanian troops part of a 10,000 man Ottoman force, sent to collaborate with British forces against the French.[8] Yet his subsequent modernisation policies were geared towards the development of Egypt as a separate political entity from the Ottoman Empire. In 1831, Muhammad 'Ali invaded Syria and threatened the viability of the empire itself, prompting the intervention of European powers.[9] His policy served to centralise and consolidate his own control over Egypt, thus securing his dynasty's future. Muhammad 'Ali linked the idea that a soldier of Ottoman Turkish origin, and his dynasty, could not only rule Egypt, but become an integral part of it. This was much to the dismay of the chronicler 'Abd al-Rahman al-Jabarti, who became reknown for his accounts of Egypt.[10] Soon after Muhammad 'Ali came to power he wrote:

> Oh Egypt look at your children [*Awladik*], whilst they are scattered far and tortured, you [Egypt] have been colonised by the worst of the Turks and Jews [...] they wage war against your children, they kill your heroes, they overcome your knights and destroy your role, they live in your castles, and corrupt your children. [ 19th *Dhu al-Qa'dah* /January 1807][11]

## *The Question of Religious Equality*

Muhammad 'Ali pursued a strategy for the inclusion of all the inhabitants of Egypt within its territorial entity; this was implemented through policies of religious and ethnic tolerance, commenting that 'I do not wish there to be any difference between my subjects based on difference of religion, the only difference is the way that they pray in their temples'.[12] Christians were allowed, for the first time, to ring church bells as well as to carry the crucifix in public.[13] Muhammad 'Ali also helped to facilitate pilgrimages to the Holy Land, which in previous centuries had been hampered by restrictions. A Decree issued in 1819 also eased the sanction on building churches, which had previously been subject to limitations.[14] Writing in 1954, historian Jacques Tajer claimed that Muhammad 'Ali never refused a request by Copts to build a Church; this would become a point of contention later in the twentieth century.[15] Four Copts were also nominated to the position of provincial governors in the 1830s.[16] These developments were viewed very favourably, by both Coptic commentators and European contemporaries travelling through Egypt, as one of the brightest periods in the modern history of the Coptic Church.[17]

The significance of Muhammad 'Ali's reign, with regards to Coptic religious expression, is illustrated by the changing nature of dress codes. Traditionally, the Copts had worn similar clothes to the Muslims, although it was largely distinguishable by a black, blue, grey or light brown turban.[18] By 1818, however, Al-Jabarti highlighted with some displeasure and apprehension, new developments in Coptic life which placed Copts on a more equal footing:

A gathering of the opposite sects of the *millats* [amongst whom the] Coptic and Greeks [were called upon] and [told] that they should continue wearing blue and black robes but not wear white turbans; [this was because] they had exceeded their allowance in all aspects, they turban [themselves] in coloured cashmere shawls [that are] expensive in price. They ride elegant horses and mules, [and] in front and behind them [are] servants with sticks in their hands; they hit the [local]

> people out of their [Copts and Greeks] way, it is not assumed
> by the observer that they [Copts] are any less than in the
> highest employment of the state; some go out into the
> countryside and carry arms. [*Jumada al-Ula* 1232H/ 9th March–
> 7th April 1818] [19]

Similarly, before the accession of Muhammad 'Ali, Copts and Jews
were not permitted to ride horses, but it seems that this restriction
was lifted in Egypt despite being upheld in Syria even after Ibrahim
Pasha's (1789–1848) invasion in 1831.[20] Al-Jabarti provides an
eloquent illustration of the attitude of a Muslim *'alim* towards the
improved status of non-Muslim religious groups in the early period
of Muhammad 'Ali's rule.

Another recorded case of Muhammad 'Ali's more lenient
attitude towards *millat* groups, is taken from 1844 when Sidhoum
Bishoi, a Coptic scribe residing in the town of Damietta, was
accused of insulting Islam. With popular backing, the governor of
the province forced Bishoi to convert to Islam or face a public
flogging. Bishoi chose the latter and later died from his wounds. He
was consecrated a martyr on 25th March 1844. Upon hearing of
this, Muhammad 'Ali ordered the exile of the governor for his
actions.[21] The apparent shift in policy towards the Copts, along
with other religious and non-indigenous groups, served a dual
purpose: firstly, Muhammad 'Ali's policies of tolerance assisted, to a
certain extent, to legitimise his own rule as he was keen to establish
his credentials and that of his family as the new rulers of Egypt.
Secondly, the process of state centralisation and modernisation
which was being implemented, required the integration of groups
such as the Christians who were better trained than the Muslim
population in the fields of accountancy and land surveying.

### State-Building and Modernisation

Muhammad 'Ali and his successors implemented a modernisation
program which had a dramatic effect on the inhabitants of Egypt.
Muhammad 'Ali initially regarded this policy of modernisation and
reform as a necessary process in the construction of a centralised
Egyptian state which, had nominal independence from the
Ottoman Empire.[22] Modernisation took the form of a new army,

bureaucracy and greater attention to state-sponsored education. He began the process by creating a new army; having witnessed the military supremacy of the British and French forces which had fought in Egypt, he was convinced of the need of a European-style, disciplined force.[23] The main problem lay in the manpower of the new army; the recruitment of soldiers from the Caucasus and the Ottoman Empire was not a viable option due to his hostile relations with Istanbul after he had declared himself as the independent ruler of Egypt in 1811. Between 1820 and 1824, Muhammad 'Ali recruited 20,000 men from Sudan, 17,000 of whom died in the training process.[24] With few options left, conscription of the Egyptian peasantry commenced in 1822, the officer class was drawn from the Turko-Circassian elites which had supported his rise to power.[25] His *Nizam al-Jadid* (New Organisation) was a large and costly venture, reaching a peak of 115,000 men in 1840, which constituted 12 per cent of the working-age population.[26] Copts, by virtue of their status as *dhimmi*, were not conscripted into the army.[27] As described by Lane, 'the Copts enjoy an immunity for which they are much envied by most of the Muslims: they are not liable to be taken for military service'.[28] Instead, Copts were obliged to pay the *jizya* tax.[29] In the 1830s, three different rates were imposed on the community: the richer classes in Cairo and in other large towns paid thirty-six piasters each, the poorest nine piasters, while in the countryside, the *jizya* was levied on families rather than individuals.[30]

Given the financial burdens of military modernisation, Muhammad 'Ali implemented an administrative and fiscal system to cope with the new policies. He began by creating six ministries dealing with foreign affairs, war, navy, finance, industry and education.[31] Muhammad 'Ali also divided Egypt into provinces, districts, and sub-districts, thus fostering the development of a highly centralised administration.[32] Like the army, the administration was headed by Turko-Circassians whilst Arabs served in subordinate positions. To manage all of his newly implemented reforms, it was necessary to create an efficient but, more importantly, subservient bureaucracy to serve the state.[33]

Both administrative and military reforms were paid for, in large part, through agriculture. In 1814, Muhammad 'Ali abolished the existing system of tax farming and took direct control of land.[34] Furthermore, previously large land holdings had been registered as *waqf*, religious endowment lands, in order to avoid taxation. Muhammad 'Ali scrutinised the misuse of this system, consequently turning many illegitimate claims of *waqf* into state properties.[35] He also encouraged cultivation projects through tax concessions for peasants willing to cultivate waste land and help in the construction and repair of old canals and dikes in the Delta. The aim was to increase the production of essential crops including rice, sugar and most importantly cotton.[36] The re-orientation of Egypt's economy towards the mass production of cotton was one of Muhammad 'Ali's most important achievements, as there was great demand by textile merchants in Britain. This guaranteed that Egypt, at least in the foreseeable future, had a steady means of income. By 1849, cotton accounted for 31 per cent of Egypt's total exports. Revenue was also raised through the virtual monopoly over trade imports and exports, with Muhammad 'Ali taking the profits made. In 1836, 95 per cent of exports and 40 per cent of imports were managed through the government. 'Ali recognised that foreign trade would provide him with a large cash income, a policy which had been inherited from his predecessors.[37]

The Copts were able to carve out a niche for themselves during the modernisation programs, especially in the field of finance. Whilst many did not have the medical, educational or commercial skills of other Christian communities, such as the Syrians or Greeks, they did have certain professional skills useful to the new administration. In the eighteenth and nineteenth centuries, many Copts were employed as accountants to large private landowners, land surveyors and tax collectors.[38] The demand for Copts in these roles was kept up through a system whereby the same profession would be inherited from father to son. The strength of the Copts lay in the fact that their accountancy system was highly complex and unique to them. [39] Coptic boys would from a young age, go to locally run Christian schools to acquire the basic knowledge of reading, writing, geometry and mathematics. The latter two were felt to be particularly important and were greatly promoted as useful sciences; the proportion of fields and harvests that would be lost to the Nile's annual flood could be calculated using basic geometry and mathematics coupled with the knowledge imparted to young Coptic boys from their fathers. In their teenage years, they would act as apprentices to accountants and land surveyors following in their fathers' footsteps.[40] As a result of their specialisation, by the time Muhammad 'Ali came to power Copts were in a better position to serve in their role as land surveyors than anyone else.

Similarly, Copts performed well in roles such as tax collectors. The tax recording system used by Copts was considerably different from those of the Muslims in terms of style and content.[41] This ensured that they were in a unique position to serve the administration when Muhammad 'Ali began his modernisation process, as only Copts educated in this form of collection started to be employed. Given the expenses of the modernisation program, Muhammad 'Ali closely scrutinised tax collection and revenue. *Mu'allim* Basilious Ghali was chief of the Coptic guild responsible for the collection of taxes throughout the country. A *Mu'allim*, a title given to the registrar of taxes, presided in most villages throughout Egypt. As this post was opened to non-Muslims during the French occupation, Ghali co-operated closely with Muhammad 'Ali and was thereafter considered to be his right hand man.[42] Some evidence also suggests that Ghali played a crucial role in recruiting Sudanese troops for the modernisation of the Egyptian army.[43] The potential wealth derived from such a position was considerable as suggested by the fact that by 1846 *Mu'allim* Ghali's family owned a number of villages in the Delta, one of which had over 2,000 feddans of land.[44]

Closely attached to the question of modernisation of the state and bureaucracy was the issue of education. In order to achieve modernisation, and to have an efficient bureaucratic machine, it was necessary for Muhammad 'Ali to undertake educational reforms which would supply the state with trained officers and administrators, establishing an indigenous educational system based on a European model.[45] 'Ali began sending student missions to Europe from 1813 onwards. At first the majority of students were of Turkish-Circassian origin, and were sent specifically for the purpose of military training. The focus slowly began to shift in the mid-1820s when Muhammad 'Ali also began to send future

administrators, with the aim of utilising their knowledge upon their
return and establishing specialised secondary schools with modern
systems. Primary education, however, developed at a much slower
pace, and was largely left to the traditional 'ulama'.[46] Despite
Muhammad 'Ali's foresight in reforming the bureaucracy and
military, he did not endeavour to link modern educational facilities
with the traditional. In 1869, under Isma'il (1863–1879) the
grandson of Muhammad 'Ali, a new wave of reforming traditional
schools begun.[47] There were renewed efforts to expand state
education, resulting in the reopening of the famous School of
Languages and Administration which had been founded in 1835
but closed during the reign of 'Abbas I in 1850. The *Dar al-'ulum*
(Teachers College), was also established in 1872 to train Arabic
teachers for instruction at primary and secondary school level. As a
result, state expenditure on education increased from £6,000 to
£75,000 annually, whilst education in most schools remained free.[48]
The impact of the educational policies implemented by 'Ali and his
successors on the Copts was two-fold: it encouraged the Coptic
Church to adopt similar policies, leading to the creation of Coptic
schools and the development of a Coptic intelligentsia. However,
educational policies implemented by the state also had the effect of
slowly removing Copts from the traditional roles that they played in
land-surveying and accountancy. The newly-created specialised
schools introduced new modernised forms of surveying and
accountancy, which incrementally led to the replacement of Copts
by graduates of the new institutions.

Under Muhammad 'Ali's successors, there was also a change in
personal status laws; Sa'id (1854–1863), began drafting Copts, as
well as Muslims, into the army in 1856. As suggested above, Copts
had previously been exempt from serving in the army in return for
paying the *Jizya* tax.[49] In 1854, Sa'id renounced his claim to LE
15,000 of *Jizya* that was due from the Copts.[50] The abolition of the
*Jizya* in 1855 and the drafting of non-Muslims in 1856 into the army
was in line with the Ottoman Hatt-i Humayun, the imperial edict
which confirmed provisions of religious equality within the
Ottoman Empire.[51] However, the abolition of the *Jizya* tax and the
enforcement of conscription was not favoured by many Copts. In
Asyut for example, a city in Upper Egypt with a sizable Christian

population, there were complaints that all men had been conscripted and that as a result there were no men available to support their families. The situation became so unbearable that the Coptic patriarch intervened with the government in order to have the Copts exempted from military service. This highlighted the continued role of the Church in *millat* affairs during the nineteenth century despite Muhammad 'Ali's attempts to create a more inclusive and consolidated position for himself and his successors in Egypt.[52]

## A Renaissance in the Coptic Community

The modernisation policies of Muhammad 'Ali and his successors helped redefine the boundaries of identity in Egypt bringing non-Muslim communities, and Copts in particular, into the sphere of an emerging centralised state. 'Ali and his successors' conception of identity was based on a collective solidarity and groupness which linked various people within Egypt by dismissing the notion of a fundamental and abiding homogeny.[53] In contrast, Coptic communal identities remained strongly cemented by religious ties despite the partial integration of certain Copts with professional skills into the new state structures. Under the reign of 'Abbas I (1849–1854), attempts were made by the Patriarch to reform the Coptic clergy and institutions. These attempts were partly in response to Muhammad 'Ali's modernisation policies, and partly as a reaction to the external threats posed by Christian missionaries. The reforms implemented were inward looking in nature, reinforcing the strong communal ethos which bound the community.

## *The Beginning of Islah*

The literature on the Copts, written by both scholars of religion and Egyptian historians more broadly, has described the mid-nineteenth century as an age of reform or *islah*.[54] This is in large part due to the efforts of Pope Kyrillos IV (1854–1861), also known as Abu Islah or the 'father of reform'.[55] Abu Islah has been revered as the foremost important figure in modern Coptic history, as he attempted to rescue the Church from its perceived decadence, characterised by illiteracy, maladministration and stagnation. In particular, two Copts who had been students of the patriarch wrote extensively on Abu Islah's reign and the policies he implemented, highlighting his importance as a reformer even during his own lifetime.[56] Abu Islah has therefore been portrayed as the leader of the Coptic *nahda*, or renaissance, and as the forerunner to Kyrillos VI (1959–1971), who is considered to have promoted *Al-nahda al-thaaniyah* (the second renaissance), in the Nasser period. The concepts of *Al-nahda* and *al-islah* are used interchangeably in Arabic historical literature on the Copts to discuss the period.[57]

The policies implemented by Abu Islah before and during his reign as patriarch were highly successful. In particular, those firstly implemented in the *diwan* and ecclesiastical reforms, second, in relation to iconography and third, with regard to lay educational changes. He began in 1854 by establishing an administrative system for the *diwan* of the patriarchate in order to centralise and streamline the supervision of church affairs. This included two branches, the first of which was concerned with the legal affairs related to the personal status laws of the *millat*, including marriages and deaths. The second meanwhile, dealt with reforming the ecclesiastical structures, focussing on the clergy who had long been accused of negligence in their religious duties. This took the form of a disciplinary approach, aimed at regulating the behaviour, education and dogmatic practices of the Coptic clergy, and was a reflection of their poor backgrounds and education, as the majority of clergy came from the lower classes of the community.[58] The ignorance of the clergy is perhaps best highlighted through the observations of a foreign traveller, who as early as 1799 noted:

> [T]hey keep their books, written in the Cophtic [*sic.*] language, which is compounded from a mixture of the Greek and the remains of the ancient Egyptian. Though they never read them; though they let them lie in heaps upon the ground, gnawed by insects, and mouldering in dust; they are not to be prevailed upon to part with them.[59]

Indeed, in another account by one of Abu Islah's biographers, it is stated that the poverty of the clergy was a major cause of their misuse of Church property. *Awqaf* provided the Church with extensive funds obtained from rents of lands and were subject to serious exploitation by their administrators, usually monks or bishops. The clergy were also reported to have sold their services, through performing blessing ceremonies in exchange for payment of fees.[60] Similarly, Lane in the mid-nineteenth century, reported that: '[T]he priests and monks in Cairo are seen every day begging, and asking the loan of money, which they never repay, at the houses of their parishioners and other acquaintances, and procuring brandy, if possible, wherever they call.'[61] In order to alleviate clerical financial constraints, Abu Islah introduced a system whereby priests would receive a fixed salary rather than rely on the alms donated by their parishioners. These salaries came partly from the revenue collected at Sunday mass.[62] Along with the clergy, deacons were also given attention, particularly those showing spiritual inclinations. Abu Islah provided them with appropriate clothing and instruction in Coptic chanting, as well as, education in Church dogma, and rudimentary Coptic language classes.[63]

Instruction was provided for the clergy and deacons through the creation of ecclesiastical training schools, and in 1849, as head of St Anthony's monastery, Abu Islah opened a school on a farm located in the area of Bush.[64] The school was primarily aimed at the monks in the monastery, but later took on local children; it also opened a small library at the same site, employing a local Muslim Shaykh to teach the monks Arabic grammar.[65] In 1854, when he became patriarch, Abu Islah required all the clergy based in Cairo to attend weekly classes at the Patriarchate, where theological education, along with basic literacy skills, were taught.[66] In order to facilitate many of the educational reforms for the clergy, there was a need for greater dissemination of the tenets and beliefs of the Coptic Church. This was greatly assisted by the purchase of the first private printing press in Egypt which was brought from Austria by Abu Islah and was received with great ceremony in 1859 at Bush, near the St Anthony Monastery.[67] The introduction of the printing press helped to popularise religious discourse and enabled debate to flourish, particularly as this had previously been restricted to those with access to old manuscripts in the monasteries. Abu Islah also secured permission from Khedive Sa'id I to have Coptic deacons be trained in the art of printing at the old government Bulaq printing press.[68] This began with the publication of Coptic religious tracts and grammar books, finding popular support in many of the newly founded libraries, including the expansion of the one founded at Bush.[69] Thus, the creation of two administrative units under patriarchal control, personal status codes and ecclesiastical reforms, solidified Abu Islah's centralisation in much the same way as Muhammad 'Ali and his successors.[70]

Another of Abu Islah's major reforms addressed the culture of iconography, which he vehemently and adamantly opposed. Abu Islah regarded iconography, which played a large role in Coptic belief, as a form of idolatry and superstition; this, he believed, led to the degradation of the spiritual values of the Coptic Church.[71] Whilst rebuilding the St Mark's cathedral in the Azbakiyyah district of Cairo, Abu Islah declared that no sacred pictures would be allowed in the new building: 'Behold these wooden pictures you used to honour and even worship! They can neither avail nor harm you. God alone should be adored!'[72] The culmination of this statement was a bonfire in both Cairo and Asyut, where relics were burnt much to the amusement of foreign observers who viewed Coptic iconography with distain. As reported by Mrs Butcher, who lived in Egypt:

> We should be inclined to regret this action of Cyril's [Kyrillos] if it seemed at all likely that any works of art had perished in his great object-lesson. But the art of painting had become almost extinct since the Ottoman conquest, and the pictures which had been executed for Mark's Cathedral were probably even worse daubs than those which since Cyril's time have been placed in the Cathedral which he built.[73]

The reformist message of Abu Islah was clear: the new approach focused on the enlightenment of the clergy through education, in an attempt to move away from what he believed were signs of superstition and 'backwardness'. Abu Islah's attitude towards iconography and superstition was progressive and 'modernist', the inspiration of which predated but found inspiration in the influence of Presbyterian missionaries who, particularly in Upper Egypt, declared themselves as enemies of Catholic iconography and lavishness.

قداسة البابا كيرلس الرابع
البطريرك ١١٠ ـ ١٧ أبريل ١٨٥٣ ـ ٣٠ يناير ١٨٦١

**Figure 1** Abu Islah (1853–1861).

Thirdly, Abu Islah also implemented educational reforms that were closely linked to the development of state education under Muhammad 'Ali and his successors. In the Azbakiyyah district of Cairo in 1853, he set up the first of several 'Great Coptic Schools', or *Madrasat al-Aqbat al-Kubra*, also known as the Coptic Patriarchal College. Prior to the creation of the schools, Copts had followed a very similar pattern of preliminary education to Muslim children at the local *kuttab*, where often blind teachers, *'urfan*, taught religious studies and basic literacy skills in Arabic to young boys.[74] There is evidence from western travellers that prior to the reforms, it was not unheard of for 'Copts and Muslims to be taught side by side, where they mastered religion, good manners, to read and write Arabic and Coptic'.[75] Following the creation of the Great Coptic Schools, Abu Islah continued the tradition of close interaction between Muslim and Coptic students by encouraging religious diversity. Coptic religious historian Mattewos has claimed that the Great Coptic Schools were the first civil union between Copts and Muslims in free non-governmental education.[76] Abu Islah's vision brought Copts more closely in line with the new agenda of modernisation and centralisation pursued by Muhammad 'Ali's dynasty. The schools were established using Coptic funds, which Abu Islah raised from the community, and later due to their success, were given subsidies and direct grants from the Khedival government in the form of land, farms and money.[77] Land was granted in the Al-Wadi region of the Sharqiyyah governate to help cover expenses incurred in the Schools.[78] The schools taught free of charge a number of European languages including French, English and Italian as well as Arabic and Turkish.[79] Aside from languages, a range of subjects were taught including chanting, mathematics, history, geography and logic. The teachers appointed were both foreign and Egyptian, and took charge of all subjects, whilst the *'urfan* and heads of the old *kuttabs*, were given compensation in the form of a pension by the Church following their vocal opposition to the creation of the new schools.[80] The first of these new schools, which contained both a primary and secondary school opened in 1855 and had 150 students enrolled in it.[81] Another primary school for girls was established in Harit al-Saqqayin in Cairo.[82] By the mid-1870s, this school had over 243 students and 18 teachers.[83]

These Great Coptic Schools, which were all initially concentrated in Cairo close to the old Coptic *kuttab*, graduated some of the most influential Copts that were to play roles in Egyptian history in following years; Boutros Ghali Pasha (1846–1910), the future Egyptian Prime Minister assassinated in 1910; Mikhail 'Abd al-Sayyid (1830–1914), the founder of the Coptic newspaper *Al-Watan*; and Mikhail Sharubim (1853–1912), a historian.[84] The schools also graduated two future Muslim Prime Ministers, Abdel Khalek Sarwat, who served in 1922 and 1927–28, and Hussein Rushdi, Prime Minister between 1914 and 1919.[85] Upon graduation students took a public state exam which allowed them to pursue higher education in the state institutions first created by Muhammad 'Ali.[86]

The success of the Great Coptic Schools in the capital led to the establishment of more schools outside Cairo: the first in the province of Mansura, and the second in Bush, near St. Anthony's Monastery. By the time Abu Islah died in 1861, there were a total of seven Great Coptic Schools in Egypt, including two for girls.[87] Under his successor, Pope Demetrius (1861–1870), twenty-three additional Coptic schools were built; eighteen in Cairo, two in Alexandria, two in Asyut and one in Giza.[88] All these educational institutions had boarding arrangements for those students who came from the provinces.

Abu Islah's reform policies in administration, centralisation and education of the Coptic community clearly reflected his modernist nature, complementing the reform programs implemented by Muhammad 'Ali and his successors in the state. The fear of losing consolidation over the community led to a series of comprehensive reforms aimed at solidifying and centralising the community against the external perceived threats posed by missionaries.

### Missionary Activity

The role of Christian missionaries in Egypt provides evidence as to the impetus behind some of the reforms implemented by Abu Islah and his successors in the period up to the British occupation of 1882. The main thrust of the activities carried out by the missionaries came under the rubric of the promotion of education. Two different missionary societies were particularly active in Egypt and had a sizable impact on subsequent Coptic reforms implemented by the hierarchy of the Church.

The Church Missionary Society (CMS) led one of the first waves of British missionary activity in Egypt in the nineteenth century. The CMS began meeting informally in April 1799 in London, but it was not until 1812 that the 'The Church Missionary Society for Africa and the East' was formally established. [89] In 1799, the plans of the Church Missionary Society focussed primarily on Africa, where its most evident achievements were made in the following years.[90] West Asia which included Egypt, did not feature in the agenda of the CMS until 1815 when a Mediterranean Mission was set up in Malta and which later extended to Egypt and Palestine.[91] Soon after the establishment of the Mediterranean Mission, a printing press was started and operated in conjunction with the Religious Tract Society and the British and Foreign Bible Society. The aim was to print and stock Christian scriptures in the liturgical languages of the Eastern Churches and in Arabic with a view to expanding missionary activities.[92] In charge of this process was Rev. William Jowett, who moved to Constantinople in 1816.[93] Rev. Jowett visited Egypt in 1818 to enquire about the state of the Egyptian Coptic Church and to discuss with Pope Boutros VII (1809–1852) the possibility of the Mission assisting the Church.[94] In 1825, after several contacts with the Coptic clergy and limited results, the CMS established a branch in Egypt. As the new society could not find any English missionaries, the first who served in Egypt, were neither Anglican nor English, but Lutherans from Germany.[95]

From the outset the society did not intend on proselytising amongst Copts, and instead sought to strengthen the structures of the Church. It was hoped that by raising the educational standards of both the Coptic clergy and lay community the Copts would be able to flourish in a predominately Muslim state.[96] While many of the early CMS missionaries frowned upon the ancient rituals, dogmatic practices and customs of the Orthodox Coptic Church, viewing them with oriental disdain, the strengthening of the Church was necessary in order to achieve the longer term aim of converting Muslims.[97] During the 1820s and 1830s the missionaries began studying Arabic and established their headquarters in a Coptic district of Old Cairo, with the hope of fostering good relations. It seems that the local Copts were initially wary of the intentions of the CMS, although the missionaries were well received by the Patriarch on more than one occasion.[98]

In Cairo missionary work focused primarily on the provision of educational services, and beginning with lay communal education, a number of schools were opened. In 1828–9 only five Coptic and four Greek children attended one of the newly-established CMS Schools in Cairo, the vast majority of the remainder being Catholics and Maronites. However, by 1834 there were a greater number of Coptic children in attendance along with a few Muslim boys. In the same year, a school for girls was opened, as well as a boarding school for boys. Further evidence of the early success of the CMS was that, by 1839–40, six classes on the Holy Scriptures were held per week for Copts throughout the city.[99]

In 1842–3, the CMS decided to turn to the educational and religious training of ecclesiasts. A religious seminary was established, highlighting the CMS policy of strengthening the Church. It was hoped that a new, enlightened 'modern' clergy would become vehicles for reform in the Coptic Church, encouraging the expansion of Christianity in both Egypt and the wider region.[100] Within two years, there were fifteen pupils in the institution, but the poor quality of students raised concerns for the missionaries. Leider, one of the original five missionaries, commented that, 'with few exceptions, [the recruits] have proved to be only the scum of the Church', concluding that 'it is my opinion, on account of these cases, that this institution, as it is, is not worth the great expenses to which the society is subject'.[101] Despite this, however, the seminary graduated a number of Coptic priests, including a future bishop.

The impact of lay and ecclesiastical educational programs carried out by the CMS between 1825 and 1882 had mixed results on the Coptic community. Commenting in 1850, Bishop Gobat, who had been amongst the first missionaries in Egypt, gave his estimation of the impact of the CMS on the Copts:

Besides the dissemination of the word of God and other good books in all parts of Egypt, and the scriptural though imperfect education of youth, the results of the Mission are the conversion of a few individuals, some of whom have died

in the faith, a few enlightened young men dispersed through
Egypt while many members of the different communities
have been led to doubt the truth of their superstition and
traditions. Yet upon the whole it must be confessed, that the
Egyptian Mission has not had the success which might have
been expected.[102]

On the other hand, there is considerable historical debate which
suggests that the CMS's greatest impact was on Abu Islah himself,
who was rumoured to have been a student at one of the schools
established by the CMS. Following the emergence of missionary
activity in Egypt, there was a growth in the publication of Western
travel literature, diaries and autobiographies. These observers of the
Copts believed that the notion and process of modernity was a 'gift'
bestowed upon indigenous societies by missionaries and by the
British forces that later occupied Egypt in 1882. The making of a
'modern' society rested on western influence and experience.[103] Mrs
Butcher, a British resident living in Egypt who epitomised this
perspective commented that: 'Mr Leider [of the CMS] would have
been encouraged to persevere had he known that though none of
his pupils were ordained priests, as he had hoped, his school
produced in course of time the Patriarch known as Cyril [Kyrillos]
the Reformer.'[104] It could therefore be argued that Abu Islah was
influenced not only by the process of modernisation and education
as promoted by both Muhammad 'Ali and his successors through
state practices, but also through missionary activity. On the other
hand, Coptic writer Tawfiq Iskarius wrote that it was highly unlikely
that Abu Islah came into contact with missionaries, especially
considering Abu Islah did not achieve a level of perfection in his
educational studies until well after entering a monastery at the age
of 21.[105]

Several other missionary groups established themselves in Egypt
in the mid-nineteenth century. The most important, in terms of
impact on the Copts, was the United Presbyterian Church of North
America. The American Mission was founded in 1854 with the
arrival of Rev. Thomas McCague and his wife from the US, and the
Rev. James Barnett, detached from the Mission in Syria; it was later
reinforced by the arrival of Rev. Gulian Lansing in 1857.[106]  Like

the CMS, the activity of the mission was focussed on the dissemination of education resulting in the establishment of schools for teaching and training, and the publication and distribution of scriptures. However, in contrast to the CMS, the Presbyterians promoted the conversion to Protestantism from among the Copts. It has been claimed by Arthur Fowler, a British observer in Egypt, that the American Missionaries wanted to establish an independent Presbyterian Church in Egypt.[107] The American Presbyterians became extremely active in creating a series of modern schools throughout Egypt which rivalled the traditional Coptic *kuttab*. In the autumn of 1855, the Mission opened a boy's school, with the aim of promoting Sabbath services.[108]    In Lower Egypt, the Presbyterian 1863 Annual report mentioned the existence of a boys' school and a girls' school in Alexandria, and a separate boys' and girls' school in the Azbikkiyah district of Cairo, which was in addition to a further girls' school in the district of Harit al-Saqqayin of Cairo.[109]

By 1865 it was clear that the educational aspect of the Presbyterian mission was focussing on Upper Egypt, where twelve percent of the population, and a quarter of the inhabitants of the city of Asyut, were Copts.[110] In March 1865, a boys' school was established in Asyut, with only seven students; however, by the end of the year its students had expanded tenfold, and a girls' school soon followed.[111] Women, and girls in particular, were regarded as vital bearers of the modernisers' message.[112] Historian Paul Sedra argues that the establishment of girls' schools were frequently more important than those of boys' schools in such missionary projects. In ordering family life, the Presbyterians sought to control the environment within which children were raised. The schools were regarded as a means of rendering young girls 'industrious' and 'disciplined' through instilling such values at the core of the Egyptian home. This policy of educating girls was also promoted by Abu Islah, and then later by his successors who frequently commented that prospective mothers were the cultivators of Coptic children.

Similarly, Pope Demetrius (1861–70), Abu Islah's successor, also responded to the educational activities of the Presbyterians. In particular, the role played by the missions in Asyut, Upper Egypt,

led Demetrius to establish a rival modern school in the city in 1862.
The school was funded by rich local Copts, and supported by the
Khedive in the form of land donation.[113] This school was modelled
on Abu Islah's Great Coptic Schools, which Demetrius continued
to expand.[114] In 1862, Demetrius employed a Copt who had
received his education in a Presbyterian missionary school as
headmaster for the new school in Asyut. Indeed, in an annual
report published by the Presbyterian Mission, it was noted that the
newly established patriarchal school used 'the same books in school
that we use in ours and pursues the same course of study that we
do', solidifying the link between missionary education and the
impact on Coptic reforms.[115]

The establishment of the school also reflected Demetrius'
frustration with Presbyterian attempts at promoting Protestantism
in Egypt at the expense of Coptic Orthodox Christianity, and in
particular in Upper Egypt, which had a large Christian population.
This culminated in the persecution of the Presbyterian missionaries
in Asyut in 1867. This also had the tacit support from the
government who feared that foreign intervention in Egypt would
undermine Khedive Isma'il's control:

> Isma'il, the reigning Khedive, was far-sighted enough to
> appreciate that the standards which the American missionaries
> were setting up would directly, or indirectly, result in holding
> up to criticism and condemnation of his unjust and tyrannical
> treatment of his ignorant and patient subjects. [116]

Evangelical teaching had spread exponentially among Coptic
monks who were seen throughout Asyut reading the new Arabic
translation of the Bible promoted by the missionaries. Indeed,
Watson argues that the Patriarch found his own brother reading the
new version of the Bible. Demetrius subsequently arranged an
apostolic tour among the Churches of Upper Egypt, making no
secret of his mission: the suppression of what was now regarded as
Protestant heresy. He claimed that the viceroy and Khedive had
conferred upon him the right to condemn to the galleys all those
who adhered to the Protestant faith, or to seize their children for
the army.[117]

What followed has since been termed the Coptic persecution of the Protestants. As an example of the actions carried out, there is evidence that Demetrius summoned a Coptic priest of Beni Aleig in Upper Egypt, whose brother had been a student at one of the missions' theological schools, and accused him of preaching Protestant heresy at Sunday Mass. It was arranged that the priest would be severely beaten by soldiers, and degraded of his priesthood on account of his brother's actions.[118] Demetrius, with the assistance of the state, closed all mission day-schools, as well as a theological seminary which had recently been opened. Protestant school books were collected and burnt in a public bonfire. Persecution and opposition to the Presbyterian Church was not maintained once it became clear that only an extremely small number of Copts had converted.[119] Nonetheless, the episode highlights that Demetrius feared that the expansion of the Presbyterian missions in Upper Egypt signified a growing, strengthened, educated Coptic community in Protestant doctrine, which could have a detrimental effect on the ecclesiastical structures of the Church.

## The Formation of a Majlis al-Milli (Coptic Community Council)

The issue of the Hatt-i Humayun in 1856 by the Egyptian government, a secular decree which encouraged equality, constitutionalism and representation, assisted the process of reform and modernisation.[120] One of the results of this decree was the development of community councils within each *millat* to deal with matters concerning personal status, including marriage, divorce and inheritance, as well as the administration of *waqf* lands donated to the Church for ecclesiastical and charitable purposes.[121] The actual creation of a Coptic Community Council, did not come into full fruition until 1874, and was later suspended until 1883. When the council did function, however, it embodied a shift in communal representation from clerical autonomy to a lay educated class, a process which had its foundations in Abu Islah's educational reforms, and educational policies implemented by the government.

Following Pope Demetrius' death in 1870, the affairs of the community were entrusted to Murqus, the bishop of the province of Al-Beheirah, who acted as the Vicar-General of the Church.[122] Bishop Murqus chose a number of notables to assist him in the administration of the financial affairs of the community, and thus the nucleus of the first Coptic community council was created. The notables chosen to undertake the task were Barsum Girgis Bey, Yaqub Nakhla Rufila Bey, Gundi Yusuf al-Qasabi Bey, 'Azia Manqariyus and Mikhail Habashi.[123] Indeed, two of the members of the community council had been pupils at Abu Islah's Great Coptic School, clearly solidifying the link between a new generation of Coptic notable laymen and the former patriarch's reforms.[124] With the assistance of Bishop Murqus and the approval of some of the clergy, the decision was made to formalise the arrangement in the shape of a community council, or *Majlis al-Milli*, in 1874.[125] According to Girgis Filuthawus 'Awad (1867–1955), a progressive cleric and critic of many conservative Coptic traditions, the establishment of the council had biblical sanction and as a result also had his full support.[126] Indeed, Canon Law and the writings of Ibn al-'Assal, the thirteenth century Coptic jurist, were used to justify the establishment of a *Majlis al-Milli* with specialised laymen providing advice and practical knowledge in the fields of law, medicine and accounting, which would benefit the community.

A similar question arose in the medieval period in the Roman Catholic Church, with the need to define the scope of its political institutions. Canon lawyers used the notion of 'corporation' to define the arrangements and workings of ecclesiastical organisations within the Church. This corporation in Roman Law was a partnership between a body and a legal personality, and was distinct from the character who set it up such as the pope; it was a *persona ficta*, which as such, could assume legal rights and obligations, engage in litigation, enter into obligations and hold property. The most important question that arose in the dispute in the 14th and 15th centuries for the Roman Catholic Church, therefore, was who had the right to act on behalf of the corporation. For the Papalists, the view was that the pope alone possessed this authority; the conciliar party, on the other hand, argued a council of the Church, composed of representatives of the Church from different factions, should hold authority: 'The concept of corporation thus came to involve two notions, the notion of representation and the notion of council.'[127]

This debate concerning the power balance in the Coptic community was characterised by the creation of the *Majlis al-Milli* in the late nineteenth century. The basic issue was the legitimisation of the role of the layman in religious terms. Coptic religious historian Iris Habib al-Misri (1910–1994) highlights the concerns that were prevalent regarding the new class of laymen and their roles within the Church, commenting that it was necessary, with the creation of the *Majlis*, to place safeguards: 'there is a big difference between representation that is built on love and mutual respect, and between representation of the Church carried out unilaterally by civil lay decisions'.[128] According to the 1874 constitution, the twelve lay members and twelve deputies of the *Majlis* were to be elected by general suffrage every five years and were to supervise the financial and civil affairs of the community.[129] This would include *waqf*, schools, benevolent societies, affairs of personal status and other secular functions, which would relieve the clergy and patriarch of worldly functions and transfer the power balance to the laity.[130]

Whilst all the bishops informally agreed upon this arrangement in 1873, the notables who had supported the project were keen to have the *Majlis al-Milli* recognised by the government. This was in part a reaction to other members of the clergy, whose power had remained hitherto unchallenged. With the support of Gad Shiha, a leading Copt in government, and Boutros Ghali Pasha (1846–1910), a rising politician, the Khedive Isma'il was petitioned in February 1874.[131] The petition called for the recognition of the *Majlis al-Milli*, which would consist of twelve members and twelve deputies, to meet under the chairmanship of the patriarch. On 15th February 1874, a Khedival decree was issued and the council was formed.[132]

There is considerable controversy surrounding the appointment of Pope Kyrillos V in 1874, and his relationship with the creation of the *Majlis*, especially because the seat of the patriarchy had been empty since the death of Demetrius in 1870, and only temporarily covered by Bishop Murqus. Historian Samir Seikaly has correctly noted that, as Coptic sources are contradictory, it is very difficult to determine whether the creation of the *Majlis al-Milli* in 1874 affected the election of Kyrillos V to the patriarchy in the same year.[133] There is some evidence to suggest that the state interfered in Coptic community affairs, and that Khedive Isma'il arbitrated in the long-standing dispute concerning the succession of the patriarch. Isma'il commissioned the Governor of Beheirah to bring Kyrillos V to Cairo, resulting in his consecration as patriarch in 1874.[134] The significance of these events, despite the scanty evidence, is that the state may have directly, for the first time in modern Egyptian history, intervened in the selection of the Coptic patriarch, in an attempt to reassert the legitimacy and authority of the community following the four year absence of a religious leader.

Supporters of reform, on the other hand, maintain that Kyrillos V was elected to his position after he promised several members of the council that he would work with them on the understanding that they would have his vote.[135] Indeed, in the first years of the existence of the *Majlis al-Milli*, there is evidence of co-operation between the laity and clergy as suggested by the creation of a girls' school in the governate of Sharqiyyah in 1874.[136] In 1875, Kyrillos V approved the creation of a theological college, which enrolled monks and priests so that they should receive a holistic education in the history, liturgy and dogma of the Coptic Church.[137] This interest in spiritual education was promoted further in the form of publications in religious literature, as well as personal tours to monasteries to promote literacy. Kyrillos also supported building a series of monasteries close to Cairo which had fallen into disrepair.[138]

The relationship between the new council and patriarch did not remain agreeable for long, however. By 1875, there was already evidence of what contemporary western observers, such as Mrs Butcher, termed the 'dark' and zealous clergy, solidifying traditional western perceptions of Oriental despotism.[139] According to her, the bishops managed to persuade Kyrillos that he should possess absolute power, and not govern in union with any councils.[140] The Council responded to this threat by acting impatiently, demanding their unequivocal right to deal with all civil and financial affairs.[141] The impact of the tension was dramatic, resulting in the retraction of reform policies on the part of the patriarch beginning with the closure of the theological college created that year.[142] Furthermore,

Kyrillos V subsequently refused to attend any council meetings or appoint a deputy, and for seven years the council was unable to function.[143]

Between 1874 and 1883, Kyrillos V´was left to govern the Church in the traditional, autocratic manner. This period has been described by some Coptic commentators such as the historian and journalist 'Abd al-Sayyid, as the end of the first *nahda*, which had started with Abu Islah.[144] In this period, two attempts were made to re-establish the *Majlis al-Milli* through elections, but these proved unsuccessful highlighting the fiery struggle for control and authority over the Coptic Church.[145] The establishment of the *Majlis al-Milli*, had created a schism between traditional ecclesiastical views of authority within the Church and the lay reformers who were at the head of the council. This process would lead to factionalism inside the Coptic community and the beginning of a debate that would continue until the mid-twentieth century.

# 2

# THE MAKING OF NEW NATIONAL IDENTITIES (1882–1919)

## The Impact of the British Occupation

In September 1882, British troops defeated the forces led by Ahmad 'Urabi, a colonel in the Egyptian army, who had staged a revolt against the Khedival regime at the Battle of Tel al-Kebir.[1] Britain's two main motivations behind its subsequent occupation of Egypt revolved around the security of the Suez Canal and the gold standard.[2] In the aftermath however, Britain realised that her evacuation from Egypt could only be successfully carried out after a general reconstruction of the Egyptian administration.[3] This resulted in a process which saw the imposition of institutions and methods imported from India on existing Egyptian government structures.[4] The general administrative changes implemented focussed on finance, education and bureaucracy, all of which ultimately had an effect on the Copts.

Lord Cromer (1841–1917), who had been British controller of Egypt since 1879, became Consul-General in 1883. His main role was the supervision of all administrative, financial and political changes to be implemented in Egypt, most of which was to be put under direct British control. In the Egyptian army for instance, British officers were promoted to high positions. This included the transfer of twenty-five newly trained officers to Egypt, who would in later years follow distinguished military careers in Africa and the Middle East.[5] All higher staff positions were reserved for British officers, while only half the commanders in the infantry and cavalry battalions were Egyptians; these were the highest ranks that an

Egyptian officer could aspire to during the early years of the occupation.[6]

British advisors were also appointed to Egyptian ministries, their main role was the management of differing aspects of policy. Beginning in 1883, the advisors took control over the Ministry of Public Works, followed by Justice in 1891, Interior in 1894 and Education in 1906. The nucleus of British administrative reforms however, lay in the field of finance, which was the overriding issue of importance in the first decade following 1882. Prior to the occupation, under Khedive Isma'il, the precarious financial economy of Egypt had come to a head; the process of modernisation which had begun under Muhammad 'Ali had wavered with limited success in areas such as industry, while the construction of the Suez Canal proved costly.[7] The continuous borrowing from foreign financiers had led to bankruptcy in 1875–76, and external intervention instigated by British and French investors who had a considerable share in the Egyptian economy, resulted in dual financial control. In 1876, the *Caisse de la Dette Publique* was set up in order to supervise the Egyptian budget and economy, and to ensure that share holders were paid.[8] Due to the involvement of the Ottoman Sultan, Khedive Isma'il's lack of co-operation with the *Caisse* led to his demise in 1879 at the hands of the British; Tawfiq, Isma'il's son, was instated as Khedive in 1879. Isma'il had left Egypt with a debt that totalled £100,000,000, the payment of which consumed nearly two thirds of the Egyptian budget in 1883. Ten years later, 40 per cent of Egypt's annual budget was still being set aside for debt re-payments.[9] The convention which regulated Egypt's finances was renegotiated in 1885, with more money put aside for the administrative needs of Egyptian society, and the payments of debt were reduced.[10] The most important British advisor to Egypt was Alfred Milner (1854–1925), the Under-Secretary of Finance, who was entitled to a seat in the Council of Ministers and formed the main connection between the Egyptian government and Lord Cromer. Indeed, it was claimed that the British financial advisor wielded more power than that of any other English official, barring Cromer. As part of the occupation, over 1,300 British assistants were brought to Egypt in total, taking roles that had previously been occupied by Egyptians at a fraction of the cost.[11]

Another crucial area of British administration was education.[12] Here, there was a conscious effort to avoid the mishaps of the British-led Indian education system, which was not considered to be practical enough. Cromer, in particular, was keen to promote education to run concurrently with the modernisation that was taking place in the country.[13] Thus mass education was, according to Cromer, to be rudimentary, and should consist of 'the three R's in the vernacular language and nothing more!'[14] Until 1906, there were only three government run secondary schools in Egypt, turning out less than one-hundred graduates a year in a country of eleven million inhabitants.[15] Due to the financial constraints facing the bankrupt Khedive Isma'il, state expenditure on education had reached an all time low in the years 1877–78. Total expenditure for all levels of state education was LE 29,000, this was despite the fact that education had been at the forefront of early khedival modernisation policies. Under dual control, expenditure was raised to LE 70,000 although the budget during the early years of British occupation remained tight.[16] It was not until 1890 that the financial department found itself in a position to increase the sum of money spent by the state to LE 81,000.[17] By 1906, this had dramatically increased to LE 305,000, with estimates for 1908 reaching LE 450,000.[18] While the British were keen to promote greater education, this was stunted in the early years of the occupation by a lack of funds.

A link between the education system and the bureaucracy was also formalised during the occupation: the British keenly promoted education in order to assist the modernisation of the state and fill vacant bureaucratic jobs. The Civil Service was divided into two ranks, as Egyptians increasingly regarded education as a stepping stone to a secure government position. By the early twentieth century graduates demanding government jobs exceeded the numbers available. As a result, educational requirements for government employment were steadily raised leading to a reorganisation of the structure.[19] In 1905, a decree stipulated that after 1909 the higher rank of the Civil Service was only open to those with secondary certificates; they would have a starting wage of LE 8 a month and no ceiling wage on advancement. Those with a primary education on the other hand, would merely be admitted into the lower Civil Service and could expect to earn LE 4 a month with a ceiling wage peaking at LE 10.[20] This would ensure that those working in the bureaucracy would meet certain standards, solidifying the link between education, administration and modernisation.

## The Coptic Question

The policies implemented by the British administration, vis-à-vis what they increasingly referred to as 'Egyptian minorities', are subject to controversy. The Egyptian sociologist and historian Saad Eddin Ibrahim has argued that the British government followed a policy of 'divide and rule' whereby preferential treatment was given to minorities in order to secure their support against the majority Muslim population.[21] Conversely, historian Sana Hasan has argued that the concept of divide and rule is flawed. Her main argument is that, unlike India, where the sizable ethnic and religious divisions had been used as a means of checking the emergence of a unified opposition to British rule, the Coptic population was too small to be worthy of British considerations, and consequently difficult to manipulate.[22] Further in support of Hasan's argument, the Copts were not concentrated in any specific area, nor did they form the majority of the population in any one province.

Whilst Hasan is correct to point out that the Copts were not a significant proportion of the population if compared to Muslims in India, the British government did follow a two-tiered policy of divide and rule, particularly in the period up to the First World War. Firstly, it sought to weaken communal solidarity by exploiting divisions between members of the religious establishment and laymen. This was done through attempts to co-opt priests and notables with reformist tendencies and political clout, who were welcomed by the British Residency; Coptic laymen, such as Boutros Ghali Pasha, played an important role in the formation of the *Majlis al-Milli*, and forged close ties with the British. Secondly, the British colonial administration sought to isolate the Copts through preferential treatment in the attainment of bureaucratic and state jobs.

British-Coptic relations were varied in character during the period of the British occupation. The Coptic writer Ramzi Tadrus represented many Coptic notables who had occupied a position in the state administration when he wrote in 1911 that the British occupation had brought with it:

> Positive and stabilising effects on the security of Egypt as well as a revival which would promote progress, especially as [Egypt] had become devoid of thought and was ignorant and full of corruption and without order.[23]

Cromer, the British High Commissioner, did not generally trust the Copts, and saw them as opportunists who directed their sympathies according to the situation. 'He [the Copt] wished to pose both as Anglophobe and as an Anglophile according to the requirement of the audience'.[24] In his book, *Modern Egypt* published in 1908, Cromer described the Copts as a backward community. To him, the Copt was unalterable in his nature because he was an Oriental: 'The Eastern Church, was, like the East, stationary and immutable; the Western, like the West, progressive and flexible'.[25] In this sense, he saw no difference between a Copt and a Muslim: '[T]he only difference between the Copt and the Moslem is that the former is an Egyptian who worships in a Christian Church, whilst the latter is an Egyptian who worships in a Mohammedan Mosque'.[26] This was in part blamed on the close proximity between the two religions in aspects of everyday life: 'The modern Copt has become from head to foot, in manners, language, and spirit, a Moslem, however unwilling he may be to recognise the fact'.[27] This mistrust of Copts was akin to the disdain held towards Jews.[28] As a result, Cromer preferred the support of the Syrian Christians, whom he considered to be more modern and closer to the 'European mentality'.[29]

Despite this however, Cromer did recognise that the Copts had 'developed certain mediocre aptitudes' which made them useful to both the British and their previous 'oppressive' rulers.[30] As a result, the Europeans could rely on the Copt not on account of their shared religion, but due to their utility:

[The Copt can] add and subtract, because he knows his multiplication table, because he can measure the length and breadth of a plot of ground without making any gross error in the measurement, and because, although his system of accounts is archaic, at the same time it is better to be in a possession of a bad system of accounts than, like the Egyptian Moslem [sic.], to have scarcely any system at all.[31]

Considering the development of the bureaucratic apparatus in the period of British occupation, it is clear that that the Copts were favoured over the Muslim population for employment in many key departments. While in some departments, such as finance, the predominance of the Copts was not a new occurrence mirroring the pre-occupation period, in others, such as the Ministry of the Interior, the large number of Copts was largely attributable to the British. Cromer had credited this to the fact that a large number of Copts had been educated in missionary schools.[32] The Copts were also consistently over-represented in the specialist schools of law, medicine and engineering from the 1890s. Copts had previously lacked the educational and linguistic head-start required for these schools, but after the 1890s an increase in the number of Coptic led and funded primary and secondary schools were important in escalating the number of applicants to the professional schools. Indeed, the Tawfiq Society, a philanthropic group created by members of the laity, established a professional school in Cairo in 1906. The school had 27 pupils in total, 22 of whom were Copt, whilst only 18 paid school fees.[33]

**Table 1** Religious Affiliation in Primary and Secondary Schools, 1902.[34]

| Religion | Primary School | Secondary School | Total |
|---|---|---|---|
| Muslim | 470 | 82 | 552 |
| Christian | 298 | 47 | 345 |
| Jew | 11 | 2 | 13 |
| **Total** | **779** | **131** | **910** |

Although Copts made up approximately 7 per cent of the population at the turn of the twentieth century, they produced 21 per cent of the law graduates; 19 per cent of graduates from the school of engineering; 15 per cent of graduates from the medical school, where one Copt graduated for every two Muslims, and 12 per cent of the teaching graduates, between 1886 and 1910.[35] As also shown by Table 1, the Copts were disproportionately over-represented in the state education system.

A similar over-representation can be detected in the bureaucracy. In a report on the state of the Egyptian administration, written in 1901 by Eldon Gorst (who became Consul-General in Egypt between 1907 and 1911), he stated that Copts occupied approximately 45 per cent of the posts and received 40 per cent of the salaries, while Muslims occupied 44 per cent of posts and received only 6 per cent of salaries.[36] Apart from the totally disproportionate figures between posts held and salaries received, there was also the demographic issue: Copts numbered 7 per cent of the population in 1907 but occupied nearly half of all the positions in the bureaucracy held by Egyptians.[37] Similarly, in 1905 a British commission reported that only 28 per cent of higher government posts were occupied by Egyptians, the majority of whom were Copts, and it seems that by 1911 this percentage had risen to 45.31 per cent.[38]

**Table 2** Copts and Muslims in Government Ministries, 1911.[39]

| Ministry | Copts | | Muslims | |
|---|---|---|---|---|
| | Number | Percentage | Number | Percentage |
| Interior | 3878 | 62.3 | 2347 | 37.7 |
| Public Works | 251 | 29.4 | 604 | 70.6 |
| Justice | 220 | 14.8 | 1261 | 85.2 |
| Education | 66 | 6.1 | 905 | 93.9 |
| Finance | 1032 | 44.2 | 1301 | 55.8 |
| Communications | 2500 | 48.1 | 2700 | 51.9 |
| War | 135 | 30.6 | 307 | 69.5 |
| **Total** | **8082** | **45.3** | **9514** | **54.7** |

These figures were published alongside another report issued by Gorst in 1911, and caused a great deal of controversy both in Egypt and Britain. Kyriakos Mikhail (1877–1957), a Coptic journalist, spearheaded a press campaign entitled the 'Coptic Question', which questioned Gorst's report and concentrated on the inequality of British treatment against the Copts.[40] Mikhail, having worked for a number of newspapers in Egypt, including the English language *Egyptian Gazette,* moved to London in 1908 where he opened an Egyptian information office and published a number of articles in the British press regarding the Copts.[41] Mikhail contested Gorst's figures most publicly in a book published in 1911, arguing that whilst it would appear that Copts occupied a greater proportion of jobs than Muslims, the vast majority of these were 'insignificant and such that the Muslim will not and cannot fill'.[42] Indeed, Mikhail complained that the statistics had been drawn up incorrectly and that, despite the high Coptic numbers, the figures '[P]rove, if anything, that the Copts are under and that they are plainly victims of injustice, since, although their merits have won for them this high proportion of government posts, the most important positions still remain closed', a reference to the position of *Mudir* (governor).[43]

Following the publication of Mikhail's book, the 'Coptic Question' became a hot topic in the British press. Whereas Mikhail had been concerned with the state of Copts in governmental bureaucratic positions, the British press increasingly sought to connect the 'Coptic Question' with alleged cases of violence and inequality against Copts particularly in Upper Egypt. Several cases of clashes between Copts and Muslims had been reported to the police in late 1910 and were swiftly followed by a visit in January 1911 to the region by Gorst. Upon his return to Cairo, Gorst released a statement which contradicted Coptic grievances, declaring that 'Moslems and Copts generally lived quietly together [...] and that the worst possible service to the Copts would be to treat them as a separate community'.[44] From London, Mikhail campaigned vehemently against Gorst's position, and found a great deal of support in the British press.[45] The *Daily Mail* urged that Copts be considered 'a separate community' on the grounds that they were being mistreated, while the *Evening Times* referred to them as the 'oldest body of the Cross in the world and the descendants of the Pharaohs'.[46] Indeed the Coptic Question rose to utmost prominence in the British press after the despatch of many telegrams from Copts residing in three towns in Upper Egypt which protested against Gorst's statement. These telegrams were not only addressed to the newspapers but also to the Foreign Secretary, the House of Commons, and Buckingham Palace.[47] The telegrams, signed by Coptic landowners, lawyers and politicians, complained that Gorst '[...] could not have conducted an exhaustive enquiry into such a complex question as to the treatment meted out to the Copts in such a short period of time.'[48] According to the Foreign Office, the barrage of telegrams from Upper Egypt was calculated to have cost the Copts over £250, indicating the vehement opposition to Gorst's views, as well as the highly organised nature of the Coptic community in Upper Egypt.[49] Following this display of communal solidarity, the Coptic Question was also subsequently raised in the British Parliament.[50]

Despite the uproar, Gorst dismissed Coptic criticisms and wrote to the Foreign Secretary that '[...] the present movement from among the Copts deserves no sympathy, for their position compares most favourably to Mohammadans in many respects'.[51] The emergence of a Coptic Question in Britain was triggered by several factors. The Copts behind the petitions and telegrams had endeavoured to enlist public support and that of the foreign missions, particularly the CMS, for their cause, hoping to influence opinion in America and Europe.[52] The British occupation of Egypt in 1882 had marked a shift in the nature of the relationship between missionary activists and the Copts. The CMS, who were able to operate more freely under British auspices, directed their efforts towards the evangelisation of Muslims whilst establishing a paternalistic attitude towards the Coptic community. In Britain, Mikhail had orchestrated his campaign with Anglican supporters, including Mrs Edith Butcher and A.J. Butler, who highlighted the 'commonality' between the Copts and Christians in Britain, through their shared qualities and customs. The Copts were in fact presented as co-religionists that the British public owed concern towards.[53] In A.J Butler's introduction to Mikhail's 1911 book, he wrote:

[...] so substantial and so serious are the injustices which the Copts suffer under British rule, and which in large measure have been created by British rule, that I do not hesitate to say that their position as an oppressed minority is a standing discredit and reproach to our boasted methods of government.[54]

Furthermore, Butler accused the British government of strong discrimination in favour of the Muslims, 'with the not unnatural result of turning many of them [Copts] into enemies of England and English occupation, to treat the Copts with stern disfavour, and to turn a deaf ear to all remonstrance'.[55]

The engagement of the press and the proliferation of pamphlets, books and public meetings in both Egypt and in Britain meant that the 'Egyptian Question' in general, and the 'Coptic Question' in particular, became part of the public domain. In some respects, the actions of Butcher, Butler, Mikhail and of numerous others appealed to what historian C. A. Bayly has termed Britain's 'Egyptological fantasies'. These fantasies were rooted in a new interest in ancient Egypt that created a genealogical link between the Copts and the Pharaohs.[56] The prominence given to the Muslim minority debate in India also drew attention towards the Coptic Question in Egypt, although the circumstances within the two British occupied territories differed considerably.[57]

### The Emergence of New Political Identities (1882–1914)

As a result of the modernisation policies implemented by the Muhammad 'Ali's dynasty, 'Urabi's failed rebellion, and Britain's subsequent occupation of Egypt, important changes occurred in terms of social division and political awareness of the Copts between the years 1882 and 1914. Socially and economically, Copts had already started to feature prominently as some of the major landholders in Egypt, a process that came to considerable fruition after the British occupation. Under Sa'id I a Land Code was implemented in 1858 which allowed peasants throughout Egypt to register land in their own name, while paying taxes directly to the state for the first time.[58] The *fellah*, or the Egyptian peasant, would often borrow money on the security of the land; however, with frequent crop failures in the late nineteenth century, the *fellah* was forced to concede his debt to a money-lender, usually a Copt, who subsequently took possession of the land.[59] Following the British occupation, the Ottoman Turko-Circassian classes declined in significance as landholders, and were replaced by foreigners, urban elites, and Copts who had benefitted from their traditional roles as money-lenders and surveyors. This, coupled with the Land Code, assisted many Copts in accumulating land. Following the British occupation, Egyptian agriculture was increasingly dominated by a new type of large estate ruled by notables who owed their political positions to their land-holdings and cotton cultivation.[60]

An example of the amount of land amassed under 'Abbas II (1892–1914), can be seen by the fact that the Copt Wisa Boctor accumulated over 12,000 feddans.[61] Similarly, statistics complied by the historian Samir Seikaly demonstrate that thirteen Coptic families possessed between 2,000 and 30,000 feddans, while over 100 families each possessed between 100 and 2,000 feddans. The collective accumulation of the Coptic community was approximately 1,500,000 feddans, with all other assets amounting to 50 per cent of the wealth of the country by 1914.[62] Thus, despite representing one-tenth of the total Egyptian population, Copts owned one-fifth of all agricultural land in the country as well as buildings and monetary assets. Added to this, they paid only 16 per cent of all tax on all agricultural lands, despite owning a far greater proportion, meaning that they enjoyed a comparatively comfortable life compared to their Muslim counterparts, claims of discrimination notwithstanding.[63]

By the turn of the twentieth century, Coptic capitalists were also playing a significant role in national politics due to their economic influence. Indeed, the establishment of the national economy is attributed to Tal'at Harb Pasha (1867–1941), who created *Banque Misr* (Bank of Egypt) in 1920.[64] Though not a Copt himself, Harb coerced many of his closest Coptic friends into playing prominent roles as the original shareholders of the bank. These men exclusively came from the landed Coptic gentry. The first Copt to serve on the Board of Banque Misr was Iskander Masiha, followed by Kamal Ibrahim.[65]

It was also amongst the landed Coptic gentry that a group of reformist leaders began to emerge, challenging the authority of the Church.[66] Their participation on a local level within their own community gained recognition because of their prominent roles on the national stage.[67] For example, the young Boutros Ghali who was at the forefront of demanding changes within the Coptic community in the form of a *Majlis al-Milli,* was also a Coptic landowner as well as a rising star in national politics. Similarly, the educational policies implemented by 'Abbas I and his successors, as well as by Abu Islah within the Coptic community, led to the creation of a Coptic intelligentsia who had been greatly influenced by the emergence of new political identities in reaction to the British occupation. A graduate from one of Abu Islah's Great Coptic Schools, Mikhail 'Abd al-Sayyid (1830–1914), established *Al-Watan* newspaper in 1877, a year after the foundation of the prominent Egyptian weekly, later daily, *Al-Ahram.*[68] *Al-Watan* had supported British occupation in 1882, and between 1900 and 1914, was a staunch defender of Coptic interests while being highly critical of the nationalists.[69]

Aimed primarily at the Copts as an outlet for their communal views and grievances, the editor 'Abd al-Sayyid particularly campaigned for the separation of the Arabic language from religion, 'Arabic is not only the language of Muslims.'[70] 'Abd al-Sayyid argued that the close association between Arabic and Islam led to the exclusion of Copts. As a result, *Al-Watan* attempted to distance the Copts from what it regarded as Islamic/Arab elements within Egyptian society:

> The Copts are the true Egyptians, they are the real masters of the country. All those who have set foot on Egyptian soil, be they Arabs, Turks, French, or British are nothing but invaders. The originators of this nation are Copts [...] Whoever calls this country an Islamic country means to disregard the rights if the Copts and to abuse them in their own fatherland. Not one of them would accept such a thing.[71]

*Al-Watan* was not the only Coptic paper to emerge in the late nineteenth century. *Misr* was founded in 1895 by Tadrus Shenouda

Manqabadi, an orthodox Copt who presented lay reformist views as opposed to the pro-clerical reformist stance taken by *Al-Watan*, particularly in the context of the disputes surrounding the *Majlis al-Milli*. In the early years of its publication, the paper was a staunch supporter of the British occupation, but like *Al-Watan*, in 1918 it started to support the nationalist cause.

The development of the press created a new sphere of public engagement for the community and ushered in the development of a Coptic intelligentsia which became involved in national politics. This development mirrored the consolidation of the Egyptian national press, which increasingly found new audiences among the cultural, political and literary sectors.

### *Party Politics and the 'Free Copts'*

In the early twentieth century there were two main parties in the emerging nationalist movements which had strong Coptic support. The first was the *Hizb al-Watani*, or the National Party, under the leadership of Mustafa Kamil (1874–1908).[72] This nationalist leader preached equality between Copts and Muslims and as a result had significant Coptic support. However, in the years following Kamil's death in 1908, prominent Copts who had been ardent supporters of the movement abandoned it from fear of the increasingly pan-Islamic and pro-Ottoman approach of the party.[73] This included three of the most prominent Coptic politicians; the first was Murqus Hanna (1874–1934), who had been a representative on the Egyptian University Board. Hanna was an important participant in *Al-Watani* Party and a close personal friend of Mustafa Kamil, later leading the committee to erect a statue in Kamil's honour.[74] The second Copt to abandon the party was Sinut Hanna (1874–1930), who played an important role in promoting youth education missions to France. Sinut would later take on a prominent role in the Wafd Party, as he became close to Sa'd Zaghlul, the nationalist leader of the party, and held the prestigious position of Speaker of Parliament; he was re-elected on several consecutive occasions until his death in 1930.[75] Finally, and perhaps the most prominent to leave the party, was Wisa Wasif (1873–1931), a land-owner, who was later chosen as a representative for *Al-Watani* in negotiations with the British in 1913.[76] He wrote many prominent articles in the

predominately Coptic newspaper *Misr* while also making speeches
calling for a united national struggle against British colonialism
through demonstrations of national unity against the occupation.[77]

It has been argued by modern Coptic historian al-Antuni, that
even before Kamil's death in 1908, some Copts had felt
uncomfortable with his approach, marring nationalism with Islam;
the yearly visit by Kamil to Istanbul was regarded as evidence of
Kamil's true agenda.[78] However, this interpretation fails to take into
account the fact that Kamil understood Islamic solidarity as a
political tool rather than as a source of religious discrimination.[79]
He was impressed by the European connection of nationalism and
religion, as epitomised by Bismarck's words, 'love of the fatherland
can not be separated from faith'. Moreover, Kamil appealed directly
to the Copts by invoking the image of the pharaonic past of the
country, which pre-dated Islam.[80]

The second branch of the nationalist movement popular with
Copts was the *Hizb al-Ummah*, or the Nation's Party, founded by
Hassan 'Abd al-Raziq Pasha. Its main organ, *Al-Jaridah*, was edited
by Ahmad Lutfi al-Sayyid, and played a hugely important role in
eliciting public opinion by publishing translations of major
European works.[81] Due to its ideology and nationalist goals, it was
free from the pan-Islamic and pro-Ottoman attitudes which had
been attributed to *Hizb al-Watani*. Instead, its approach was centred
on Egypt as a unique cultural and political entity.[82] Supporters of
*Al-Ummah* included prominent Coptic notables such as Sinut
Hanna, having deferred from *Al-Watani*, and Fakhri 'Abd al-Nur
(1881–1942). 'Abd al-Nur had started his career as a diplomat, and
joined *Hizb al-Ummah* in 1908, later also playing an important role
with Zaghlul.[83] Despite the appeal of *Al-Ummah* to certain Copts
because of its ideology, it lacked the popular base and support
network of *Al-Watani*. Nonetheless, the association of Copts with
both nationalist parties served to highlight the common goal: the
independence of a united Egypt made up of Muslims, Copts and, to
an extent, Jews.

In March 1908, a Coptic political party was formed in an attempt
to counteract the perceived failings of the newly-created nationalist
parties, particularly after Kamil's death. The Coptic Reform
Association, established in 1907, aimed to promote a lay-led *nahda*,

resulting in the formation of the Independent Egyptian Party. Four main aims were to be promoted by the new Coptic Party, including the promotion of Coptic middle class care; the defence of Coptic rights within greater Egyptian society; the accessibility of education; and the promotion of communal affinity through the endorsement of the Coptic faith.[84] In April 1908, the Independent Egyptian Party was founded, as the main political organ to promote the associations' aims.[85] In particular, the party would act as a mouthpiece for greater Coptic concerns of inter-communal hostilities. The leader of the party, Akhnoukh Fanous, had formally been a member of *Hizb al-Watani* but left during what he described as the emergence of 'sectarian differences', stemming from the perceived Islamic colourings of the nationalist movement, following Kamil's death.[86]

Fanous called for greater Coptic positive action within the community that would primarily take place through the promotion of education; he argued that only through this would the entire Coptic community benefit, and, there was indeed a conscious movement within the lay Coptic community in the early twentieth century to promote education. [87]

Fanous had initially come under fire for attempting the creation of a religious party, naming it *Al-Ahrar al-Aqbat*, (The Free Copts); this resulted in a sudden and more inclusive change of name to the 'Independent Egyptian Party', reflecting Fanous's earlier roots in *Hizb al-Watani*. Fanous's party, which lasted between 1908 and 1911, had several clear-cut demands, regularly aired in the monthly *Al-Firu'an* newspaper owned by Tawfiq Habib (1880–1941). Habib played an active role in the *Majlis al-Milli* until his death.[88]

The constitutional demands of the Independent Egyptian Party included the formation of two uniquely representative bicameral chambers. The first (lower) chamber, with legislative powers, was to be composed of members, half of which were to be elected from foreigners who had resided in Egypt for at least five years, the other half to be Egyptian. The second (upper) chamber would be for general control, and was to be composed of deputies elected by Egyptians only, in such a way as to represent each community.[89] Analysing Fanous's party, it is clear that its initial aims had been born out of internal communal reform, as evident by the common aspirations of the *Majlis al-Milli*, as well as Coptic fervour in the face of a perceived Islamic threat within the nationalist party after Kamil's death. Thus, Fanous's party combined an assertion of Coptic communal identity and reform, along with political interests, which were couched in nationalist colourings, but safeguarded by the presence of foreigners in the constitutional chambers.

### The Coptic Congress and the 'Akhnoukian Throne'

It was also following Kamil's death in 1908, that the Coptic *Al-Watan* newspaper participated in a civil war of words with *Al-Liwa*, *Hizb al-Watani's* mouthpiece, revealing deeply imbedded inter-communal tensions prevalent in the nationalist movement. *Al-Liwa*, (The Standard), printed its first edition in June 1900 under the guardianship of Mustafa Kamil, who primarily used journalism as one of several means, along with oratory and correspondence with foreign leaders, to effect political action.[90] In 1908, *Al-Watan* wrote an article in which it accused the Islamic conquest in 641 AD of oppressing Egypt. *Al-Liwa* replied with insulting and derogatory remarks aimed at the Copts entitled 'Islam, a stranger in its own country'.[91] Suspicions towards the Copts on the part of the Muslims, as well as perceived Coptic collusion with British imperialism, was confirmed with the appointment of Boutros Ghali Pasha (1846–1910) as Prime Minister in 1908. Under the British, he had been Minister of Finance (1893) and Foreign Affairs (1895).[92] Ghali was considered an Anglophile by both contemporaries and some historians, who regarded his only priority as keeping his LE 3000 annual salary.[93] Two years after his appointment as Prime Minister he was assassinated, by nationalist Ibrahim Nasif al-Wardani.[94] There is considerable controversy among historians as to the motives of Al-Wardani and the assassination: some historians, such as Vatikiotis, have argued that Al-Wardani belonged to an Islamic-nationalist trend which saw the collaboration of the British and Ghali Pasha as justification for his assassination.[95] Recent Coptic historiography, published in the last twenty years, has tended to view Ghali in an extremely positive light however, claiming that he was an ardent nationalist and hero.[96] It is argued that Ghali saw any uprising by Egyptians against British rule as unproductive, since, even if they were successful, it would only result in the return of the 'corrupt Turks'.[97]

On the other hand, from a non-religious perspective, there is also a purely nationalist case which can be cited as motivation for the assassination. In the two years between his appointment in 1908 and his assassination in 1910, Ghali had infuriated Egyptian public opinion.[98] This was particularly the case during the Dinshawi trial which saw the detention of 52 Egyptians.[99] Ghali presided over the special court which tried the men and in June 1906 four Egyptians were executed whilst others were imprisoned with hard labour or received a publicly-viewed flogging.[100] Ghali also signed the Sudan Condominium agreement, and was known to favour the extension of the Suez Canal concession, which was briefly opposed by the nationalists in the General Assembly.[101] In this light, Ghali's assassination was seen by members of both the nationalist movement and the general public as a just move against an unpatriotic and pro-British agent.[102] Gorst later commented that 'the leaders of the nationalist movement are morally responsible for the murder of Boutros Pasha'.[103] Historian Malak Badrawi who has examined police investigations of the time, concludes that Al-Wardani when questioned claimed that he was a Muslim and that Boutros Ghali was a Coptic Christian, but that religion had no bearing on his motives for the shooting of the Prime Minister whom, he considered a traitor.[104] Nonetheless, some anti-Christian sentiment was expressed by a small fringe following the assassination. Storrs, the Oriental Secretary at the British Residency in Cairo, reported that groups of Muslims roamed the city celebrating 'Wardani, who killed the Nazarene'.[105] Yet the vast majority of demonstrations, chanting and newspaper articles in the immediate aftermath of the shooting saw Al-Wardani's actions as an 'inescapable truth', a reference to justice having been served.[106] Many Copts, including some progressive elites and religious men, blamed the 'Islamic' colourings of *Hizb al-Watani*, to which Al-Wardani had belonged for Ghali's murder, in an attempt to ensure the latter's martyrdom. Indeed, Coptic newspapers referred to Al-Wardani as 'wicked' and 'low', although were cautioned by the Ministry of Interior in an attempt to prevent further straining of communal relations.[107]

Soon after Ghali's assassination in April 1910, a gathering was organised by *Hizb al-Ummah*, and held at the headquarters of its newspaper *Al-Jaridah*. The attendees consisted of moderate Coptic landowners, who sought to quell the fragile community relations which had been exacerbated following the murder. Murqus Fahmi (1872–1955), a prominent Coptic layman, spoke of unity in Egyptian demands for constitutionalism. Another Copt declared that he personally knew Al-Wardani, and that he was not fanatical but patriotic.[108] Despite these attempts however, Coptic grievances were highlighted and resulted in a Coptic Congress being held in the city of Asyut in March 1911. The Congress was partly established as a response to Gorst's ongoing claims that the Copts were not discriminated against and partly addressed the Egyptian nationalist movements, particularly following the assassination of Ghali.

The Coptic Congress, numbering 500 members or more according to official reports, formulated the grievances of the Copts. The most important demand made was the recognition of aptitude as the sole test for admission to government appointments a direct reference to the Coptic Question. In a substantial speech given by the lawyer Tawfiq Doss, who later played an important role in the Liberal Constitutional Party, calls were made for a meritocratic system in line with the 'noble Egyptian nation'.[109]

Gorst along with many nationalists claimed that the Coptic Congress had no mandate to speak on behalf of the 706, 322 members of the Coptic community. Indeed, the Coptic patriarch himself also reportedly disapproved of the proceedings.[110] The Coptic Congress was met with a plethora of comments from the Muslim nationalist press; Shaykh 'Ali Yusuf, the leader of the Constitutional Reform Party and editor of *Al-Mu'ayyad*, founded in 1890, published the text of the Coptic demands, as set out in the manifesto of the Congress. In a subsequent editorial, he commented:[111]

> My God! We look at the attitude of the Copts now when they are still a minority of 6 per cent and who have been ruled over for 1300 years and find that 60 per cent of the government employees are Copts and yet they summon their masses and

conspire both openly and secretly against the Muslims and they raise their complaints to the England that they are oppressed.[112]

The tendency for the press to view the Coptic Congress as an issue which could have larger sectarian ramifications was apparent in the commentary of *Al-Ahli* newspaper, which ran several articles under the heading 'The Coptic Religious Conspiracy'.[113] Indeed in another editorial, published in *Al-Mu'ayyad* a few days after the Congress, Shaykh Yusuf argued that the Copts had turned the occupation of Egypt into a united Christian movement against the Muslims of the country.[114] Despite the tendency of some papers to view the Coptic Congress as evidence of a growing rift between Islam and Christianity in Egypt, others, including *Al-Liwa*, considered the Congress as a threat to the nationalist movement, calling it 'A plot against patriotism and Egyptian unity, not a Congress'. The same editorial also highlighted that the British policy of divide and rule would not, in the long term, benefit the Copts.[115] Akhnoukh Fanous, the leader of the Coptic led Independent Egyptian Party, played an important role in the Congress, and came under fierce personal criticism. *Al-'Alam* published a double page article, entitled 'The speech from an Akhnoukhian throne', in which the writer depicted imaginary scenes with Akhnoukh Fanous as the Coptic emperor, who established a kingdom inside Egypt with its capital in Asyut from where he directed operations against his Muslim neighbours.[116]

In late April 1911, an inter-confessional Egyptian Conference was held to counteract the Coptic Congress. The proceedings were characterised by moderation and quiet enthusiasm, in direct contrast to the meeting held in Asyut. The Coptic Congress's claims were calmly refuted, and thereafter relegated to the background, as economic and social questions concerning the occupation were addressed.[117] Over 2,000 people attended, including a number of Coptic members of the various nationalist parties, one commentator enthusiastically declaring: 'not a single influential Coptic notable or man of standing, did not join the Egyptian conference at least in spirit if not in name'.[118] While this was an exaggeration, the main thrust behind Coptic grievances lost

momentum in the run-up to the First World War. Akhnoukh
Fanous's party closed in 1911, as more Copts gradually moved
towards the nationalist movement, particularly after the end of the
war. Indeed, by 1914, the Coptic *Al-Watan* newspaper adopted on
an anti-occupation line.

The creation of a new Coptic intelligentsia and landed elite
played a significant role in the emergence of a Coptic politically-
active class and the way in which various members of the Coptic
community were able to mobilise mass gatherings to respond to
perceived fears which were embodied by the Coptic Question. The
1911 Coptic Congress in Asyut demonstrates how traditional
historical portrayals of the Copts as a passive and 'beleaguered
minority' should be scrutinised more carefully. Instead, the Coptic
Congress provides evidence of how individual Coptic actors, such
as Akhnoukh Fanous, defended and articulated Coptic communal
rights in pre-war Egypt. The activity of the lay Coptic community,
particularly through the press also highlighted the increasing
rhetoric of periodicals as a way of disseminating views and
opinions.[119] In particular, the Coptic press played an essential role
as a form of nationalist and communal contestation, revealing the
developments through Egypt as a whole.

### Coptic Participation in the 1919 Revolution

In 1914, Sa'd Zaghlul, a former Minister of Education (1906–1910)
and Minister of Justice (1910–1913), established himself as the
leader of the opposition against the government, and the British
power which stood behind it.[120] Zaghlul had always been closer to
*Hizb al-Ummah*, favoured by many Copts, rather than to *Al-Watani*,
which had been led by Mustafa Kamil. Towards the end of the war,
Egyptians began to discuss the possibility of forming some sort of
representative delegation to present Egypt's case for independence
at the peace conference to be held in Paris. Woodrow Wilson's 14
points, which were later articulated into the Treaty of Versailles
following World War I, translated Wilson's policies of democracy,
self-determination, open agreements, and free trade into the
international realm.[121] An Egyptian delegation, or 'Wafd', was
established in order to present its demands to the British and
negotiate its independence. Two days after the armistice, on 13th

November 1918, Zaghlul and two other members of the Wafd called on the British High Commissioner and asked to go to London to present Egypt's case to the British government.[122] This request was denied and was shortly followed by the fall of Prime Minister Rushdi's government (April 1914–April 1919).[123]

Tensions grew in the following months, and Zaghlul, along with some supporters, were arrested on 8th March 1919 and deported to Malta on 1st April.[124] Widespread disorder broke out across Cairo, beginning with students of higher colleges, the majority of whom had left in order to participate in demonstrations; Zaghlul, one time Minister of Education, was popular among students. On the first day, the rioters were dispersed with some difficulty by Egyptian police and 310 arrests were made; at least one person was killed:[125] rioting and pillaging spread, including in the vicinity of the historic Al-Azhar mosque. According to British reports, the nationalist movement, which had at first been purely political, was 'now taking a religious turn'. The centre of the religious disturbances was at Al-Azhar, where the British claimed that 'seditious and inflammatory speeches are made all day and night'.[126] Owing to the sacred character of the mosque which was revered throughout the Muslim world, its demonstrators could not be restrained by force. Muslim nationalists were not the only frequenters at Al-Azhar; Coptic priest Qommus Sergius also led demonstrations from the same mosque. The disturbances took the British by surprise and an armoured car on patrol was, on one occasion, compelled to use its machine-gun wounding and killing some demonstrators in the process.[127] The High Commissioner, Francis Reginald Wingate (1917–1919), was replaced by Edmund Allenby, who had occupied Jerusalem in 1917.[128] Zaghlul was subsequently released and allowed to go to Paris to plead his case before the Peace Conference; twelve Muslims featured in the mission, as did three prominent Copts: Sinut Hanna (1873–1930), George Khayat (1862–1932) and Wisa Wasif (1873–1931). [129]

### Qommus Sergius: The Al-Azhar Orator

Egyptian and Western historiography has portrayed the 1919 revolution as a moment of Egyptian national unity with the image

of the cross and the crescent flag intertwined.[130]  Writing on the
revolution, Coptic historian Milad Hanna argues that:

> March 1919 instilled feelings that are prevalent in the
> conscience of every Egyptian until today and these are that
> 'religion is for God, and the nation is for all' [as well as] the
> slogan 'long live the crescent [entwined] with the cross'.[131]

Similarly, Mustafa al-Feki, in his book *Copts in Egyptian Politics*,
highlights Coptic politician Makram Obeid's role, and brandishes
an intertwined cross and crescent on the cover of his book.[132]
There are several problems with the nationalist portrayals. First, the
cross and crescent flag that is so commonly portrayed and used on
the cover of books, in films and in literature to represent 1919, is
scarcely found in photographs of the events.  Very few eyewitness
accounts of the riots with flags exist, although an Italian publicist
wrote in 1919: 'For the first time in history the banners flowen
showed the Crescent interwoven with the Cross'.[133] The flag
appears to be more significant as a symbol of the supposed spirit of
1919. This however, is not to negate the existence of the flag which
is increasingly seen in photographs and writings after 1922. Indeed
the prominent Egyptian Feminist, Huda al-Sharawi, discusses in her
memoirs how she and her fellow Egyptian female delegates hung
an intertwined cross and crescent flag at the Feminist Congress
held in Rome in March 1923:

> I remember how on this occasion when we went to the
> Conference [in Rome] we found that the flags of all the other
> nations hanging in the main hall, and that we were unaware of
> protocols of conferences. For that reason, we asked some of
> the women of the delegation to prepare an Egyptian flag
> which contained the crescent and cross. They made the
> biggest sized flag and when we gathered around it to look at it
> they commented that Egypt was the greatest of nations so
> should have the biggest flag.[134]

Beth Baron in her book *Egypt as a Woman* found that photos of
women who had participated in nationalist demonstrations and

which were published in *Al-Lata'if al-Musawwarah* were doctored when republished in books so that the flags showed the cross and crescent symbol.[135]

A second problem is that the events of 1919 and Coptic participation within it, are largely presented as monolithic; all Muslims and Copts were united in the Egyptian national cause. Instead, various Coptic stances can be identified, just as was the case amongst Muslims. A third problem with the portrayal of 1919 is that most histories are concerned with Zaghlul's interactions with British officials rather than the nature of grassroots mobilisation during the crucial period of March to April 1919.[136] None of these portrayals specifically address Coptic participation at the grassroots, but instead focus more on the wider political scene.[137] The pitfalls of failing to highlight Coptic representation in 1919 are symptomatic of deeper flaws of the representation of Copts in Egyptian historical literature.

The role played by Coptic ecclesiast Qommus Sergius during the riots of March to April 1919, is significant as it was related to several different issues. Firstly, Sergius's activities highlighted the impact of the educational reforms implemented since the mid-nineteenth century on a new class of religious reformers, who became involved in communal and nationalist politics, linking a religious *nahda* with a political one. According to Sergius, freedom from occupation, corruption and the old order were the key to a modern reformed society.[138] Sergius's nationalist activities in 1919 earned him a great deal of respect from 'ordinary' Copts who later went on to support him as a promoter of communal reform and modernisation within the Coptic Church. This case study also suggests that, whilst the Church hierarchy may have supported the nationalist activities in 1919, they were more cautious in their advocation out of fear of antagonising their position as *Ahl al-Kitab* within the established political order.[139]

Qommus Sergius was born Malti Sergius 'Abd al-Malik in Girga in Upper Egypt in 1883, and came from a well established clerical family.[140] In 1889 he joined the clerical college on the outskirts of Cairo established by Kyrillos V. The college promoted spiritual enlightenment of the clergy through education of languages and religious text. Whilst the creation of the clerical school appeared to be in line with reforms that had been promoted in the nineteenth century by Abu Islah, the institution was largely led by the same ecclesiasts it sought to exclude.

Sergius finally graduated with honours in 1902 and became a teacher there in 1903. He began to advocate more radical reforms in the Church, gaining the reputation of a revolutionary among more conservative clergymen. In 1903, he was instrumental in the organisation of a student strike, where he made key demands with considerable student support concerning the quality of theological education to be received at the clerical school. Sergius' demands, which included a more drastic overhaul of the Clerical College, were dismissed by Kyrillos V, who regarded such changes as an encroachment on his own authority as patriarch. Parallels can therefore be drawn between the patriarch's attitude to the lay *Majlis al-Milli*, and the clerical reformers such as Sergius, who subsequently organised a march on the patriarchate. Sergius clearly demonstrated the personality of a demagogic activist through his ability to mobilise Coptic clerical reformists.[141] An investigative committee was established after the strike, made up of Coptic notables including Boutros Ghali Pasha, as well as the head of the clerical school, Yusuf Bey Manqariyus; it was agreed that as penance, Sergius should be forced to marry and be ordained a priest, thus effectively stunting his career in the ecclesiastical path of the Church and forcing him into the mainstream clergy.[142] He was subsequently ordained a priest in 1904.[143] This episode of Sergius's early ecclesiastical life revealed two main issues: firstly, Sergius's ability to mobilise popular Coptic ecclesiasts in the face of perceived failings in the clerical school and, secondly, the practical position of the Holy Synod and the patriarchate regarding the actual nature of reform, how it was to be carried out, and who was to initiate it.

From his new position as a clergyman, Sergius continued campaigning for reform within the Church, resulting in his trial by a clerical board. Sergius was ordered to retire at the age of 21 and returned to his hometown of Girga.[144] In 1907, Sergius was reinstated and appointed priest for an Asyut church after befriending Bishop Macarius of Asyut (who later became Pope). Later the same year he was promoted to the rank of Qommus or

Canon. The relationship between Qommus Sergius and Bishop Macarius was to continue until the death of the latter in 1945. By 1912, Sergius had earned a reputation beyond Egypt for his religious reforming tendencies. His achievements were published in an article entitled 'The Voice of Truth', and prompted the Coptic Bishop of Khartoum to request Sergius for his personal services.[145] Sergius remained in Khartoum for two years, where he produced, edited and wrote in a fortnightly magazine entitled *Al-Manarah al-Murqusiyah*. The magazine, which was 16 pages on average, discussed religion, literature, and social issues for Copts in Sudan as well as Egypt. He produced over 30 issues in Sudan although *Al-Manarah al-Murqusiyah* was banned from being distributed in Cairo for fear of its editorial pieces, which were both highly acclaimed as well as criticised for their 'revolutionary' and inflammatory views.[146] Among the central issues discussed in the early years of the magazine was the question of whether the ecclesiasts or the Coptic people were responsible for the downfall of the Church. This debate culminated with the issuance of a seven-point decree condemning the simony of the Coptic Church.[147] By 1914, however, the patriarchate in Cairo had had enough of the actions of the populist Sergius in Sudan, placing him on trial on sixty counts, all of which revolved around his editorials. Having failed to induce Sergius to plead guilty, the Holy Synod dropped the charges and allowed Sergius to return to Sudan where his popularity increased among Muslims and Christians due to his increased attention to social injustices prevalent in society.[148]

Sergius' grassroots popularity was based on a mixture of religious fervour and nationalist credentials as advocated by his campaign against what he perceived to be the unjust colonial occupation of both Egypt and Sudan. In May 1915, the British authorities deported Sergius from Sudan to his native Girga.[149] Evidence of his intense popularity can be seen in the fact that, whilst in Girga, Sergius' monthly salary continued to be sent from Sudan, despite being effectively unemployed.[150] Indeed, his faithful Sudanese congregation helped finance the construction of a Church in the Qulali district of Cairo, where Sergius was reported, according to Copt Ibrahim al-Guindi, editor of *Al-Watan*, to have given fiery demagogic speeches.[151] This is particularly important as it reveals that not all Copts were against the British occupation. Indeed Al-Guindi's newspaper *Al-Watan*, in fact promoted the benefits of British occupation, particularly for the Copts up until 1919 when it switched to support the nationalists. Nonetheless, Qommus Sergius commented that: 'Whether I am in Sudan or in Egypt, I am in my country, I will not stop telling the people to protest against you until we free our country from your [British] presence'.[152]

Sergius' nationalist fervour was most clearly apparent, however, during the 1919 revolution. Sergius himself described his participation in the events of 1919, and the significance of being a man of religion taking an active role in nationalist politics.[153] When the first demonstrations broke out in March 1919, Sergius was visiting a Coptic family near the Fajallah Church in Cairo. When he heard chanting in support of Sa'd Zaghlul he reports: 'I felt a strange shaking and my blood was boiling in my veins. I left the family and found my feet taking me straight to Al-Azhar!'[154]

Sergius became the first Coptic Christian priest in the history of Al-Azhar mosque to stand and preach at its pulpit.[155] During the riots that followed in March and April 1919 Muslims and Christians gathered in the 'Abbassid quarter of the mosque. This became the central meeting point for devising plans concerning the organisation of the anti-British demonstrations with Sergius commenting that: 'We were the leading instigators who would organise and participate and who were aware of the demonstration secrets.'[156] There was therefore a central clique during the rioting and Sergius was clearly part of this. News of Sergius's popularity and actions were significant, as they prompted 'Adli Yakan Pasha, the Interior Minister in Rushdi Pasha's government (April 1914–April 1919), to contact Sergius during the crisis in late March 1919. He urged Sergius to use his ability to enter Al-Azhar and his popularity to deliver a speech to the masses calling for calm and order. Sergius's one and a half hour speech drew clear lines of where Egyptian identity lay: Copts and Muslims, Sergius argued, were united against the British. Sergius delivered speeches for 59 consecutive days at Al-Azhar's pulpit between March and April 1919.[157] Indeed, it was as a result of such speeches that the epithets of 'Orator of Al-Azhar' and 'Orator of Egypt' were bestowed upon him by the 'father' of Egyptian nationalism, Zaghlul.[158]

In the Azhar the Cross and the Crescent were raised/ With thanks to Sergius's call

Long-live the country and its people and its king/ Long-live the shaykhs and the priests[159]

Sergius's contribution to the nationalist cause was not limited to speeches in mosques and churches, but extended to the squares of central Cairo, including Al-Opera and 'Abdin, where many of the demonstrators would gather, and where Sergius would make demagogic speeches invoking the natural spirit of Egypt using the image of Egypt as both a woman and motherland.[160] In one demonstration attended by Sergius, troops were dispersed, injuring some attendees and killing one British civilian.[161] Along with the demonstrations and nationalist speeches, Sergius also assisted in fundraising for the Wafd Party after Zaghlul returned to Cairo in 1919, and in the city of Rahmania in the governate of Sharqiyyah, Sergius collected LE 35,000 in just one evening of fundraising for the Wafd.[162]

The role played by Sergius as a promoter of national unity and political agitator during this period led to his removal from Cairo by the British authorities.[163] He was sent to Al-Qasr al-'Aini Camp, where he spent a few days and was later transferred to a camp in Palestine.[164] The questionable legality of British actions against Sergius revealed friction between the Patriarchate, Ahmad Fu'ad (1868–1936), later King Fu'ad I, and the British. The pope claimed that the British authority had no right to question a religious man, let alone arrest and detain him. In a letter from Kyrillos V to Ahmad Fu'ad, the patriarch urged action be taken on behalf of Sergius.[165] The pope claimed independent jurisdiction over the clergy in the following terms:

[A]ccording to the special and distinguishable rules that are applicable to men of religion we had the right to decide whether or not he exceeded the line [...] Perhaps the authorities are ignorant of these religious privileges or perhaps they are aware of them but are enforcing emergency laws, nonetheless this is no excuse for by passing the privileges available to us.[166]

In this letter, no mention is made of Sergius's nationalist position, nor that of the Church. Instead, Kyrillos V appeared to be defending Coptic rights as a traditional *millat* and the sanctity of their clergyman. In other words, he invoked the special status of the Copts as *Ahl al-Kitab*. Given the unavailability of sources from the higher echelons of the Coptic Church, only tentative conclusions can be drawn regarding their position vis-à-vis the events of 1919. However, clearly by invoking the Church's distinctive status within traditional society, Kyrillos V was distancing the Church, and himself, from the nationalist movement. This is confirmed by 'Ali Fahmi Muhammad, a journalist, who wrote a pamphlet in 1911 arguing that the Copts had a tendency to lend only nominal support to the nationalist movement out of fear, commenting that 'merely because they could not do otherwise else they would have been crushed into the thick of the night'.[167] These actions, and the rare letter from the patriarch to Fu'ad however, stand in complete contrast to the portrait of Kyrillos V presented by his official Coptic biographers, and historians who view him as a nationalist figure and supporter.[168]

Following these pressures, Sergius was later released, along with a number of Muslim shaykhs who had also been detained by the British for their anti-occupationist stance.[169] Despite these iconic nationalist actions, Sergius, 'the unknown soldier', has been neglected in both the nationalist literature as well as in Arabic and Western historiographies focussing on 1919.[170] This can partly be attributed to Sergius's direct opposition to and confrontation with the patriarch, which lead to his third excommunication in 1952. Indeed, in 1944 Sergius sarcastically commented, in response to a re-printed article on his actions in 1919, published in the *Akhir Sa'a* Magazine,[171] 'Why all this patriotism suddenly? [...] Everyone has forgotten these actions long ago. Is *Akhir Sa'a* pre-empting my obituary?!'[172] Despite this, the role of Segius's activities in 1919 provides evidence of actual Coptic grassroots nationalist activity, in contrast to official diplomatic efforts by Copts who had joined the ranks of the Wafd, serving to highlight one example of the various political, religious and social Coptic identities that emerged in the period following the British occupation of Egypt.

# CONSTITUTIONAL POLITICS
# AND POLITICAL ISLAM
# (1922–1946)

## Copts in Constitutional Politics

In 1922 the British unilaterally declared Egyptian independence; a constitution was drawn up in 1923 as well as the promulgation of a new electoral law for parliament.[1] In September 1923, Sa'd Zaghlul, the leader of the Wafd Party, was permitted to return from exile in the Seychelles and following elections led the first independent Egyptian cabinet (26 January–24 November 1924) into negotiations surrounding Britain's four provisos to independence.[2] These clauses included the security of imperial communications; the defence of Egypt from all foreign aggression; Sudan; and most importantly, the protection of foreign interests and minorities.[3]

The Wafd was the most important party in the interwar years, and had been established by Sa'd Zaghlul in 1919 in an attempt to secure Egyptian independence.[4] The party was identified with the national cause because it harnessed the spirit of the 1919 revolution.[5] Between 1919–1952 the party only held power for a total of seven years, yet, it was undoubtedly the dominant political force whenever free elections were held, and not marred or undermined by the King or the British. The history and centrality of the Wafd to the so called 'liberal experiment' in Egypt, embodied by secular constitutional politics, lasted until 1936;[6] thereafter, the Wafd went into decline, losing their main political drive.[7] The Wafd's history can therefore be split into three separate phases: 1914–1927, ending with the death of Zaghlul; 1927–36, with the second generation of Wafd politicians coming to power, the Anglo-

Egyptian Treaty of 1936 and the end of the liberal experiment; and finally, 1936–1952 which was epitomised by the decline of the Wafd and coincided with the rise in strength of radical nationalist parties including, *Misr al-Fatat* (Young Egypt) and *Al-Ikhwan al-Muslimin* (The Muslim Brotherhood). The three different phases of constitutional politics in Egypt leading up to the revolution of 1952 had an immense social, political and economic impact on the Copts.

Zaghlul and the first generation of Wafd leaders were a closely interrelated group of landed aristocrats and wealthy professionals. This included several Copts for example, Sinut Bey Hanna (1874–1930), who had travelled with Zaghlul to Paris in April 1919 as part of the Wafd delegation, had extensive lands in Asyut.[8] The first generation of Wafd politicians were committed to democratic forms of government based on parliamentary western models.[9] Egypt's first independent cabinet under the leadership of Zaghlul in 1924 had two Coptic ministers, Murqus Hanna Bey, Minister of Public Works and Wasif Boutros Ghali Bey, Minister of Foreign Affairs, as well as one Jew, whilst the head of the Chamber of Deputies was a Coptic barrister, Wisa Wasif (1873–1931).[10]

The Wafd's ability to secure massive popular support, particularly between 1919 and 1936, was due to their focus on ousting the British and not, as historian Janice Terry correctly observes, on radical societal changes: 'The British were viewed as the primary enemy [...] so long as the British remained the focal point of hostilities, the Wafd was not under heavy pressure to formulate a domestic policy'.[11] The Wafd's strong anti-colonial stance meant that the British were unwilling to negotiate with the party. Instead, the Wafd concentrated on promoting the image of national unity in the face of colonial occupation while neglecting the wider social, economic and political shifts occurring in Egypt during the interwar years. Historian Erlich Haggai has commented that the 1930s constituted a watershed, a reference to the shift in the operations of the parliamentary system.[12]

By the mid-1930s, the Egyptian political and social scene had altered radically from the immediate post-war years. To begin with, the promotion of state education under British occupation, was highly successful, and marked by an unprecedented growth in the number of professionals such as doctors, lawyers, civil servants and bureaucrats. While this highlighted the success of the modernisation policies, it also had the effect of increasing unemployment rates among the new graduates who were unable to be absorbed by the existing bureaucratic and state machines. The expansion of the civil service grew at a slower rate from the late-1920s which meant that only 10 per cent of new secondary school graduates could find employment in government departments.[13] The creation of this new class of urban educated unemployed intelligentsia, would manifest itself in an organised political fashion in opposition to the Wafd in the following years. These new political movements not only sought to fight British colonial occupation, but would also address the socio-economic problems, including, unemployment facing Egypt during the inter-war years and immediately after.

The emergence of new radical ideologies during the 1930s also constituted a watershed in the history of both the Wafd and parliamentary politics as a whole. Historians Israel Gershoni and James Jankowski have argued that Egypt increasingly turned towards Arabising the Egyptian character; indeed, they argue that even the Wafd Party acknowledged the idea of 'Arab brotherhood' as a euphemism against Western Imperialism.[14] Closely connected, is the argument maintained by historians such as Sayyid-Marsot and Vatikiotis, who argue that from the late-1920s Egypt increasingly turned towards Islamic rhetoric as evidence of the end of the liberal experiment. The emergence of *Islamiyyat*, or popular Islamic literature, saw Egyptian intellectuals like the writer and politician Muhammad Husayn Haykal (1889–1956) alter their original ideologically liberal stance, and shift to Islamic 'intellectualism', resulting in what has termed as a 'Crisis of Orientation'.[15] This has been taken as clear cut indication that these intellectuals had 'abandoned modernisation and Western orientation, turning their backs on rationalism, liberalism and humanism and dispensing of the principle of separation of religion and state.'[16] The growth of *Islamiyyat*, along with the emergence of popular nationalist radical parties who advocated militarism, social reform and national independence, such as *Misr al-Fatat* (Young Egypt) and the Muslim Brotherhood, also had a grave impact on the support and ability of the Wafd to operate. Instead, the party remained pre-occupied with its nationalist vision, ignoring social and economic problems prevalent in Egypt in the later inter-war years.

By the mid-1930s, even Britain, which had hitherto followed a position of 'neutrality', changed its focus. It has been argued that the British no longer viewed Egyptian political parties as split between the 'extremists', such as the Wafd who had advocated active struggle against the British, and 'moderates' like the Liberal Constitutionalists who had been nominated by the Palace and were against the adoption of anti-British policies.[17] Instead, the British were more concerned with the Italian and German ideological threat.[18] They increasingly viewed the Wafd and its leadership as the national authority to negotiate a multilateral treaty, ultimately resulting in the 1936 Anglo-Egyptian Agreement.[19]

The Agreement required Great Britain to withdraw all troops from Egypt, except those from the Suez Canal, as well as assist the Egyptian army in the case of war. This was met by a mixed reception as it had still failed to achieve the Wafd's objectives despite the prolonged negotiations. Selma Botman argues that for most of the population of Egypt, the Wafd's negotiation of the 1936 Agreement constituted no more than a long-standing symbol of colonialism, with little substantial change.[20] Disillusionment with the Wafd's failure was expressed by a mixture of anti-Wafd sentiment, at the conditions negotiated in the treaty, along with criticisms of the quality of leadership, which was viewed as drastically weakened and 'moderate' in comparison to the previous nationalist leadership of Zaghlul. The interwar years, which had been marked by unprecedented growth in the number of professionals, also had an impact on the Wafd's popularity. High unemployment and dissatisfaction with Wafd negotiations in 1936 led one British observer in 1937 to comment:

> This decline [in the Wafd's popularity] is now making itself seriously felt, and is adding to the general unpopularity of the present [Nahhas] Ministry which has spread [...] soon after the advent to power of the Wafd, the Ministry was kept fully occupied with treaty negotiations and routine work was allowed to slide and accumulate [...] after the signing of the

ratification of the treaty, the Ministry had more time to attend to the internal administrative matters[…] instead of tackling this problem, Nahhas Pasha and his colleagues have been fully occupied with countless interviews and social functions, with the result that the accumulation has not been dealt with but has increased in bulk.[21]

Fractures within the party also emerged, resulting in the creation of a splinter party, the Sa'dists, led by Ahmad Mahir and Muhammad al-Nuqrashi, who had been driven out of the Wafd in 1937. The growing unpopularity of the Wafd was made particularly clear during the Second World War, when the Wafd was immobile and the British were held responsible for both shortages in food and substantial price increases in the cost of living.[22] The growing popularity of radical political parties, the perceived Islamisation of Egyptian society, high unemployment and continued British occupation led to the weakening of the Wafd. These conditions also directly impacted the Copts, raising pertinent questions within political and communal discourse concerning the community's identification with the nationalist cause.

## *A Case for Proportional Representation*

The 1920s saw a rise in Coptic political participation. This was significantly influenced by the debate which arose surrounding the Declaration of Independence in 1922. In this declaration, the British claim to protection of foreign interests and minorities was of particular importance, substantially revealing British attitudes towards the Copts.[23] The protection of minorities was to be facilitated through the right of proportional representation in the Egyptian Parliament. In a draft constitution, early in 1922, Copts were guaranteed four out of seventeen seats in the Legislative Assembly. This was a far greater proportion than their numbers, and took its precedent from the 1917 assembly, in which Copts were given 23 per cent of seats in the Assembly despite numbering 8.06 per cent of the population.[24]

The Wafd Party, which had enjoyed grassroots popularity in the immediate period following 1919, rejected the stipulations in the Declaration of Independence as well as the suggestion that a system of proportional representation should be implemented in parliament. At the forefront of the Coptic proportional representation debate was Murqus Hanna Pasha (1872–1934), a Copt who served for an interim period as chairman of the Wafd Party. He argued that to give Copts proportional representation was the equivalent to approving the fourth clause of the 1922 Declaration of Independence which dealt with the protection of minorities: 'If a minority which includes Egyptians [i.e. Copts] is so protected by England they will be outside the elective pole, which is a monstrous idea'.[25]

On the other hand, the Liberal Constitutional Party, in opposition to the Wafd, were keen advocators of proportional representation. Their position was consolidated by the king, and serves as a useful example of Palace opinion and political views. The notion of proportional representation was exemplified by the prominent Liberal Constitutionalist and Copt Tawfiq Doss (1875–1950) in 1920.[26] In Doss's scheme, which was loosely based on the Belgian model, the Copts would be given 20 per cent of all seats in parliament, again a far greater percentage than their population numbers. Doss's aim was supported by the Jewish community, represented by Yusuf Qatttawi Pasha, by the Coptic Church and *Al-Watan* newspaper.[27] Despite Doss's plan however, the policy of proportional representation was rejected by the vast majority of Copts who had joined the ranks of the Wafd, indicating a visible split of the community in national politics.[28] This denunciation was based on two main principles. Firstly, in adopting proportional representation the Wafd argued that the nation was tacitly accepting that the Copts were a subsection within Egyptian society, thus effectively excluding them from the national struggle.[29]

Secondly, the Wafd correctly argued that proportional representation would divide the country along ethnic and religious lines. It was feared that a policy of proportional representation would deepen sectarian differences, fragmenting the process of nation building. Pitting the majority Muslim population against the minority Copt would have the implicit undertone that the majority epitomised the nationalist idea of an Egyptian independent nation, and thus the legitimate citizens. Conversely, the minority, if not absorbed in the majority, would form a special status as a national minority, effectively divorcing the Copts from popular sovereignty and re-establishing *millat* lines with the new label 'minority'.[30] Such minorities, however, would be unable to claim special privileges or status, since the logic of popular government, led by Zaghlul, required equality of all citizens. Labelled as a 'minority', the Copts would be a fixed and separate entity, effectively securing their *un*-equal status and inability to fully participate in the national discourse.

Salama Musa, a secular Coptic writer with no particular party affiliation, saw no advantage of forming a separate Coptic faction in parliament as it could still be outvoted by a Muslim majority.[31] Acknowledging these arguments, the Wafd therefore made attempts to secularise discussions and keep the agenda political rather than religious. Similarly, a number of Copts had gathered under the leadership of the prominent lawyer Salama Mikhail, to present a paper to the Constitutional Commission which assembled in 1923. In the paper, the special treatment of the Copts was rejected as incompatible with the sovereignty of the state, and that the Copts did not, nor should they have, different interests to their fellow countrymen.[32]

With Copts voting against the concept of a 'state within a state', the *millat* status of the Christian community had been defiantly given up, despite formally lasting well into the inter-war years;[33] Copts were to be integrated into the political forum alongside their Muslim counterparts. Elections without positive discrimination proved to be beneficial when in 1924, Copts gained more seats than they would have received had they adhered to a policy of proportional representation.[34] In the years following the 1924 election, Copts affiliated with the Wafd faired well. Zaghlul set a precedent whereby there were always two Coptic Ministers in the Cabinet, a policy which continued until 1944.

### The Diminishing Role of Copts in Public Employment

Government employment was regarded as a prized job due to its security, and was therefore sought by Muslims and Copts alike. As discussed, better-educated Copts had long occupied a greater proportion of the bureaucratic posts than their percentage of the population justified before 1919. However, the dual impact of a greater proportion of educated middle-class graduates vying for governmental bureaucratic jobs, as well as the emergence of a shift towards an increased Islamisation of intellectuals and popular opinion, had an impact on the role of Copts in the Civil Service and public employment in the interwar years.

The decrease of Coptic representation in certain branches of administration from the effective monopoly of the early years of the twentieth century under the British protectorate, to a figure more closely proportionate to the population-ratio of Copts to Muslims in Egypt, was an inevitable result of an extension of educational facilities implemented since the mid-nineteenth century by the state. Indeed, Hugh Jones, the British financial advisor, commented in 1936 that 'the Egyptian resolve to educate their own people [is] exhibited in the increase from 163 to 786 in the teaching staff since they got the first instalment of independence in 1922'.[35] Economist Adel Beshai has argued that, whilst the share of Copts in the Civil Service declined, the actual number of Copts occupying such positions increased due to expansion in the Civil Service following the Anglo-Egyptian Agreement in 1936.[36]

Between 1922 and 1945, the highest percentage of Copts were to be found in the Ministries of Public Works (29.4), Finance (44.2), and Postal and Telegraphic Services (48.1). In other ministries, Copts were employed in the departments where their traditional expertise was high; accountancy, record-keeping and translation. In these departments, Copts were employed as directors and assistant directors, while in other departments they were rarely promoted.[37] The British financial department based in Cairo argued that the process of removing Copts from positions of influence in government departments had steadily increased in the 1920s, reaching an apex by the mid-1930s. The financial department, which continued to oversee financial affairs on behalf of the British Residency, argued that the political complexion of the government made little difference to the situation of the Copts in government jobs.[38] Nonetheless, by 1933 it was the general opinion of the British Residency that nothing could be done 'to check this tendency in Egypt without a return to a modified form of *Cromerism* which would enable us to control the recruitment and promotion of government officials.'[39] This was a clear reference to Cromer's belief that the number and flow of graduates should be firmly controlled in order to cap unemployment and disorder and that Copts showed a particular aptitude in the fields of finance and accountancy.[40]

In the Finance department, the change had been effected gradually by the introduction of Muslims from other departments to replace retiring Englishmen or other foreign Christians, mainly Syrians and Jews. In 1922, there were 2392 foreign civil servants, but by the 1936 Anglo-Egyptian Treaty, this number had almost halved to 1226.[41] Muslims were selected in order to understudy the remaining Copts in high positions, with the result that, whereas most of the heads of sub-departments in the central administration had been non-Muslims during the 1910s and early 1920s, very few were left by the early 1930s.[42] In the Direct Taxes Department, traditionally the stronghold of the Copts, only one Copt remained at the headquarters in a position of any importance by 1932. [43]

In the Ministry of Agriculture, more drastic results in the administration were evident. By 1932 there was not a single Copt with any influence left in the Ministry, and in the junior ranks, Copts had little hope of progress. While the overall increase in educated graduates could perhaps be attributed to the diminishing role of Copts in the higher levels of the civil service, the Islamisation of Egyptian society was attributed to the unequal distribution of public funds, particularly in education.

## The Distribution of Public Funds

During the interwar years claims were made by the Anglican Church, with the support and backing of Coptic officials in the Egyptian Government, that Copts were being discriminated against as disproportionate amounts of public money were being granted in aid of Muslim religious endowments. Formally, the respective *waqf* of each religion solely maintained the religious works and funds that were allocated. However, Percy Loraine, the British High Commissioner to Egypt, claimed in 1933 that: [44]

> [T]he development of Al-Azhar; the Sharia tribunals; the growing attention paid to the upkeep of mosques; the decrease in the returns of the endowments owing to the

general fall in agricultural values; and King Fu'ad's policy of
giving importance to Islamic institutions, all contributed to
making it necessary for the government to provide increased
sums of money from the public treasury to supplement the
inadequate return of the *awqaf*.[45]

The specific example cited by Loraine was the construction of a
mosque in Alexandria, at the cost of LE 11,000 in 1933. Normally,
*waqf* revenue and other private donations met such expenses but, in
this case, the government's treasury had to provide funds for the
project. According to Loraine, who reflected an opinion which
seems to have been widespread within the British community, the
Egyptian government had not shown the same solicitude for
Christian religious institutions and works, especially as large sums
of public money, the product of the taxation of both Muslim and
Copts alike, was being used to fund such programs.[46]
    The British Residency increasingly regarded the Islamisation of
public funds as a real threat. Indeed, Hugh Jones of the financial
department attributed this shift in public spending to Galal Fahim
Bey, the Assistant under Secretary of State, who was supposedly
trying to capitalise on his Muslim status. Jones stated that:

> He visited the holy places in Hijaz this year, is regular in his
> attendance of 'zikrs', and announces his intention of making
> pilgrimage next year. That an able man like Galal should think
> all this worth doing, is confirmation in itself that Muslim
> fanaticism pays in government service.[47]

Whilst it is certainly true that the massive deficit in the public
treasury was increased by the upkeep and restoration of Muslim
religious heritage, there is also evidence that public money was used
for the benefit of the Coptic Church in the same manner. In 1932,
the Egyptian government provided LE 3,000 to help in the
payment of priests' salaries, which had fallen into arrears owing to
inadequate funds at the disposal of the *Majlis al-Milli*, combined
with maladministration of resources. In 1933, a further LE 2,000
was granted by the Egyptian government to the Coptic
patriarchate.[48] This policy was continued into the post-

revolutionary period when, on two occasions, President 'Abd al-Nasser supplied funds to the depleted Church finances to pay for salaries.[49]

More importantly, the question of public spending was closely related to the issue of religious education in government schools. Evidence suggests that Coptic officials in the Egyptian government in 1933 believed that, given a large proportion of taxes were paid by Christians, as tax was raised on income, it was unreasonable for the government to spend such extensive amounts on Islamic education.[50] With the expansion to universal education in 1933, religious instruction became an area of controversy. In June, Law 46 was introduced whereby elementary education was made compulsory for boys and girls between the ages of 7 and 12; religious education occupied more than one-third of the total teaching time. The law did not however, contain any provisions for the instruction in the Christian faith for Coptic children. This despite that fact that the constitution laid down the principle of equality between the two sections of the community, and guaranteed freedom of religion. This was in contrast to the previous policy upheld by the Egyptian government, which had prescribed the teaching of Christianity in various government schools since 1867.

Contestation over religious instructors also evolved around the issue of Muslim teachers. Mr Morrison, Secretary of the CMS, claimed that Copts believed that there should also be a reasonable proportion of Christian teachers in elementary schools; these same demands had been voiced before 1922.[51] In 1933 all primary school teachers were Muslim, as teachers generally provided instruction in all subjects which included Islam, a subject which a Copt was considered unable to teach. Any attempt to alter the system would have involved a large increase in the teaching staff, and consequently, additional expenditure for the government. The Copts felt that, even if the hours of religious instruction were reduced, the fact remained that their children were under the influence of Muslim teachers, the result being that, on average some 600 Copts converted to Islam every year, according to some reports.[52]

Alongside the question of time spent on religious instruction was the nature of the academic instruction itself, which was also subject to fierce debate. The Ministry of Education had included in its 1912 syllabus for primary and secondary schools the study of passages from the Quran through memorising them. Although this was never obligatory for Christian students, a new syllabus introduced in 1935 increased the numbers of passages required, thereby making them compulsory for Christian students due to examination requirements. The same year, the CMS, which was actively involved in educational campaigns, suggested to Minister of Education Hilal Bey, that Christian students should be offered alternative passages taken from Arabic literature. Whilst Morrison's anxiety appeared reasonable, Hilal argued that this innovation had been introduced for examination purposes. Previously, examiners had been able to distinguish Christians from Muslims on the basis of their knowledge of the Quran; the Prime Minister argued that the government had wished to abolish distinctions between Muslim and non-Muslim children. Moreover, Hilal emphasised that there was no better Arabic than that of the Quran, and therefore it was the best possible method for language instruction. Following intervention by the British Residency however, Hilal decided to revoke the new regulation and revert to the old system.[53] The clause in the 1922 Declaration, which maintained British influence for the protection of minorities, was cited as justification for intervention against the government on the Copts behalf.[54]

### Makram Obeid and the Black Book Scandal

The role of Makram Obeid, the most prominent Coptic politician in interwar politics is critical in charting the rise and fall of Coptic secular participation within the Wafd Party. Born in 1888, William Makram Obeid studied at the American Mission School in Asyut in Upper Egypt, completing his higher education at Oxford and returning to Egypt in 1906.[55] In 1919 Obeid was a key participant in the general strike of labourers and as a member of the Wafd delegation left for London alongside Zaghlul.[56] In December 1921 he was arrested and exiled to the Seychelles with the nationalist leader and upon his return in 1924, was elected Wafd deputy for the city of Qena in Upper Egypt.[57] Following the death of Zaghlul in 1927, Obeid became General Secretary of the Wafd.[58] Alongside Mustafa Nahhas, Obeid emerged as the second most prominent leader of the party. In Nahhas' cabinet of 1928, Obeid was appointed Minister of Communication later holding the position of Minister of Finance in 1930 and 1936. Obeid's most important role within the Wafd however, was his position as the primary negotiator of the 1936 Anglo-Egyptian Treaty. Obeid's centrality to the negotiations is highlighted in a lengthy speech which he delivered at the Fu'ad I University in November 1936.[59] Recounting the process, Obeid's party loyalty was apparent, repeatedly praising Nahhas, who was in the audience, and defending the Treaty which was strongly opposed by *Al-Watani* Party, among others, due to the vagueness of its terms.[60] Two main themes should be noted in relation to Obeid: first, Obeid's centrality in mobilising popular support for the Wafd Party through active recruitment among the youth and educated. Second, Obeid's demise from the Wafd in light of attitudes held by new radical nationalist parties towards the party secretary as both a Copt and the chief negotiator of the 1936 Agreement.

In the mid-1930s, Obeid's role within the Wafd was closely linked with enlisting popular support for the rank and file of the party. As the Wafd Secretary, Obeid led the party's youth activities on Fu'ad I University campus, and was at the vanguard of formulating Wafd policy towards the youth. Obeid had begun to focus his attention on Egyptian youth in 1934, with the establishment of a newspaper called *Nahdat al-Shabaab*, (Awakening of the Youth), which gained widespread popularity for its blunt use of nationalist rhetoric, an aspect of the Wafd Party that was robbed by the Treaty. Active student support for the Wafd decreased however with the growing prominence of a more organised national socialist militarism, in the form of *Jam'iyyat Misr al-Fatat*, or the Young Egypt Society, founded in 1933.[61] *Misr al-Fatat* broadly appealed to educated, unemployed youths, who increasingly felt disenfranchised by the Wafd's lack of formulated policy for broader social and political problems prevalent in Egypt, such as increasing food prices. Obeid's solution, in December 1935, was to create *Al-Fariq al-Shabaab*, an updated version of their ailing youth movement, which also became known as the 'Blue shirts'.[62]

[T]he Wafd realised that their influence over the students was no longer as it used to be […]the greenshirt group [*Misr al-Fatat*], which had grown very active amongst the students, were becoming more and more influential and it was said that they were being supplied with pistols and might start political murders, thus endangering any understanding with the British […] in the above circumstances, the Wafd considered that the only way open to them to regain their lost control over the students was to create their own group of youths. Thus the blueshirts came into being. Makram Obeid took a special interest in initiating the movement.[63]

**Figure 2** Makram Obeid Pasha.

According to British figures, membership of *Al-Fariq al-Shabaab* in Cairo alone in 1936 reached 2,000, although it was estimated that only 15 per cent were students; in contrast, historian Marius Deeb has argued that membership reached an estimated 5–6000.[64] This number seems grossly exaggerated however, given that the vast majority of support for its rival, *Misr al-Fatat*, or the blueshirts, was also largely urban based, and had no more than 700 members in Alexandria in the same year.[65] Despite Obeid's attempts however, *Al-Fariq al-Shabaab's* activities were in no way comparable to *Misr al-Fatat*, with many loyalist Wafd supporters on university campuses switching their support, particularly following the 1936 Anglo-Egyptian Treaty.[66] Indeed one Christian student, Luwis 'Awad, commented that in the academic year 1935/6 the overwhelming majority of those frustrated with the Wafd moved to the right, coming under the influence of other rivals of Western-modelled parliamentarianism:

> Many of our young leaders opted for different ways some for Young Egypt, some for the Muslim Brethren, others for one of the small parties and others for the oligarchic pashas [...] divided by different demagogic voices but united by one thing in common, that was the hatred for the Wafd and the burning desire to fight against it. [67]

Obeid's attempt to build more grassroots support serves as evidence of his integral role within the party, which was based on the secular beliefs of the Wafd, established since Zaghlul. Despite this, the popularity of *Misr al-Fatat*, which increasingly adopted Islamic colourings, grew. *Misr al-Fatat* modelled itself as the antithesis to the Wafd's leadership, especially as personal corruption charges against specific Wafd leaders increased. Obeid in particular, was increasingly attacked by the para-military organisation for being a Copt and playing such a prominent role in the Wafd. Accusations of Coptic dominance over the Wafd were voiced in one of *Misr al-Fatat* mouthpieces, *Al-Thaghr* magazine. When the Wafd were dismissed from office in 1938, *Misr al-Fatat* used stronger language, claiming that '90 per cent of the Wafd's supporters were Copts' and that it was a 'Coptic Clique'.[68] *Misr al-Fatat* blamed Wafdist ministers for the spread of crime in the country and the Copts as the 'supporters' of the Wafd were, as a result, indicated as the inciters of the violence: 'The Wafd and its Coptic element were well on their way to being excluded from any concept of national unity'.[69]

Aside from attacks from *Misr al-Fatat*, Obeid's integrity and reputation were also damaged during Nahhas' fourth term (February 1942–October 1944), which has been described as riddled with rivalry and corruption.[70] The affair was named after *Al-Kitab al-Aswad* (the Black Book) which Obeid wrote following a dispute with Wafd Party leader Nahhas, in May 1942. The failure of the 1936 Anglo-Egyptian Treaty had resulted in a weakening of the Party, including several splits by various previously-active party members. A rumour circulated that Nahhas had asked Obeid to resign from the Cabinet, which the latter had refused to do; Nahhas, as a result, dissolved his Cabinet and reformulated a new one which excluded Obeid.[71] In retaliation, Obeid wrote a long exposé of his former Wafdist colleagues, accusing them of corruption and abuse of power, this became known as the 'Black Book'. Nahhas in particular, was accused of serious violations of misconduct.[72] Nahhas was forced to answer parliamentary questions in April 1943 concerning the nature of the Black Book, and published a counter-response to Obeid in the form of a 'White Book'.

Historian and politician, Mustafa al-Feki, who has carried out extensive research on Makram Obeid, has described the Black Book as 'his cardinal political mistake after a long and active political life.'[73] Fellow politicians who agreed with Obeid in principle, disagreed with the impulsive manner in which he carried out his response.[74] Muhammad Husayn Haykal, the leader of the Constitutional Liberal Party, however, argued that Obeid only erred in publishing such a long list of names in the Black Book.[75] Obeid's book ultimately resulted in both his expulsion from parliament and imprisonment until October 1944, when Nahhas' government were forced out of office and Obeid was appointed Minister of Finance in Ahmad Mahir's new cabinet (October 1944–February 1945).

Al-Feki argues that the Black Book affair meant that Obeid 'failed to fulfil his dream of becoming a Coptic Prime Minister of Egypt. His split from the Wafd relegated him to second place.'[76] Whilst Obeid never claimed to be representing the 'Coptic voice' in parliament, his departure did intensify discussions concerning the composition of the Wafd. Unlike Prime Minister Boutros Ghali, who was considered a leader of the Coptic community due to his connections in the *Majlis al-Milli*, Obeid had deliberately refrained from playing the role of sectarian leader. This was partly due to the fact that Obeid had never really participated in Coptic organisational and Church disputes. Al-Feki argues that many Copts viewed Obeid as an uninterested spectator in Coptic affairs, and considered him merely as an ambitious Copt in Egyptian politics. At the same time, however, Obeid always believed that the Wafd and Nahhas had somehow considered him to be the representative of the Coptic community within the Wafd: 'Aware of this view, Ebeid [sic.] never gave the chance to any other Copt politician to hold a distinguished place in the Wafd.'[77] Historian Tariq al-Bishri argues that Obeid's split form the Wafd did not alter Coptic support for the party.[78] Despite this however, it should be noted that given Obeid represented the only significant Coptic player in the Wafd, (and indeed Egyptian politics), his departure marked the loss of a highly competent and charismatic Coptic representative in both the nationalist movement and constitutional politics.

## The Threat of Political Islam

Coptic discussions surrounding discrimination in public employment and the distribution of public funds, along with the demise of visible Coptic political participation in constitutional politics in the interwar years, was fuelled by a debate concerning the rise in Islamism. This was in part influenced by the end of the so called 'liberal experiment', and the perceived shift towards an increasingly Islamic outlook. However, tense Coptic-Muslim relations were not a new phenomenon as the years 1908–1911 were characterised by spouts of violence, claims of discrimination and large-scale wars of words between various Coptic and Muslim newspapers. The 1930s and 1940s also saw similar intensified debates taking place largely in the Coptic press. The press served as a forum for debating issues which pre-occupied the educated middle-classes, particularly the issues of political and social reform, cultural orientation and communal identity.[79] These debates revolved around discrimination, placing particular emphasis on the rise of Islamic extremism, along with assertions that non-Wafdist governments lent their tacit support to organisations which followed Islamic agendas. This, along with the continued anti-colonial struggle and increased campaign for independence against the British, led to a series of attacks against Western and Christian targets following the failure of the Wafd Party and the 1936 negotiations.[80]

In 1928, the foundation of *Al-Ikhwan al-Muslimin*, (the Muslim Brotherhood), in Ismailiyya, near Suez, led by Hassan al-Banna, had a profound impact on religious and national politics in Egypt.[81] Al-Banna, who was initially concerned with the defection of the educated youth from the Islamic way of life, led the early movement with an eye to reassert core Islamic values through the propagation of *Al-Da'wa* (the message).[82] It was not until 1934 that the society entered the political arena.[83] The aim of the Muslim Brotherhood, like many lay and religious Coptic reformers, was to promote a *nahda*, which would remedy all aspects of Egyptian life, including political, economic and social ills. Robert Landen has argued that in many respects, the organisation offered a blueprint 'for social and economic reorganisation according to commonly understood Muslim principles, and worked as a vehicle of resistance to foreign control.[84] Indeed, the Muslim Brotherhood played an active role in providing for the material and economic needs of the urban poor which also increased their popular base. Throughout the 1930s, the Muslim Brotherhood also offered an attractive religious alternative to the ailing constitutional politics practised by the Wafd and traditional political parties. In 1936, Al-Banna wrote a pamphlet entitled *Nahw al-nur* (*Towards the Light*) in which he expressed the practical means of an Islamic revivalist society which encompassed a socialist political ideology.[85] Al-Banna's *Nahw al-nur* provides clear evidence of an attempt to modernise within an Islamic framework, and thus serves to challenge those historians who viewed the emergence of *Islamiyyat* and the shift from liberal constitutional politics pre-1936 as an abandonment of modernisation. Indeed, in the fields of social and everyday political life, Al-Banna clearly stated in *Nahw al-nur* that he wished to promote institutional progress and educational programs for girls, albeit within an Islamic framework. [86] Similarly, Al-Banna promoted reform of the law, so long as it was entirely in accordance with Islamic legal practice.[87] By the late-1940s, the popular support base for the Muslim Brotherhood numbered over two million members.[88] It was under these conditions that the Coptic press increasingly sought to defend their interests, which they believed were being eroded.

## Salama Musa and the Coptic Press

The most prominent Coptic newspaper in the period 1919 to 1952 was *Misr*, founded in 1895 by Tadrus Shenouda Manqabadi (1857–1932), an Orthodox Copt. He had initially presented a Coptic reformist view in opposition to the Coptic-owned *Al-Watan* (founded in 1877), and was a staunch supporter of the British occupation. *Misr* changed its position during the First World War converting to the nationalist cause and becoming a lucid organ and advocate for the Wafd. After Obeid's departure from the party in 1944, the paper's support for the Wafd waned and increasingly becoming communal in character, sponsoring prominent Coptic journalists including Salama Musa to publish regular editorials. Musa, who had in his youth experimented with socialism, had increasingly by the mid-1930s adopted a stronger secular tone and became one of Egypt's most iconoclastic writers.[89] A discussion on Musa is significant as it highlights how he represented the opinion of educated Copts who, had been alienated by the demise of the Wafd as well as the growing prominence of more radical nationalist parties like *Misr al-Fatat* and the Muslim Brotherhood. While fully supporting Egyptian independence, Musa developed an aversion to the idea of a nation bound together on religious terms or ideology.[90] He argued that religion practiced through the state, was imperialistic and adverse to the social progression of Egyptian society, just as British policy was detrimental to its empire.[91] For Musa, there was therefore a clear connection between independence based on secular beliefs, and the progression and modernisation of Egypt which was being stunted by what he saw as religious fanaticism.

In regular editorials appearing in *Misr* throughout the 1940s, Musa argued that he could see the fanaticism of the Muslim

Brotherhood emerging and spreading in organisations throughout Egypt. In particular, Musa paid close attention to the judicial system. He argued that judges of the Sharia Courts were being influenced by calls of the Brotherhood that the 'sons of the Nile Valley should have one religion'.[92] Musa pointed to a number of incidents including one in which a Sharia Court pronounced a verdict that it was not permissible to hold any *waqf* property attached to the churches.[93] In Musa's opinion, this highlighted the fact that the Coptic Church and community were under serious threat, and would be unable to survive with a radicalised Sharia Court in operation. In another incident, a Sharia Court pronounced a verdict that a Christian wife should join her divorced husband who had embraced Islam.[94] Musa vehemently and articulately argued that the suppression of the Sharia Courts was necessary on the belief that they could otherwise tamper with cases concerning Christian civil liberties.[95] It was also on this basis, that it was necessary for the Copts to ask for an amendment to the Constitution which would separate religion from the state. The Copts, Musa argued, could not feel assured regarding the survival of their religious and other institutions so long as the Sharia Courts cancelled decrees of the Coptic *Majlis al-Milli*, and considered *waqf* dedicated to the churches as unlawful.[96] In April 1946, *Misr* became the first newspaper to put a full-page advert calling for the equality of all citizens in Egypt by amending the 1935 Egyptian constitution. This would be based on a restoration of 1923 constitution, while also disbanding all religious parties.[97]

Aside from the perceived Islamic fanaticism that Musa saw within the Sharia Courts, the Muslim Brotherhood were also considered by *Misr* to be the predominant instigators in cases of discrimination against Copts. In sensationalist articles, the authorities were painted as having leant their tacit support to the promotion of an Islamic agenda. The Coptic lawyer 'Azmi Mansour, for example, wrote in *Misr* that the policy of the government under Nuqrashi Pasha (February 1945–February 1946) and Ismail Sidqi Pasha (February 1946–December 1946), both non-Wafdist anti-liberal governments following the fall of Obeid, was to encourage various Muslim associations such as the Muslim Brotherhood, *Shabaab Muhammad* and *Misr al-Fatat* to set out against the Copts. While Mansour did not provide any evidence, he did argue that the Copts were being persecuted with the knowledge of the government. A series of other incidents were reported in un-authored articles in the days that followed in *Misr*.[98] In the village of Drao, in Upper Egypt, *Misr* reported that the Muslim Brotherhood had attacked Coptic property and cattle in the presence of the *ghaffir* and shaykh of the village who, in turn, did nothing to prevent this.[99] In another case, Coptic notables were killed near the police station in Luxor following a riot between Muslim Brotherhood sympathisers and Copts. The Brotherhood were reported to have called for the Copts to choose between Islam, the sword or the *Jizya* tax.[100] Discrimination against the Copts was said to be so rife that while a Coptic Church was closed in the village of Sheshta in the Gharbiyya province for preaching religious sermons too loudly, the Muslim Brotherhood were permitted to drive rented cars with loudspeakers around Alexandria calling for one religion.[101] It is difficult to verify these specific cases, particularly as there is little evidence to corroborate the claims. Nonetheless, the fact that such a widely read and popular newspaper such as *Misr* should take such a hard-line stance, particularly given its previous nationalist credentials, suggests an element of legitimacy.

Salama Musa also highlighted his own dissatisfaction towards Isma'il Sidqi's second ministry (February–December 1946) which had conceded to the demand of the Muslim Brotherhood over the issue of the creation of a daily newspaper. Musa argued that the government had not paid the same solicitude towards the demands of the Copts on the issue of newspapers.[102] Musa had applied for a licence to create a Coptic journal in 1929 but was obstructed by the state. The newspaper *Al-Misri* was finally given permission to publish in 1930, only to close a year later.[103] Musa went on to attack the Brotherhood for what he regarded as their reactionary attitude towards the Copts, stating that he was in favour of the attitude that had in the past been adopted by Nahhas' Wafd government (February 1942–October 1944), when they closed the offices of the Brotherhood.[104] Nahhas had considered Muslim Brotherhood fanaticism as counteractive and would demolish national unity.[105]

The British Residency also commented on that fact that in the late-1940s it was common for the 'leftists', which included Musa and *Misr*, to have expressed their apprehension that the palace and the Sirri government (September 1949–July 1950) were preparing a fascist regime in order to fight the Wafd with the help of the Muslim Brotherhood.[106] Some modern Coptic historians, such as Sami Zaki, have argued that an alliance existed between King Farouk and the Muslim Brotherhood.[107] Facilitated through Shaykh Al-Azhar, Mustafa al-Maraghi (1935–1945), Zaki argues that both the Brotherhood and the King had common enemies; the Wafd and the Copts. The Wafd, he argues, were accused of bias and Coptic fanaticism by the Brotherhood, a reference to the role played by Makram Obeid. Similarly, Zaki argues that the palace was displeased with the Wafd due to the party's aversion to the King's role, particularly during the Anglo-Egyptian Treaty negotiations. The Wafd also refused to coalesce in religion and politics. The most vivid example of this was during the coronation of King Farouk in April 1936 when the Wafd sought to forestall religious ceremonies in state affairs, and boycotted the coronation; in retaliation, a delegation of the Brotherhood insisted on attending.[108] There is some evidence that the Muslim Brotherhood fostered closer relations with the King in 1936; however, by the time of Al-Banna's assassination in 1949, the Ikhwan had turned against the monarchy.[109]

While journalists and guest writers in *Misr* directly accused the government of sponsoring an Islamist approach against the Copts and standing idly by as cases of discrimination and violence perpetrated by the Muslim Brotherhood occurred, the government's Press Office retaliated against the barrage of articles coming from the paper during the mid-1940s. A decree was issued in 1946 stating that there would be no government advertisements placed in *Misr*. The Press Office argued that the editors had, through their commentary, caused incitement of sectarian and religious differences without obtaining lead for justice or consulting with the government for their consideration.[110] The assertion was that through drawing attention to the worsening situation and pursuing a discussion, *Misr* was hindering the image of national unity.

By mid-1946, more pro-active calls were made by *Misr* to curb the Brotherhood's activities using retaliatory and defensive mechanisms: this call highlighted the strengthening shift in urban educated middle-class attitudes from the earlier demands made by Musa, and calls were made for the Coptic Community to take direct action: 'cowardice and fear will no longer do any good [...] we should be ready for any sacrifice as did our ancestors in the past'.[111] This was a clear reference to the popular Coptic discourse that the community was in a constant state of persecution, a process which could be dated back to the Era of Martyrs in 284 AD. Demands for being pro-active included a call by Musa to invite Copts to set up a rival Christian organisation and take-up arms. The society which would be called the Coptic Brethren, would have a youth section named Jesus's Youths and would be in direct contrast to *Jami'yyat Shabaab Sayidina Muhammad* (The Society of Our Master Muhammad), more commonly known as *Shabaab Muhammad*, created in 1939–40.[112] While the sincerity of Musa's call can be questioned, particularly given his strong anti-religious/clerical nature, the call nonetheless highlighted two points; firstly, that in the face of a perceived threat Musa, as a secular Copt increasingly sought to identify himself within the framework of the religious community. Secondly, the activities of *Shabaab Muhammad* and the Muslim Brotherhood highlighted the vacuum that had be left by the Wafd, and galvanised a communal-led response to a perceived threat. Indeed, this was not the first call to create a Christian based youth society with paramilitary connotations. The 'Soldiers of the Christian Army' were a group of young men formed in Upper Egypt, who took part in social, religious and political activities.[113] They stood in direct contrast to a number of Muslim Youth Movements with political connotations, which also found prevalence in the interwar period.[114] The Society of the Christian Army believed that Coptic spiritual weakness was responsible for the inability of the community to defend itself against the Muslim Brotherhood.[115] The role played by an educated Coptic paramilitary youth organisation was to have an immense impact on Coptic communal mobilisation later in the post-revolutionary period.

## Ode to the 'Fezzed Shaykh'

In contrast to Musa's calls for government intervention by changing the constitution and promoting equality of citizenship through the secularisation of politics, Qommus Sergius took a more populist line of action from early on to highlight what he perceived to be the Islamic threat. This was articulated in his religious periodical *Al-Manarah al-Murqusiyyah*, which was founded by Sergius in 1928 after he had become renown for his nationalist activities in 1919.[116] *Al-Manarah* was an influential advocate for Church reform; popular with Muslims and Copts alike in its early days, Sergius's journal expressed views with little tact or journalistic etiquette, and was the bane of the patriarchate until Bishop Macarius's victory as pope in 1944. In 1935, the magazine changed its name to *Al-Manarah al-Misriyyah*, reflecting its greater focus on Egyptian-wide issues; nonetheless, it continued to express indiscreet criticisms of the Church, and later the state until its suspension through military order in 1953.

Throughout the 1940s, a series of articles on the Muslim Brotherhood and their actions became regular features in *Al-Manarah*. Initially, Sergius had shared Musa's view of constitutionalism. In 1944 he had made a personal request to Prime Minister Ahmad Mahir Pasha (October 1944–Februrary 1945) for the implementation of a constitution which would 'literally and spiritually equalise between all Egyptians in their rights and duties and provide food and shelter for all people'. Qommus Sergius also requested that Prime Minister Mahir make a statement to 'certain Muslim sectors to calm them and lessen their anger towards Christians'.[117]

By 1947 however, Hassan al-Banna, the spiritual guide of the Brotherhood, had become the prime target of Sergius's populist editorials. In contrast to Musa, who only alluded to Al-Banna as the head of the Muslim Brotherhood, Sergius remained intent on attacking the organisation, exploiting Al-Banna's iconic image as the leader of the Brotherhood. Sergius used the figure of Al-Banna in his editorials to epitomise all the ills of the organisation, while simultaneously creating a puppet caricature figure of the spiritual guide for ridicule. In May 1947, Sergius wrote a series of articles that ran for several months entitled: 'Death is better than a state under Hassan al-Banna', in which Al-Banna was portrayed as a donkey.[118] Sergius, who had been the voice of reason, co-operation and religious unity in 1919, became increasingly insulting towards the Islamic values that were associated or promoted by the Muslim Brotherhood's guide.[119]

In late 1947, Sergius accused Al-Banna and the Muslim Brotherhood's actions of leading towards 'nation breaking': Al-Banna was a tool manipulated by the British easing their prolonged occupation, and was as a result a 'clown for rent'.[120] Sergius's criticisms were clearly an allusion to the ties between King Farouk and the Brotherhood. It is apparent that Sergius did not associate Al-Banna and the Muslim Brotherhood with a progressive anti-colonial nationalist force, and used *Al-Manarah* to adamantly air his opinion. Historian Ami Ayalon has argued that, during the inter-war years and immediately after, the use of the press was marked by its vivid linguistic imagery: contemporary journalists recalled arguments which 'often involved mothers, wives and sisters. These are not newspapers, these are hagglers' stalls'.[121] This was certainly the case throughout the late-1940s, and provides evidence of the way in which a specific class of Copts, having been marginalised from the new wave of radical ideologies, were able to vent their expressions. This process would continue in Egypt even after the revolution.[122]

*Al-Manarah* also became the organ of a series of inflammatory poems written by Nathan Tadrus Obeid focussing on the Muslim Brotherhood in Egypt. The poem below, entitled 'Oh Fezzed Shaykh: A Poem on Good Construction', is a clear indication of the ways in which the written word, and in this case poetry, was used as a subversive means to criticise popular authorities. The poem which was published without Arabic diacritics, is carefully constructed so that many of the stanzas have a dual meanings depending on how one reads or pronounces the text. For example 'A Poem on Good Construction', or *Husn al-Bina*, if read as an adjectival-noun, would ironically be a play on Hassan al-Banna's name.[123]

# يا أيها الشيخ المطربش !

يا أيهــا الشـيـخ المطربش    أفتنا
بعد التعوذ من هوى الشـيطان
واسرد أحاديـث الائمــة   صادقاً
واشرح فقد غمضت على الاذهان
هل فى كتابك    سورة او آية
تدعو إلى التقتـيل والطغيان
هل فى الحديث عن البخارى (مرشداً)
ينحط بالانسـان    للحيوان
الله   بالمعــروف   دومـاً   آمـر
لكنه  ناه   عن  النكران
فلاى دين    تنتمى يا ناشــراً
وباء الهلاك وطاوى الاحسـان
وتقول فى طول  البلاد  وعرضهـا
بيدى سأرفع راية القرآن
وتبيح فى هـذا  السـبيل  طرائقاً
شـتى من التدمير والعـدوان
وتروح تنفث من سمومك ناقماً
فتزيد من وحشية ( الاخوان )
سمومك بنــاء  وإنك معـسـول
للهـدم لكـن لست للبنيان
لا تحسبن الله عنك بغافل
فالظالمون مصيرهم لهوان
ناثان تاوضروس عبيد

Figure 3  'Oh Fezzed Shaykh' (Arabic).

Oh Fezzed Shaykh!

Oh Fezzed Shaykh give us fatwas/After seeking protection from the devil

Narrate the Imam's teachings truthfully/And explain, for your (teachings) have closed people's minds

Is there in your book a Surah or Verse/Advocating killing and oppression?

Is there in Bukhari (as a guide)/The degradation of humans to animals

God has always demanded us to do good deeds/But of bad ones he never sanctions

So to what religion do you belong as you spread/Plague of destruction and fold away goodness

And you say throughout the land/With my hand I shall raise the banner of the Quran

And you permit in achieving this aim/All varieties of destruction and enmity

And you spew your venom/Augmenting the brutality of the "brotherhood"

Your highness is a constructor but you are a mallet/For destruction and not building

And do not think that God is unaware of your [deeds]/For the oppressors fate is misery

Nathan Tadrus Obeid

Poem on Good Construction

**Figure 4** Hassan al-Banna.

The title of Obeid's poem is derogatory and critical of Al-Banna and the Brotherhood in several ways. Firstly, by naming the poem after the 'Fezzed Shaykh', it becomes abundantly clear that Obeid is referring to the prominent iconic figure of Al-Banna, dressed in a suit and fez. Al-Banna did not conform to the traditional dress code of an Islamic shaykh with a *'ama* and turban, and yet commanded the authority of the Brotherhood and supposed path of Islamic religious values and politics. The fez, signified not only a piece of attire, but was also closely associated with the *effendiyya*. This class in the nineteenth century had attended professional schools as part of Muhammad 'Ali's modernisation program. By the twentieth century, and particularly in the 1930s and 1940s, the *effendiyya* came to represent 'a new urban society, new social institutions, and new ways of life. The effendi was now an engineer, a lawyer, a doctor, but also a journalist and, increasingly, a political activist'.[124] In this respect, the fez signified modern habits and practices. Lucie Ryzova has argued, 'The culture of "being modern" functions here as a value judgment and as a gatekeeper to social status and mobility'. [125] Yet, in highlighting Al-Banna's attire Obeid had aimed to mock the guide. The tone of the poem is one of sarcasm; Al-Banna may have worn a fez but he failed to represent the 'emerging secular elite [...] known as the *mutarbishun*, "tarbush-wearers", who would eventually clash with the *mu'ammamun*, the "turban-wearers"'.[126] Al-Banna was a false effendi.

Similarly, the word *mutarbish*, interpreted as a passive participle, or the one wearing the fez, can also be taken to mean the one who has lost his mind or is confused, taken from the Arabic *derwish/muderwish*. Obeid had therefore portrayed Al-Banna not only as a fake Shaykh in a fez, but also one who has lost his mind.

In the second stanza, 'Narrate the Imam's teachings truthfully/ And explain for your (teachings) have closed people's minds', Obied suggests that the meanings and teachings of the true Imams have escaped people, including Al-Banna, who did not or could not understand and has, as a result, relayed them incorrectly. Thus, not only is Al-Banna depicted as an illegitimate religious scholar, but also a misinformed guide. Similarly, with the final stanza of the poem there is a notion that Al-Banna's actions will be held accountable by God given he has not acted in correct accordance with the teachings of Islam. There is thus an implicit acknowledgement that there are commonalities between Islam and Christianity which follows the rules as set by God. What Obeid portrays throughout the poem is a legitimate Islamic practice, accepted within the Christian/Coptic communal discourse, from which Al-Banna and his followers had strayed.

While the poem questioned the 'Islamic-ness' of Al-Banna and the Brotherhood, it also questioned his actions with regard to the nationalist discourse. The play on words concerning 'construction' can be interpreted as the creation, or building of a nation, comprised of Muslims and Christians, in which Al-Banna is not portrayed as a builder *Banna*, but rather as a sledgehammer or 'mallet' of destruction. This falls in line with Ryzova's discussion on effendiyya, who in the interwar years emerged in moments of crisis as the 'defenders of Egypt's independence and speakers for the nation'.[127] Here, the false effendi and illegitimate Shaykh is viewed as an obstruction to independence and a tool for prolonged occupation by the British.

Poems, articles and commentaries against Al-Banna by Coptic owned newspapers and magazines led to the Brotherhood's spiritual guide issuing a formal personal complaint to Pope Yusab II (1946–1956) in 1946.[128] In an open letter, Al-Banna accused the Church of publishing false allegations against the Brotherhood, highlighting the extent to which Coptic remonstrations, pleas and activities were an effective means of demonstration. Whilst *Misr* had a largely Coptic readership, and *Al-Manarah* an almost exclusive one, their actions serve as useful tools of understanding the ways in which various actors within the Coptic community were able to articulate their grievances in light of perceived marginalisation by the state. The fact that Al-Banna had felt it was necessary to make a formal complaint to the patriarch reveals the extent to which Sergius and Musa warranted Coptic opinion, as well as Al-Banna's perception of hierarchy and where authority in the Coptic community lay.[129] Both Musa and Sergius therefore highlight the ways in which Copts articulated and defended the community against threats of discrimination and the Islamisation of the Egyptian state on the part of the Muslim Brotherhood, challenging traditional perceptions of a 'meek' and 'beleaguered' minority.

# PART II

# *INTRA*-COMMUNAL RELATIONS: THE COPTIC COMMUNITY FROM WITHIN (1882–1954)

# 4

# BENEVOLENCE AND PHILANTHROPY (1882–1945)

The emergence of benevolent societies in the late nineteenth century contributed to a wider debate closely linked to the dispute regarding the creation of the *Majlis al-Milli*, the administration of *waqf* (religious endowments), and the role played by lay and ecclesiastical members in Coptic social and political affairs. The emergence of a politically active elite who promoted the *Majlis al-Milli* from 1874, created a new set of circumstances which transformed the ways in which Coptic lay notability, including landowners, viewed their role within the community. The most important manifestation of this trend was the establishment of charitable, benevolent and philanthropic societies which cared for the educational, social and material welfare of the Copts, thus providing a source of support as an alternative to both the Egyptian state and Church.[1] By the early twentieth century these societies had developed broader agendas which not only encompassed the pastoral care of the community but also embodied increasingly nationalist aims and ideologies.

## Coptic Benevolent and Philanthropic Societies (1880s–1940s)

The late nineteenth century saw the creation of philanthropic groups throughout Egypt which established orphanages, educational and medical facilities. The majority of activities were placed within a religious framework which cared for the poor, but was also closely tied with the emergence of nationalism and the spread of capitalism by the early twentieth century.[2] Elite Egyptians sought to fill the gap that had been left by state and communal failures, and in doing so laid claim to the role as the vanguard of national obligation.[3] Traditionally Christians and Jews in the Middle East provided for their own needy within their respective *millat*. The centralisation of government which had begun under Muhammad 'Ali had resulted in the creation of the *Dabtiyya*, the central police force, which oversaw the management of poorhouses and meant that there was increasing interaction between different religious communities who found themselves in the poorhouses. Thus, in the late nineteenth century there is evidence that some Christians and Jews were recipients of state sponsored charity.[4] For example, the Armenian Ibrahim al-Fayun was once resident in the *Takiyyat* Tulun, a poor house in the district of Ibn al-Tulun in old Cairo. Similarly, lists of shelter residents for 1859–1861 include at least one Copt, Girgis 'Abdul-Masih.[5] However, the state only provided in part for non-Muslim religious communities, and as historian Mark Cohen argues, in the case of the Jewish community, they were expected to provide and support Jewish newcomers to Egypt from other regions within the Ottoman Empire.[6]

Non-state sponsored charity was also increasingly promoted during the late twentieth century. This linked charity with social and educational obligation on the part of the respective religious communities. Shaykh Muhammad 'Abduh (1849–1905), a theologian, reformer, political activist and later Grand Mufti of Egypt, had long been a proponent of encouraging philanthropic and educational facilities within not only the Muslim community but also the Coptic one.[7] In 1881 he wrote a series of newspaper articles about the growing problem of families loosing their children to other faiths because of the emergence of foreign schools in Egypt, a clear reference to missionaries.[8] Indeed he warmly welcomed the participation of Copts in his weekly study circles. An example of one of his disciples was the Coptic poet Francis al-'Itr, (1882–1974) who was the son of a well-known Coptic priest and a regular participant in the study circles of 1902.[9] 'Abdu sought to provide poor Muslim children, families and orphans with spiritual and moral guidance.[10] There is therefore evidence of cross-communal solidarity at an elite level concerning religious and social obligations, charity and education of the poor.

Similarly, in order to understand the emergence of social networks of support such as benevolent and philanthropic societies, it is necessary to understand which members of society were targeted or intended to be the recipient of such support. Definitions of the poor were often flexible enough to allow benefactors to decide how inclusive or exclusive they wished to be.[11] A 'poor person' could be defined as someone in a state of need, although such a definition is invalid until the concept of 'need' itself is defined; similarly, a 'poor person' could be defined as someone who did not possess a specific amount of wealth in surplus of what was needed in order to support and protect the life of their dependants.[12] With the proliferation of benevolent societies and missionary activity, the understanding of who came under the category of 'poor' developed. For example, the concept of 'deserving poor' as opposed to those who were un-deserving, the able-bodied, or those who had taken up 'voluntary poverty', such as the ascetic Sufis or Monks, became a way to define entitlement and obligation of charity.[13] The diversification and broadening of the definition of poor in the late nineteenth century came to benefit individuals who, for example, fulfilled various religious functions such as a shaykh.[14] This tradition had developed in Islamic theory; the justification being that in the case of *fuqaha*, poverty was inherent in the group since the occupation of knowledge, or *'ilm*, prevented them from earning.[15] This was not the case in the Coptic Church, priests were not regarded as part of the poor, although there is evidence that in Jaffa, Palestine, Muslim *qadis* permitted Christian *waqf* to benefit Christian priests and monks, thus providing them with a salary.[16] According to Miriam Hoexter, the case of Jaffa provides evidence that the *qadi* drew a parallel between the priests/monks and various *'ulama'* who came to be regarded as 'poor' by definition.[17] Several other categories of people also benefited from the emergence of benevolent and philanthropic societies.

### The Great Coptic Benevolent Society (1881–1921)

The first Coptic charitable society was the Great Coptic Benevolent Society, *Al-Jam'iyyah al-Qibtiyyah al-Khayriyyah al-Kubra*. Its creation was based on the vision of Kyrillos V who supported the poorest segments of the Coptic population of Cairo during his early visits in the 1840s.[18] The patriarch had in 1875 begun to pay a monthly stipend of LE 90 into a fund for the care of the Coptic community; the money was collected from the congregation of the Coptic Cathedral and a special account for the poor was kept at the Patriarchate. However, the monthly sum did not prove to be sufficient to meet the needs of the poor. This resulted in the interference of Copt, later Prime Minister, Boutros Ghali Pasha, who decided to set up a special society for this purpose. The social principles which underscored the activities of the society were not strictly religious but humanitarian based on the ideas of *insaniyyah*, or humanitarianism.

At a meeting held in January 1881 in the house of a Coptic notable of Cairo, Youssef Effendi Muftah, it was decided to form the Coptic Endeavour Benevolent Society, which later changed its name to the Great Coptic Benevolent Society in 1908.[19] Many laymen attended as did a number of influential Muslim *'ulama'* including Shaykh Muhammad 'Abduh. The aims of the society following its inception was varied in character and included to help the poor; to find work for those who were in need and were able to work on the condition that they should be persons of good character; to defray the costs of burying the poor; to bring up and educate poor orphans; to open schools in Cairo and its suburbs; and to serve other benevolent purposes for the welfare of the Coptic community in particular and Egyptians in general.[20]

The aims and activities therefore served to highlight several aspects of the society. Firstly, the society provided financial and charitable assistance. This was funded in part through religious endowments, yearly membership dues and fundraising parties. The benefits of which, helped finance individual projects, building on the religious principle of a community's obligation towards the needy. The society therefore firmly re-enforced bonds between Copts, first and foremost, whilst also ensuring assistance to those in need.[21] Secondly, the cross confessional nature of the organisation continued, having been influenced by its early association with the Muslim Charitable Society of Alexandria and Muhammad 'Abduh. For example, in 1921 there were 8,892 people who received assistance from the Coptic Benevolent Society; 4,937 were Copts, 3,939 were Muslim, and 16 were foreigners listed as *khawaja*.[22] Thirdly, the philanthropic and educational rubric of the organisation, which was in line with modernisation policies implemented since the nineteenth century by both the Church and state, enabled this, amongst other later societies, to emerge as vehicles for the modernisation of the community.

## Religious-Led Societies (1882–1940)

The British occupation of Egypt in 1882 not only brought about political and economic changes in the country, but also reinvigorated missionary activity by both the British-led Church Missionary Society (CMS) and the American Presbyterian Church.

The activities of the CMS flourished following the arrival of Rev. Klein to Cairo in 1887, who had formerly been a missionary in Palestine; this marked the beginning of a new policy to be followed by the CMS. Rev. Klein's instructions were to direct his efforts towards the evangelisation of Muslims, whilst simultaneously maintaining a friendly approach towards the Coptic Community.[23] The work of the CMS was mainly divided between Cairo and Old Cairo. In Cairo, two schools were established. By 1899 the boys' school had 129 pupils; its make-up was a third Copt, a third Muslim and a third Syrian, Jew and Armenian. The girls' school in the Bab al-Luq district of Cairo had 46 pupils. In Old Cairo the CMS had also established two schools which between them in 1899 had over 150 pupils, as well as a hospital where over 500 patients were being regularly treated.[24]   As well as education, the CMS founded a medical mission under the auspices of Dr Frank Harpur in March 1889. The hospital began in a private house but moved site eight years later where the Old Cairo Hospital became known as the Harmul hospital, a corruption of Harpur's name.[25] The work of the American Presbyterian Mission also flourished under the protection of the British authorities. In 1893, a missionary station was opened in Tanta whilst others were established in the governates of Benha and Zaqaziq the following year. By 1894, the work of the

Presbyterians embraced 33 organised congregations, with a total membership of 4,554.[26] The Anglican Church greatly criticised the Presbyterian Mission for their approach, accusing them of targeting Copts.[27] Indeed it was claimed that the leaders of the Presbyterians would openly discuss their objective of founding a native Presbyterian Church in Egypt, much to the dismay of the Anglican Church.

The educational, medical and philanthropic work carried out by missionaries, had a profound impact on the emergence of a group of Coptic-led pious societies prior to the First World War who were concerned with the spiritual welfare of the community. The emergence of these religiously motivated societies was the result of what the founders believed was a void in the pastoral care of the Church. This was particularly in light of the prolonged disagreements concerning the dispute of the *Majlis al-Milli*. Thus, unlike the Great Benevolent Society, these groups who were largely closely associated with the Anglican missionaries, did not concern themselves with intra-communal institutional politics and power struggles but rather religious welfare.

One of the first successful religious societies was established in 1908, *Asdiqa' al-Kitab al-Muqaddas,* the Friends of the Holy Bible Society (FHBS) was founded by the Copt Basili Boutros Effendi (1882–1922).[28] Basili had graduated from Kyrillos V's clerical school in 1901 and immediately took up posts in Minya (1902) and Tanta (1903) for the theological and moral educational welfare of the governates.[29] His activity was varied and included publishing a number of opinion pieces in the newspapers *Al-Ahram* and *Al-Watan.* Basili Boutros championed issues of equality of women, advocating the establishment of a school for girls in the 'Abassiyyah district of Cairo in 1909.[30]

The main aim of the society was the representation of Coptic students. This would occur through increased services in predominately Coptic communities and the promotion of active membership within it. They urged members, mainly students and school boys, to pray and study the scriptures through spiritual work with the intention, in the long run, of helping to promote a longstanding revival in the spiritual well being of the Coptic Orthodox Church.[31] Modernisation and reform within the Church would therefore be achieved, according to *Al-Asdiqa'*, through the educational enlightenment of the youth of the Coptic community. The relationship between *Al-Asdiqa'* and the CMS was close, highlighting the ethos of the CMS which sought to encourage Coptic modernisation, education and philanthropy.[32] The Reverend Douglas Thornton, of the second CMS mission, first suggested the proposal of creating a society to Basili Effendi in 1907.[33] During the period of its formation, as well as in later years, the society received the wholehearted support of Canon Temple Gairdner an active CMS member.[34]

The methods of work followed by *Al-Asdiqa'* were numerous and varied covering a wide range of activities, including daily Bible study and open forums of religious discussion and prayer. This was an attempt to ensure that the youths participating would have a more direct understanding of God in their everyday lives.[35] Similarly, the promotion of Sunday schools along with weekly meetings for the public and a monthly magazine, was an attempt to reach out into the broader community. Communal work was also carried out in rural areas where members of the *Al-Asdiqa'* would make weekly visits to families. This included preaching to Coptic *fellahin* in villages where there were no churches or religious societies. On a more tangible level, *Al-Asdiqa'* also provided hostels for students from the provinces, opened summer camps, and sponsored annual regional conferences.[36]

This encompassing set of aims, from religious to philanthropic directed towards young members of the community, helped *Al-Asdiqa'* grow in popularity. In 1909 there were 40 members who regularly met in the house of one of their fellow members. By 1910 however, money was raised and the local Young Men's Christian Association (YMCA) building was used until 1919 with as many as 500 people regularly attending.[37] By the 1940s, the society had expanded so considerably from its early days that it had more than 35 branches with a membership of over 4,000. There were also seven branches dedicated exclusively to the direction and management of Coptic ladies and young women, thus echoing Basili Boutros' original aspirations.[38] In 1939, a special branch of the society was opened which was aimed to provide supportive care for female students studying in the capital away from their native towns.[39]

The work of *Al-Asdiqa'* was mainly sponsored by contributions received from its friends. Its main successes were amongst the students of universities and the pupils of secondary schools in Cairo and Alexandria between the years 1910–1945. This was through their direct dealings with students, providing term time lodgings in the big cities.[40]

Also closely connected with the *Al-Asdiqa'*, Basili Boutros and the work of the CMS, was Qommus Ibrahim Luqa of St. Mark's Church, Heliopolis (1897–1950). Luqa was born in 1897 to a wealthy religious family and gained a secondary school certificate in 1915, later graduating from the clerical college in 1918.[41] Having been prevented from going to study at a theological school in Russia, Luqa went to Asyut and worked with Bishop Macarius, who was later to become Pope Macarius (1942–44). Like Sergius in 1907, Bishop Macarius also ordained Luqa a *Qommus*, (Canon) in 1924.[42] The two Canons had an intense personal rivalry with one another mainly due to their ideological differences. Qommus Luqa closely met with Anglican representatives in Cairo throughout the 1920s and 1930s, forging an intimate working relationship which was positively viewed by the British Residency.[43] In contrast, Qommus Sergius viewed co-operation with the Anglican Church as collusion with the occupying British forces and therefore in direct contradiction to his strong nationalist beliefs which had been vociferously expressed in 1919. Sergius later went on to whole heartedly support Bishop Macarius as a candidate for patriarch in 1944, whilst Luqa supported his rival, Bishop Yusab. An intense cold war between the two continued until Luqa's death in 1950.

Luqa's life-long work based from his Church, St. Mark's in Heliopolis in Cairo, provides evidence of local activities of fundraising and community awareness for spiritual, religious and benevolent needs of not just Heliopolis, but other projects throughout Cairo and Lower Egypt. A charity box was set up in the church and its spendings were published in Qommus Luqa's personal monthly publication *Al-Yaqazah* magazine.[44] For example in May 1928, it is possible to see that the majority of funds procured were from donations and subscriptions, while money was paid out for the pastoral care of the Coptic community throughout Egypt:

**Table 3** Inventory of Expenses, May 1928.[45]

| Total In | LE |
|---|---|
| Credit from previous year | 250 |
| Monthly donations | 50 |
| | 50 |
| | 100 |
| | 300 |
| Monthly subscriptions | 100 |
| | 20 |
| | 100 |
| | 100 |
| | 50 |
| **Total** | **1120** |
| | |
| **Total Out** | **LE** |
| Payment of family debts in Cairo | 200 |
| Monthly Care funds to families in Cairo | 400 |
| Monthly Care funds to families in Upper Egypt | 200 |
| Student travelling grants | 100 |
| Student help grants | 100 |
| **Total** | **1000** |
| **Total Credit** | **120** |

As evident from the table above, Luqa's collections acted as benevolence for those from poorer Coptic families, while also serving to assist the education of students, forging a link between religious charitable obligation and education. Appeals for contributions and donations were regularly placed in *Al-Yaqazah*, for example in 1943 a request was made for the Coptic Sunday School Orphanage in Shubra, 70 Rod al-Farag Street.[46] Similarly, requests were placed in the newspaper for the urgent maintenance of St Mark's Church in Heliopolis. These requests would be made in the form of a flyer or perforated donation slip in *Al-Yaqazah*.[47]

Construction is currently underway in the St. Mark's Church in Heliopolis for the strengthening of the fence and stairwell. This operation will cost LE 400 and we ask Christ to encourage readers of *Al-Yaqazah* for their donations for this project, in so much as their circumstances permit. All donations should be addressed to the treasurer 'Azuz Effendi-Salah al-Din Street, Building number 5, Heliopolis, or in the name of Qommus Ibrahim Luqa, Heliopolis. And may God bless all those who answer this call for assisting the completion of this project for the House of God.

------------------------------------------------------------------------------

Excellency,

Greetings and best wishes: Enclosed is the following amount --- Piasters, --- Pounds [LE] for the upkeep of the Church.

Name and Address: ---

Here, we have very clear evidence of the ways in which magazines, and newspapers were used by various organisations and pressure groups to encourage donations; *Al-Yaqazah,* amongst others, was a means for procuring beneficence and charity, whilst simultaneously acting as an organ for transparency by publishing accounts and guaranteeing the sanctity of silent donations that were received. For example, in October 1943 a receipt was published confirming that a donation had been received and that *Al-Yaqazah* would act at the mediator.[48]

Finally, one of the most successful religious-led benevolent societies to emerge was *Jam'iyyat al-Iman al-Khayriyyah,* or the Iman Benevolent Society, established by a group of clerics in 1899. They began by creating small branches which taught the Coptic language and printed books, whilst also delivering religious advice concerning the community which was published in their monthly circulation, *Al-Fata al-Qibti.*[49] The main aim of the society, as stated in its manifesto was to:

Gather through the Iman Society all the Coptic communities under the faith of Our Saviour. This will be done through religious education, Coptic language, its magazine *Al-Fata al-Qibti*, and the spreading of love and brotherhood among the individuals of the Coptic nation [*Ummah*][50]

By 1907 there were five branches of the society located in Tanta in the Delta region; Batanoon; Shabeen al-Qom in the governate of Minufiyyah; Daqadus, and Qena in Upper Egypt.[51] In 1908, a new branch of the society was opened in the governate of Sharqiyyah, located in Hiya. This branch had been established following the wishes of the overseer of the Church in the area, Philips Androus, and a local landowner, Hanna Effendi 'Abdulqudus, who was also the head of the local school. The Church in Hiya raised over LE 200 towards the society and was inaugurated in March of the same year.[52] The Iman Society in Hiya was extremely active in the community; indeed in the space of one year alone, it paid for the education of more than thirty poor Coptic children in schools. Similarly, a monthly salary or benefit was given to the poorest families to help with their upkeep.[53]

In 1908, the central branch of the society moved out of its original headquarters, to a more spacious building which included gardens and was located in the Fajallah district of Cairo, opposite the Coptic Church in Elias Sosa Street, where weekly religious ceremonies were held every Sunday afternoon.[54] The main body of the society and its six main branches in the early 1900s, were largely concerned with religious education and the re-affirmation of the Coptic language; they were mainly set up by local landowners and church parishes, clearly solidifying the link between the upper class and 'benevolent activity' towards the poorer Coptic parishioners in the area.

While religious societies had initially sought the support of foreign missionary groups such as the CMS, there is evidence that links fostered increasingly cooled by the mid-twentieth century. This was particularly evident with the greater activities of the nationalist movements. The religiously motivated societies, despite in large part being led by ecclesiasts, remained nonetheless distant from ongoing debates concerning the nature of the Church and role to be played by the *Majlis al-Milli*.

## Lay-Led Societies (1890–1945)

Unlike the religious societies which were concerned with the spiritual development of the community, emerging organisations funded by the laity were less inclined to seek the support of Anglican and missionary donors basing themselves instead, on the blueprint of the Great Coptic Benevolent Society. Their main aims were only marginally focussed on the spiritual religious revival of the Church, choosing to focus on the promotion of education in line with the advancements occurring within the Egyptian state; philanthropy and modernisation were therefore at the forefront of the activities promoted by these groups.

A census carried out by the Coptic community in 1909 revealed that only one in every five Copts could read and write.[55] Both boys and girls were encouraged to participate in active education, with calls made to establish a new girls' school.[56] In several magazines, including the monthly free *Al-'Ailah al-Masihiyyah*, (The Christian Family), special sections were devoted to how to read and write in classical Arabic; this was much to the dismay of certain Coptic revivalist magazines who argued that the use of Arabic was a foreign language on the tongues of Copts, calling for greater promotion of the Coptic language in everyday use.[57]

In particular, *Jam'iyyat al-Mahaba*, (The Mahaba Society), which was created in 1902, aimed to promote Coptic secular education of young women free of charge. In June 1909, *Al-Mahaba* established its first free girls' school in the Darb al-Ibrahimi district of Cairo. Twelve of the neediest girls who already received a monthly grant from *Al-Mahaba* were accepted; they received books, tools, handcrafts and clothes. Within the first month, the school had a total of 35 girls who were taught by two Coptic female teachers; after three months, the school was divided into two classes consisting of 75 girls in total. In October 1910, the school was relocated to a larger venue in Cairo, another class was established and a headmaster and third teacher were also appointed. The improvements and changes to the structure of the school heavily impacted the finances of *Al-Mahaba*, whose spending of LE 315, far outweighed its capital of LE 221 for the academic year 1910–11.[58] Despite this however, the relative success of *Al-Mahaba* in its early years, resulted in a steady increase in the amount of money that the society received in donations and grants from charitable committees:

**Table 4** *Al-Mahaba* Society Donations, 1910–1912.[59]

|  | Date | Amount |
|---|---|---|
| **Institutional Contributions** | | |
| The Great Coptic Benevolent Society | December 1910 | LE 15 |
|  | April 1911 | LE 20 |
|  | June 1912–October 1912 | LE 12 |
|  | December 1912 | LE 5 |
|  | November 1912– September 1913 | LE 27 |
| **Individual Contributions** | | |
| Boutros Ghali Pasha | March 1910 (Posthumous) | £15 (UK) |
|  | April 1910 (Posthumous) | £ 15 (UK) |
| Naguib Pasha (Honorary President) | Annually | LE 5 |

It is worth noting that *Al-Mahaba* received donations and support from the larger Great Coptic Benevolent Society. By the early twentieth century, the society which had been the original blueprint for Coptic philanthropic organisations, increasingly sponsored other similar societies to promote and carry out projects related to education and philanthropy, so long as they adopted a similar ethos.

*Al-Mahaba*'s success continued well into the inter-war years, having established an orphanage. By 1944, the society was able to buy a new large building in Zahour Street in the Shubra district of Cairo for LE 6,000, with the aim of educating and providing orphans with a skill. *Al-Mahaba* had managed to raise the majority of the costs from donations, revealing the sizable impact that the society had on the community, as well as the role played by ordinary lay Copts in assisting the establishment of institutions for the advancements and benefit of the community.[60]

The most significant lay-led society to emerge however, was *Jam'iyyat al-Tawfiq* created in 1891, approximately ten years after the establishment of the Great Coptic Benevolent Society; however unlike the latter, *Al-Tawfiq* was not founded by landowners, *'ayan* and politicians, but all initial twenty-one representatives of the society were Coptic educated young-men, mainly civil servants, under the age of forty.[61] Their initial motivation had been two fold, the creation of a reforming leadership, primarily aimed at the social inequalities prevalent in Coptic society and, they also viewed themselves as a reaction to the British occupation of Egypt. However, *Al-Tawfiq* faced difficulties, all their initial plans in 1891 were to be carried out on a miserly budget of forty-four piasters.[62] Historian Ahmad Shalabi Hilmi argues that *Al-Tawfiq* was 'nothing more than a small drop in the ocean' in comparison to the formation of other social and benevolent societies that were being set up by both Copts and Muslims in the late nineteenth century. Their main aims, he argues, was to address the issue of the vast social and economic divide between classes.[63]

Nonetheless, *Al-Tawfiq*, despite their initial small budget, were extremely successful in stepping up their work within the Coptic Community, printing and distributing a number of pamphlets dealing with reform. For ten years they also issued *Al-Tawfiq* magazine which ran until 1910.[64] This became their mouth-piece concerning a variety of subjects including education, finances and inventories as well as charitable donations, thus ensuring transparency which *Al-Tawfiq* accused the patriarchate of failing to do.[65]

In 1894, the focus of the society expanded as education of the community was added to the register of activities. *Al-Tawfiq* opened a primary school for boys in 1895 and one for girls in 1897.[66] By 1907, the schools had 512 pupils in total, 391 boys and 121 girls; just under a fifth of the school received a free education, whilst 45 Muslim children were also in attendance with 2 'others', presumably Jews, highlighting once again, the inter-confessional nature of lay-led Coptic benevolent societies.[67] In order to cover spiralling costs of schools and expenses, the society increasingly thought of ingenious ways in which to raise revenue. This included the creation of a car hiring firm: *Al-Tawfiq* rented wedding and funeral carriages annually and then provided a service with chauffeur for the occasion resulting in an annual profit to be spent on schools and other expenses of approximately LE 750.[68]

**Table 5** *Al-Tawfiq* Society Inventory, 1900–1902.[69]

| | LE | Piasters |
|---|---|---|
| **Total Out** | | |
| General Administration | 2165 | 654 |
| Printing Costs | 1451 | 859 |
| School Expenses | 1934 | 246 |
| Funeral Cars | 1234 | 693 |
| Wedding Cars | 303 | 369 |
| Contingency | 395 | 788 |
| Miscellaneous | 59 | 57 |
| Remainder | 191 | 142 |
| **Total** | **7,755** | **808** |
| | | |
| **Total In** | | |
| Incoming Money | 1569 | 739 |
| Printing | 1163 | 595 |
| School Fees/Donations | 2183 | 535 |
| Funeral Cars | 1789 | 952 |
| Wedding Cars | 183 | 869 |
| Contingency | 573 | 575 |
| Miscellaneous | 5 | 258 |
| Remainder [1900] | 285 | 785 |
| **Total** | **7,755** | **808** |

The society expanded its work spreading its influence in 1912 by founding a secondary school for boys and in 1929 one for girls. In terms of attendance, the impact of *Al-Tawfiq* schools achievements were very clear. In 1894 the total number of pupils had grown from the initial 66 to 1,323 in 1948; 30 per cent of all pupils at the school were admitted free of charge.[70] It was not an easy task to keep funding; in 1910, when the society closed the publication of its magazine *Al-Tawfiq*, the society fell into a period that saw a lack of funds mar their activity. Nonetheless, Shalibi, argues that after the

1919 revolution, the society's drive altered somewhat. It took onboard a dual ambition which connected religious and social reform within the Coptic community with the nationalist cause.[71] Indeed the fiery Al-Azhar Coptic orator, Qommus Sergius himself gave a speech to *Al-Tawfiq* members in 1919 to encourage the association of educational and social activities of the society with the nationalist ideology prevalent.[72] Shalabi argued that the social make up of *Jami'yyat Al-Tawfiq*, along with the drive for transparency against corruption within the Church, meant that support for the end of the occupation was a natural occurrence.

In December 1921, *Al-Tawfiq* wrote and published an open letter in which it criticised the Egyptian authorities for the detention of Sa'd Zaghlul and the infringement on the rights of the 'Egyptian *ummah* and people'.[73] Indeed the society went even further, and apologised to Shaykh 'Abdulaziz Khawish of *Al-Liwa* newspaper attached to *Al-Watani* Party for *Al-Tawfiq* magazine's criticism in 1908 over the Coptic Question. It stated that *Al-Tawfiq* recognised the contribution that was made by both *Hizb al-Watani* and *Al-Liwa* as organs of nationalist opinion and opposition to British occupation. *Jam'iyyat al-Tawfiq* therefore provides clear evidence of a philanthropic society, which although initially purely interested in education and societal ills prevalent within the Coptic community, had by 1919 increasingly placed its activities within the emergence of nationalist ideologies regarding modernisation of the Church and of the greater Egyptian society as a whole package.

The emergence of benevolent, philanthropic and charitable societies in the late twentieth century played differing active roles in the promotion of education, modernisation and philanthropy within the Coptic community. The Great Benevolent Society, initially established by notables, sought to play a more direct role in the palliative care of the Coptic community through the promotion of education. This was later mirrored by societies sponsored by an emerging Coptic middle class like *Al-Mahaba*. Similarly, religious-led societies like *Al-Asdiqa'* and Qommus Luqa's St. Mark's Church, sought to bolster the spiritual failings of the youth through their charitable actions, highlighting many of the perceived failings of the Coptic Church. Despite differing ideological positions, the lay and religious led societies recognised the immediate need for reform

reform within the Coptic community, which had hitherto remained within the realm of the Church. In creating societies, the lay and religious Copts were indirectly accusing the patriarchate and the upper echelons of the Church of serious mal-administration and neglect whilst challenging its traditional authority.

## *Waqf* as Beneficence

In early May 1883, renewed efforts were made by Coptic elites to revive the *Majlis al-Milli* which had been made redundant after the continued deadlock with the new patriarch since 1875.[74] The 1883 amendment of the *Majlis* constitution proposed that the new council would be made up of twelve representatives and twelve deputies.[75] The *Majlis* would also take under its control Coptic *waqf*. This would include all Coptic lands, including patriarchal, monastic and charitable properties, as well as the administration of Coptic schools, printing, publishing and the oversight of the poor and orphans.[76] However, soon after these renewed efforts in 1883 a stalemate occurred once again. At the centre of the new dispute between the patriarch and the *Majlis* was the question of the control of the *waqf*.[77]

The lay segments of the *Majlis al-Milli* had wished to gain control of the *waqf* as they claimed that the income of properties was often misappropriated by clergymen and monks resulting in large profits and corruption; this was contrary to the concept of 'voluntary poverty' which the monks as ascetics had undertook. Up until this point, *waqf* had generally been divided into two types; endowments that arose from the monasteries and those related to specific churches in the forms of lands and houses. Those who advocated the role of the *Majlis al-Milli* demanded that revenue should be channelled directly to the community.[78] Thus the aim was to ensure that *waqf* revenue financed the maintenance of churches, schools, hospitals, public works, libraries and tombs directly, as opposed to the extravagant and lavish lifestyles led by many monks and bishops. In sum, the *Majlis* wished to ensure that *waqf* sustained the foundations of Coptic society.

Failure to agree on the 1883 constitution led to a standoff. The upper echelons of the clergy and monks largely sided with Pope Kyrillos V in order to protect their own interests, while the lay

*Majlis* and newly formed Coptic Benevolent Society stood in opposition.[79] Many of the same individuals who played an active role in the *Majlis al-Milli* were also closely attached to the Great Coptic Benevolent Society, including, Boutros Ghali Pasha. By 1891, the intra-communal dispute concerning *waqf* came to head when popular demonstrations erupted. These protests were sponsored by the newly formed *Jami'yyat al-Tawfiq* with the implicit support of the Great Coptic Benevolent Society and the *Majlis al-Milli*. Unlike the Great Coptic Benevolent Society, *Al-Tawfiq* was largely comprised of young educated Copts, solidifying the link between the popular support for greater lay participation in the *Majlis al-Milli* and reform of *waqf*. *Al-Tawfiq* began by issuing pamphlets in the hope that they could encourage educated Copts to participate and support the society's claims for reform. Popular Coptic press also played an active and important role as a means of articulating not only opposition to the patriarch, but also as a resource to advertise the actions and opinions of pressure groups whilst soliciting donations. For example, articles demonising the Patriarch were placed in *Al-Haq* newspaper, as well as in *Al-Islah*, and *Al-Tawfiq* magazines. The articles claimed that Kyrillos V was regressive through his unwillingness to co-operate with the *Majlis al-Milli*, accusing him of being against the improvement of the education of Copts as had been advocated by Abu Islah.[80]

Indeed, British observer Mrs Butcher claims that the popularity of *Al-Tawfiq* gained so rapidly that the patriarch and clergy feared its effect.[81] This sparked off the creation of a counter society in the same year, led by the clergy, bishops, heads of monasteries and the Holy Synod, under the auspices of the patriarchate, it was named *Jam'iyyat al-Aqbat al-Urthodoxiyyah*, (The Orthodox Coptic Society).[82] The main aim of the society was to de-legitimise *Al-Tawfiq* and re-establish the spirit of deference and authority to the patriarch, claiming that *Al-Tawfiq* was working as an agent for the protestant missionaries and that their aims were treasonable. *Al-Tawfiq* however, unlike *Al-Asdiqa'* and Qommus Luqa, had no connections with any foreign missionary activity. This defamation led to a popular demonstration instigated by members of *Al-Tawfiq* in the spring of 1891; speeches were made in an attempt to urge Kyrillos to assemble a functioning *Majlis* for the urgent need of reform.[83]

Appeals and pressure from *Al-Tawfiq* and from the Great Coptic Benevolent Society, along with the *Majlis al-Milli* to the new Khedive, 'Abbas Hilmi Pasha (1892–1914), finally resulted in action being taken on the laymen's behalf. Kyrillos was forced to concede, and in 1892, the government brokered an agreement whereby the monasteries were forced to present their accounts to the patriarchate but would retain, after deductions, all profits arising from the *waqf* properties under their control.[84]

Most importantly in the new agreement however, was the change in the composition and structure of the *Majlis*. The 1892 agreement stipulated that the clerical affairs of the Church would not be supervised solely by the *Majlis al-Milli* and that there was to be co-operation with members from the Holy Synod under the leadership of the patriarch.[85] This effectively diluted the monopoly held by the laymen over the *Majlis al-Milli*. A third of the members were now to be drawn from the clergy whilst the rest were to remain from the laity.[86] From the government's perspective, this helped to restore the balance of power between the two factions.

On 17 July 1892, a Khedival Decree was issued making this agreement official whilst the patriarch, in protest, simultaneously petitioned the Khedive.[87] The petition received in late July 1892 addressed to the Council of Ministers, advocated the Church's traditional freedoms and the role of the patriarch as the highest authority of the community. The patriarch widely publicised the petition, the contents of which appeared in several newspapers.[88] Kyrillos V also convened a meeting at the patriarchate with all bishops, and called upon the governor of Cairo for protection to what he regarded as traitorous acts.[89] In retaliation, the members of the *Majlis al-Milli* under the leadership of Boutros Ghali Pasha, managed to convince the youthful Khedive 'Abbas and Prime Minister Mustafa Fahmi (May 1891–January 1893) to remove the perceived obstructive patriarch and his secretary of the Holy Synod, Bishop Yu'annis of Beheirah.[90] The Khedive, in accordance with the demands, consented to the historically unprecedented dismissal of the patriarch from his duties. Both the Pope Kyrillos V and Bishop Yu'annis were removed from office and sent to the Wadi Natrun al-Baramusi Monastery by Khedival decree in September 1892.[91]

In protest, the priests and bishops of the provinces, members of *Jam'iyyat al-Aqbat al-Urthodoxiyyah*, along with a number of influential politicians, both Christian and Muslim, including the new Prime Minister, Riyad Pasha (1893–94), petitioned the Khedive.[92] The Prime Minster, a conservative Muslim, had according to a British observer, Leeder, been genuinely shocked at the rebellion against the legitimate hierarchal authority.

> Riaz [Riyad Pasha] saw that the vast majority of the Coptic people, whatever the reformers might think, were desolated by the removal of a man who was still their head. And then too, Cyril's [Kyrillos V] parting thunders of excommunication had brought the whole Church to a standstill, drying up the comforting wells of absolute and benediction [...] the result is an irresistible hunger made itself felt for restoration of the hierarchy; and the only man who could have prevented the recall of the Patriarch [Lord Cromer] felt that the quarrel had gone far enough.[93]

Mrs Butcher does not discuss this event but provides a personal comment over the deeds of the Great Coptic Benevolent Society, *Al-Tawfiq* and the lay members of the *Majlis al-Milli* stating that they committed 'not only a crime but a blunder'.[94] The reason, she argued, was that ordinary Copts within the community had felt that the situation had gone too far with the exile of Kyrillos V.[95] *Jam'iyyat al-Aqbat al-Urthodoxiyyah*, led by ecclesiasts, played a major role in rallying the support of the 'ordinary' Copt which Mrs Butcher described as being behind the exiled patriarch.[96] Kyrillos' banishment was clear-cut evidence of what many within the community could not accept, the infringement of laymen in the spiritual duties of the Church. Whilst the *Majlis al-Milli* as an institutional development, and the work of the benevolent societies were welcomed, the banishment of the pope, it was argued, tainted the image of not only the patriarch as the spiritual leader of the Copts, but also of the community as a whole.[97] Indeed in the days following, Khedive 'Abbas bestowed on Kyrillos a medal of the highest order.[98]

Following these remonstrations, the Khedive issued a proclamation to reinstate the patriarch, who returned to Cairo escorted by a government envoy in February 1893. Upon arrival, the crowds were reportedly so great that Kyrillos struggled to get into his horse and carriage; he was blocked by Coptic onlookers and well wishers who carried palm leaves and olives in celebration for Kyrillos' symbolic return to the city.[99]

There are mixed interpretations by Coptic historians and foreign observers concerning the events of 1883–1893. For example, whilst Mrs Butcher had clearly regarded the banishment of Kyrillos V as the result of an intra-communal struggle between the *Majlis al-Milli* and the newly formed lay societies on the one hand, and the patriarch and bishops on the other, Coptic historians have been more inclined to view the episode in a different light. Religious historian Iris Habib al-Misri, is keen to highlight the role of the British occupation, describing this period in terms of a dual battle fought by the Coptic community; on one hand against the British occupation in 1882, and on the other hand the intra-communal battle concerning who would control the affairs of the community.[100] Similarly, Father Bishoy al-Antuni, a modern religious historian has dismissed claims that banishment of Kyrillos V to the monastery was due to the *Majlis al-Milli* and its supporters. Instead, he claims that Kyrillos V was exiled by the British for opposing Protestants and other Christian sects who arrived in Egypt; thus Kyrillos is firmly brought into the fold of the nationalist narrative. Bishoy argues that Kyrillos' exile was due to his patriotic opposition to the British occupation and missionary Christian denominations which allowed a person to 'to steal without being interrogated and abuse the people, the land and the wealth on Egypt with no limitations'.[101]    British observer Leeder, has argued that the mass scenes of jubilation upon the return of the Patriarch should be seen as an act of defiance against the British occupation and Cromer who had sent Kyrillos into exile on the *Majlis'* recommendation. Indeed many Muslim crowds also turned up at the station to meet Kyrillos.[102]

The period 1883–1893 saw great turmoil within the Coptic community. The formerly defunct *Majlis*, failed to regain its posture and hold the patriarchate accountable to what it perceived as necessary reforms within the structure of the Church. For the *Majlis*, *waqf* served as a vehicle to finance Coptic society by making it into an institution which could maintain churches, schools, hospitals and libraries, thus ensuring that it sustained the foundations of Coptic society. Through the support of the newly formed Coptic societies who were concerned first and foremost with charity and beneficence, the role of the *Majlis* was slowly re-established and increasingly, from 1893, brought the issue of *waqf* and its abuse to light. Thus, the alliance between the *Majlis* and the societies, working together to act as a pressure group on the traditional forces within the Church highlight the growing forces of reform and modernisation within the Coptic community. Similarly, the response of the patriarch with the creation of a similar charitable structure in the shape of *Jam'iyyat al-Aqbat al-Urthodoxiyyah* to defend the position of the Church, highlighted the increasing factionalism prevalent within the Church, a theme which would continue until the mid-1950s. The state also played an important role by intervening in order to consolidate their own position as the broker within the community.

## Debating the State of the Clergy (1893–1927)

During Kyrillos V's papacy, particularly in the years 1893 and 1927, several changes took place in the constitution of the *Majlis*.[103] Following Kyrillos return from exile, an agreement was made after negotiations took place between the patriarch, the government and the *Majlis al-Milli*. The patriarch was to convoke the *Majlis al-Milli*, which he had previously declined to do, but in doing so he curtailed the rights and privileges of the institution.[104] The management of *waqf* property was no longer to be within the competence of the *Majlis al-Milli*, but was to be considered the private concern of the patriarch and bishops: 'By a mixture of stubbornness and subtle diplomacy the pope eventually obtained a repeal of the legislation which had restricted his rights in favour of the *Majlis al-Milli* and kept reforms at bay almost to the end of his papacy'.[105]

In 1912, this arrangement, which had been in force since 1893 though never sanctioned legally, received legislative authority through Law No 3 of 1912. This introduced two important modifications in the provisions of the Decree of 14 May 1883:

firstly, the *Majlis al-Milli* which had up until now been an elective body of twenty-four representatives, was reduced to a committee of twelve members, four of whom were ecclesiasts nominated by the patriarch and the remaining eight were laymen, elected by the community. Secondly, in questions related to property, articles 8 and 9 of the 1883 Decree, which gave the *Majlis al-Milli* exclusive jurisdiction over all Church property, was abrogated and replaced by a new text, which left in the hands of the *Majlis al-Milli* the management of the *waqf* property attached to the churches and schools, but with the exclusion of the second type of *waqf*, the property of the monasteries, which was by far the richer. [106] This latter property was to fall under the patriarchal prerogative thus increasing his ability to exert and exercise power over the community.

Those who supported the patriarch, including the bishops and Holy Synod, argued that the patriarch was perfectly sincere in believing that his duty and responsibility had always been to guard the Church from schismatic changes, leaving the Church to its successor as he found it.[107] Kyrillos' critics, mainly comprised of the *Majlis al-Milli* and Benevolent society members however, believed that this reform fell short of the Church's necessary commitment to modernise the Coptic community.

Kyrillos V himself had a conflicting image as a reformer and patriarch. Cromer called Kyrillos 'the greatest reactionary force in Egypt', a reference to his dispute with the *Majlis al-Milli* and unwillingness to modernise.[108] Nonetheless this image was not shared by all; British observer, Leeder, argued that Kyrillos' private life was well-known and was full of 'purity, great simplicity and self-denial with his personal expenditure not exceeding more than LE 60 a year'.[109] Kyrillos V is also accredited with the renewal of many aesthetic areas of the Church. For example, in terms of building restoration and repairs, he was responsible for repairing the doors, windows and delicate ornate frames for St. Mark's cathedral in the Azbikkiyah district of Cairo.[110] He also supported the construction of new churches including St. Mark's in Giza in 1877 and the Angel Gabriel in Al-Saqaqqin alleyways in 1881. Annual repairs were made to monasteries and churches, the patriarchate and diwan.[111]

With regards to the education of the clergy, Kyrillos established a clerical school on 13th January 1875, although it closed less than a month later, reopening in 1893 following the end of the first phase of the *Majlis* crisis and moving to larger quarters in 1902.[112] Kyrillos V also attended and supported the opening of new Coptic schools, mainly based in Cairo, although they were not funded by the patriarchate but by the newly emergent benevolent societies; in March 1903, he inaugurated a new trade school.[113] Kyrillos also greatly supported the education of women, opening a girls' school in the Fajallah district of Cairo in January 1908. Indeed writing in an article in *Al-Ummah* newspaper, Kyrillos called for others to follow his personal example of a LE 100 donation to ensure women's education became a priority.[114]

Despite this image of a reformer however, much criticism was made towards the state of the clergy and their education during his papacy. Tawfiq Habib (1880–1941) was an active member of the *Majlis al-Milli* and had established *Al-Fira'un* (The Pharaoh) newspaper in 1902. In an article Habib stated that deacons had no salaries and were being replaced by children who chanted the words without understanding or knowing the meaning, thus serving to highlight some of the failings in education and modernisation of the Church:

> The Church has been ignored and is loosing its credibility in Eastern Churches due to the conditions of priests which is worse than the monks since most of them do not receive wages nor can they get the basic necessities for their families to the extent that some beg and lose their family honour and respect to support their family.[115]

Most of the charity that Coptic priests in Egypt received came in the form of donations of corn or wheat for bread. This was barely adequate to cover their expenditures, particularly as their average salary was, at the turn of the twentieth century, only LE 3 a month. Indeed, even priests' salaries that were paid were a form of charity, or *sadaqqa*, that were supplied by the Great Coptic Benevolent Society. Salaries were not a guaranteed income, and priests were paid only three to four times a year as the Great Coptic Benevolent

Society did not always have enough funds for all salaries. Chanters were in the worst position however, with their average wage at 80 piasters a month, the vast majority resorted to begging. All this, Tawfiq Habib reported, was when the average spending for a priest and his family stood at 15 to 20 piasters a day in 1912.[116]

Habib, amongst others, argued that there was clear disparity between the state of the lower clergy and that of the monks in the monasteries and bishops who were accused of misappropriating *waqf* funds which had remained in their control:

> Monks used to be in the past years very poor, just as the Coptic people were poor, as were the heads of the monasteries [...] has the situation remained the same however? The reality today is that Bishops now live in palaces and they eat heavily all the best foods and between their hands are the papers and administrative control [of *waqfs*] be they a bishop of administration or a diocese.[117]

In 1912, in light of the debates concerning misappropriation of money, Coptic newspapers also began scrutinising the personal expenditure of Pope Kyrillos which far exceeded the humble figure of LE 60 stated by Leeder, instead amounting to LE 616 in 1907.[118] Similarly, patriarchal food costs for the same year were a staggering LE 614, in comparison to the LE 235 subsistence costs for a fully operational Coptic orphanage under papal jurisdiction.[119] It was argued by a number of Coptic newspapers in 1912, including the two dailies *Al-Watan* and *Misr*, that a solution to the *waqf* problem was necessary as it would not only alleviate the state of the clergy, but also encourage the Coptic Church to modernise its structures internally and externally.[120] A suggestion was made in late 1912 that Coptic *waqf* should follow the direction of Islamic endowments which were to be transferred to a new ministry.[121] Indeed one article in *Al-Watan* argued that *waqf* should be looked after by the British: 'Coptic *waqf* should be administered by a Ministry of *awqaf* like Muslims. It is surprising that the government is ignoring non-Muslim *waqf* whilst non-Muslims are asking for it'.[122] The Coptic Youth Association, a loose federation of lay youths, in Asyut, Upper Egypt, also supported the plan of a Coptic Ministry of

*Awqaf*.[123] Both *Misr* and *Al-Watan* newspapers published on open letter to this effect in October 1912 proving the popular lay led opinion behind such a reform taking place.[124]

In addition to monetary spending, a calculation of some of the largest *waqf* holdings revealed that the Patriarchate and monasteries held substantial amounts of land in 1912:

**Table 6** Patriarchate and Monastery *Waqf* Holdings, 1912.[125]

| Plot | Size (Feddans) |
|---|---|
| Patriarchate | 3124 |
| St. Anthony Monastery | 931 |
| Anba Bula Monastery | 680 |
| Abi Majar Monastery | 94 |
| 'Resurrection' *Waqf* | 800 |
| Al-'Azra Monastery, Barmousi | 156 |
| Al-Muharraq Monastery | 1980 |
| Anba Bishoi Monastery | 78 |
| Al-'Azra Monastery, Siriyan | 80 |
| Al-'Azra Monastery, Jabal Teer | 45 |
| Mar Girgis Monastery, Harit Zawila | 31 |
| Al-Masa' Benevolent Society, Cairo | 286 |

This was in addition to the other small feddans in the provinces which were thought to be worth LE 1.5 million. This lead *Al-Firu'an* to comment in 1913 that:

> [I]f one-tenth of all *awqaf* are spent on schools and churches, then nine-tenths are spent by the monks on themselves. One hundred and ninety-five monks should be on an approximate wage of 40 piasters a month but this is not the reality.[126]

Numerous other newspaper articles appeared criticising the policy of leaving such substantial sums of money in the hands of a minority of monks who could manipulate the *waqf* funds. In one case, it was only after local Copts complained about their neighbourhood monastery and monks that Kyrillos V investigated. It was found that one monk had frivolously spent LE 160,000 in just a few years. When the monk was asked for receipts, he presented only LE 11,000 worth; LE 149,000 had just disappeared.[127] Similarly, the *waqf* of Al-Qiyama and Lady Dimyana monasteries were also disputed. In 1907, the monasteries were placed under patriarchal control including 300 feddans of Dimyana land and buildings in Cairo. Despite this, the vast majority of *waqf* belonging to the monasteries were disputed. It was discovered after an inventory that 500 feddans were personally written under the name of Anba Themothas, the overseer of the monastery. Themothas claimed that he had brought the land with his own money despite *waqf* records proving the contrary.[128]

The protracted dispute concerning *waqf* which, had been taken up by not only large Coptic newspapers such as *Misr*, but also those associated with benevolent societies like *Al-Tawfiq*, highlighted the importance of the loss of revenue in lay-led discussions concerning Coptic educational and social reforms. By promoting the rubric of education and philanthropy, organisations and newspapers initiated debates on Coptic *waqf*, whose reform was widely perceived as a necessary step, in the modernisation of the community and also serving to highlight the existing widespread corruption. Indeed an inventory of patriarchal *waqf* in 1907 highlighted that incompetence alone lost over LE 35,000 in annual revenue thus serving to further contribute to the long-standing debate.[129] The formation of these new Coptic societies therefore played an invaluable role in challenging the traditional authority of the Church in all aspects related to the administration and governance of the community. Both lay and religious societies also offered legitimate alternative avenues for exposing discontent concerning the existing structures of the Church.

# FACTIONALISM AND CORRUPTION (1882–1945)

The short reign of Pope Macarius III (1944–45) epitomised factional politics which marred the Coptic Church in the years preceding the Free Officers Revolution in 1952. Following the ongoing debates concerning the lack of Coptic representation in constitutional politics and their diminishing role in government employment, secular and religious reformers placed greater emphasis on the role of the Church as an institution to embody and represent Coptic qualms. The events which surrounded the election of Pope Macarius in 1944, highlighted a process which, for the first time in Coptic history, was conducted as a modern political campaign reflecting developments in national politics. This process brought to the fore the existence of factions within the community, and emphasised how the press and political rallies became part of a new repertoire of political mobilisation.

## An Invitation to Unity

Amid discussions concerning the question of inter-communal tensions prevalent in Egypt throughout the interwar years, and particularly after the 1936 Anglo-Egyptian Treaty, questions also arose concerning the role to be played by the patriarch and the Church. This debate was exacerbated by the deficiency of the Coptic Church as a unified institution which failed to represent a community under perceived systematic discrimination and attack.[1] Instead, it was argued by Qommus Sergius, Salama Musa and benevolent and religious organisations like the Christian Soldiers

Society, that intra-communal disputes and the lack of reform and modernisation had rendered the Church unable to fully act for the community on a wider Egyptian political level as well as embody the many different factions internally. As stated by Qommus Luqa, the religious reformist, in the editorial of his monthly magazine *Al-Yaqazah*:

> Spiritual life is weak, manners and social behaviour is ruined [...] our national unity is broken [...]our churches have become empty, and the lambs have run away. The authority of the Church has weakened [...]the Church has lost its glory and honour in every direction. Our issues are now subject to the scrutiny of others. After we were a head, we have now become a tail.[2]

The disenchantment with the natural authority of the Church and its ecclesiastical as well as administrative structures manifested itself most visibly by the mid-1940s. The result was that by the death of Pope Yu'annis XIX, Copts from a variety of backgrounds no longer viewed the Church and clerical hierarchy as the sole legitimate representative of the community. Qommus Sergius in *Al-Manarah* wrote:

> The Copts have very little interest towards the Pope or the role he plays which has resulted in a lack of responsibility when it comes to his election. The Patriarch's image is one of an old man with rosary beads and no action. People do not get involved as they have no reason to choose [a new patriarch]. People have become spiritually disheartened and the Church as a result has weakened. Every Pope that has died has been unable to achieve reform. The result is that people are waiting for the following one [new patriarch] to achieve what the previous could not. This has resulted in the departure of 10,000s of people from the religion and Church.[3]

It was for these reasons that issues of the spiritual and administrative reform of the Church were at the forefront of the election of a new patriarch in 1944. As Qommus Luqa commented,

'Our Church today is in great need of people who feel responsible towards it'.[4]

In 1942 Pope Yu'annis XIX (1928–1942) died, leaving the See of St. Mark vacant.[5] Yu'annis had been closely associated with corruption in the Church, limited reform and prolonged disputes with the *Majlis al-Milli*.[6] King Fu'ad (1917–1936) was said to have interfered in the appointment of Yu'annis, as Article 142 of the Egyptian constitution of 1930 gave the King the right to appoint religious leaders.[7] Walter Smart, the Oriental Secretary at the British Residency wrote that Yu'annis' election had been favoured 'by a present of bags of gold' to the King.[8] The Anglican Bishop in Egypt, Llewellyn Gwynne (1920–1937), concurred that: 'Through the connivance of an unprincipled lawyer, two or three rich monasteries were forced to supply him [Yu'annis] with funds; with these he bribed the highest officials in the government to obtain the post of patriarch.'[9]

Historically, the election of a patriarch was secured through a variety of methods. According to tenth century Coptic scholar Ibn al-Muqaffa', Pope Abilius (d.80 AD) was picked by all those who had converted to Christianity following St Mark the Evangelist's death, thus ensuring a consensus through a public forum. There is also evidence that in the fourth century a patriarch would select his successor upon his deathbed.[10] By the eighteenth century however, a more consistent method of selecting a patriarch developed. This involved the nomination of a number of candidates, to be chosen by the Holy Synod for the patriarchy and later put to a vote. Initially, only high ranking bishops could vote, however following the creation of the *Majlis al-Milli* this expanded to include prominent notables sitting on the council. During the election process of 1942, calls were made to expand the amended voting regulations of 1928 which stated that those with an income higher than LE 120 per annum and owned property would be eligible to vote. Yet the call for universal Coptic suffrage in patriarchal elections failed to materialise until after the revolution.

Also related to the elections, was the debate concerning which candidates were eligible for nominations to the patriarchy. Traditionally, all patriarchal candidates were chosen from amongst the monks who were regarded as uncorrupted by worldly and administrative affairs, these were instead roles that had been undertaken by bishops. As a result of their seclusion, monks were traditionally viewed as more pious and thus more suitable for the position of patriarch. It was therefore agreed by certain traditionalists, although this debate continues to the present day, that to nominate a patriarch from amongst the bishops was sacrilegious, and that the customs of the Church were based on long founded traditions of monasticism; the nomination should be from amongst the monks, whose rank did not exceed that of Qommus.[11]

In 1927, after the election of Bishop Yu'annis, who had been a close aid to Pope Kyrillos V, nomination laws were changed. It was agreed by the members of the Holy Synod and *Majlis al-Milli* to promote a bishop to the rank of Patriarch if, 'no monks were deemed suitable for the position'.[12] The declaration was signed by a number of bishops, including the four who were nominated to the position of patriarch in 1944.[13]   Some commentators, including Qommus Ibrahim Luqa of the Heliopolis St. Mark's Church, argued that this decision would not have been agreed upon by the Holy Synod in 1928 unless all bishops were in full agreement with the theory of electing a pope from amongst the bishops.[14] Despite this however, the debate concerning the nomination of monks over bishops gained widespread coverage in the Coptic press throughout January 1944. An open letter written by five bishops was published in *Misr* and *Al-Watan* in early 1944 dismissing the 1928 law.  The bishops claimed that there was no precedent for the amendment other than that of the recently departed Pope Yu'annis.[15] This was also supported by a series of consecutive articles, again written by bishops, which appeared in *Misr* arguing that it was against Coptic tradition to elect a bishop to the See of St. Mark.[16] In particular, the bishop of Minya declared that the Coptic people should be steadfast in their traditions; this despite the fact that he himself had been appointed in 1930 to his Bishopric by Pope Yu'annis, a former bishop.[17] In response to these articles in *Misr*, Qommus Sergius sarcastically replied in his own paper *Al-Manarah al-Misriyyah*, that the bishop of Minya should resign given he accepted his bishopric 'from such an illegal patriarch!'[18]

Whilst the debate concerning whether the new patriarch should have monastic or clerical roots was of considerable religious significance, the selection from either of these backgrounds also had crucial social and political implications; the candidates who had been chosen from amongst the bishops had a formal understanding of the nature, issues and threats that were facing the Coptic Church, whilst those of monastic origins would have been, at least theoretically, secluded whilst in hermitage. Differences between the two types of candidates can also be identified in the ways in which they ran their election campaigns in 1944. The bishops adopted modern forms of political lobbying, with manifestos, agendas and the extensive use of the press as a propaganda tool. Conversely, those who came from monastic roots, were less inclined, prepared and indeed capable, to be absorbed into the world of political lobbying.

In early January 1944, a meeting was held by the Papal nominations committee. It was chaired by Bishop Yusab of Girga, the Acting Patriarch, and attended by five members of the *Majlis al-Milli*, plus five bishops.[19] Elections for the new patriarch were scheduled for early February and nominations were put forward for four bishops and two monks; the winning candidate would gain over 50 per cent of all votes cast, or a new contest would be scheduled to be held between the two highest candidates on 18th February.[20] What subsequently ensued in the coming month was an election campaign for the nomination of candidates which had increasing political overtones. Each candidate promoted a different agenda and was supported by a faction of the community vying for certain reforms, changes or extensions in powers.[21]

Only two monks were nominated by the committee; Athnasious of the Muharrak Monastery and Francis Shenouda. The former came last in the elections with only 5 votes, having failed to establish an effective electoral and lobbying base amongst Copts eligible to vote.[22] The latter, Monk Shenouda, was the youngest candidate and had received his education as a lawyer in the mixed courts, and only joined the ranks of the clergy three years earlier. Whilst practicing as a lawyer, Shenouda had allegedly swindled a client who threatened to sue him; Shenouda in atonement became a monk, and his client subsequently dropped the case.[23] Shenouda's nomination was pushed by a number of Coptic lawyers, young Coptic thinkers and the bishop of Minya, whose sole objective was his candidature for the patriarchate.[24] Unlike Monk Athnasious, Shenouda's connections outside the monastery as a former lawyer proved useful in rallying a campaign on his behalf and securing his place in fourth position in the elections.

The top three candidates who received the most votes in the election, and operated strong publicity campaigns in the press, were all bishops; all three had different support bases, with specific views on the future of the Church. In third place was Theofilos, the bishop of Jerusalem and the Diocese of Sharqiyyah, with 160 votes.[25] It was reported by both British and Egyptian commentators, that he was an 'energetic man', although somewhat of a materialist rather than spiritualist. His wealth, which was considerable, was said to be spent on buying votes for support in the elections.[26] During a rally in a school in the predominantly Coptic area of Shubra, in Cairo in February 1944, Theofolis' spokesman warned the audience of 'malicious personal rumours' against the bishop.[27] For Theofolis, his campaign rested on the question over *waqf* which, he argued, should remain in the hands of the monasteries and monks revealing his traditional approach to the question of the nature of the Church. Theofolis symbolised the voice of the extreme right wing of the Church represented by the majority of the Holy Synod of bishops. The Holy Synod wished to strengthen the institution of the Church with an absolute patriarch, whose spiritual and administrative roles were so interwoven that one was absorbed by the other, thus making the role of the lay *Majlis* obsolete. The Anglican bishop in Cairo viewed Theofolis' agenda as evidence of his serious personal mismanagement, pointing out that he was 'the most malignant enemy of reform in the Coptic Church'.[28] Despite this however, Theofolis received considerable support from his Diocese in Sharqiyyah where the majority of his votes came from. Theofolis' status as the bishop in Jerusalem, was also used as a rallying point, claiming that he would ensure a 'return to Christianity and its principles'.[29]

In second place, was the Acting Patriarch and favourite, Bishop Yusab of Girga with 736 votes.[30] Yusab stood on a platform of religious and administrative reform which would enable the ecclesiastical structures of the Church to return to spiritual duties. Yusab's campaign was promoted by Qommus Ibrahim Luqa of St. Mark's Church in Heliopolis, particularly through the use of his newspaper *Al-Yaqazah* as a means of advancing Yusab's campaign. It will be recalled that Qommus Ibrahim Luqa played an important role in promoting charitable alms, to the needy through the creation of a funds box in his Church. Luqa, who had sought to distance himself from the more secular benevolent societies, which were closely aligned with the *Majlis al-Milli,* had established good relations with the Anglican Church and wished to promote a religious *nahda* based on communal participation. He urged his readers to unite in searching for distinct specifications that should be present in a new Coptic patriarch. The pope, he claimed, should be highly educated and speak foreign languages, whilst upholding religious, moral, civil and social responsibilities.[31] Bishop Yusab, Luqa argued, fulfilled all these qualities having great piety as confirmed by a number of letters of recommendation.[32] Yusab was highly educated, literate in Coptic, Arabic and Greek; whilst his primary concern was the Church, having promoted good relations with other institutions and solidifying Coptic-Ethiopian relations.[33] This, along with statements of support by the prominent Coptic lawyer, Saba Habashi (1897–1995) the doctor Naguib Mahfouz (1882–1972) and the lecturer Sami Gabra (1893–1979) proved, according to Luqa, that Yusab should assume the role of patriarch.[34] Luqa's campaign for Yusab was therefore based on the promotion of spirituality and encouragement of responsibility towards the Church; these qualities would promote Christian values which should, he argued, be at the forefront of the campaign rather than a 'popularity competition'.[35] Yusab gained substantial support from educated religious and lay Copts many of whom had close personal working relations with the Anglican Church and the Residency who, like Qommus Luqa, wished to promote a spiritual and religious *nahda,* and were less concerned with the question of the administration of *waqf.*

On 4th February 1944, bishop Macarius of Asyut won the election for the Coptic patriarchy with a clear mandate of 1221 votes.[36] Macarius' manifesto for election was largely based on his reform legacy which he had developed in his early years as Bishop in Asyut. His prominent success occurred after discovering that Presbyterian missionaries were making strong gains through converting a number of Copts in Upper Egypt. In an attempt to quell this, Macarius built fourteen new churches. He also restored and renovated a number of old churches, including spending a total of LE 90,000 on the Tasa Monastery in Upper Egypt, LE 35,000 of which was raised from local communal fundraising.[37] With regards to education, Macarius established a progressive program which included a range of non-religious subjects in the curriculum. He created the Great Coptic Boys School in Asyut in 1900, followed in 1909 by a school for girls which boasted a British Oxford graduate as its head-teacher. His program to increase education proved successful as he set up over thirty elementary schools for the poor throughout Asyut, as well as charitable institutions which were subsidised by the community.[38] Through the extension of education, Macarius sought to rally the allegiance of Coptic congregations in Upper Egypt in order to counter missionary efforts in line with the earlier policies of Abu Islah.[39]

Macarius' election campaign was also efficiently run as a political operation with a series of popular rallies and statements of support including and led by Qommus Sergius.[40] Sergius, like Qommus Luqa had been promoted to the rank of canon by Macarius whilst he was still a Bishop in Asyut.[41] Despite the mutual connections with Macarius however, both Sergius and Luqa took opposing opinions and techniques in the campaign. Sergius' fiery, demagogic speeches and commentaries regularly appeared in his own fortnightly magazine *Al-Manarah al-Misriyyah,* where he personally attacked both Luqa, and his candidate Yusab.[42] On 1st February, three days before the patriarchal election, Sergius ran a special edition of *Al-Manarah,* in which he pre-empted the victory of Macarius with a full front page cover spread.

The edition, which was solely dedicated to Macarius's anticipated victory ran several articles including a biography, speeches in favour and even mockingly announced that Qommus Luqa had 'come to his senses' and supported the nomination of Bishop Macarius. Sergius's techniques provide a good example of the ways in which factions with particular agendas were able to articulate and disseminate their opinion to various other groups within the Coptic

community. This was particularly important, given that Qommus
Sergius felt the community had been disenfranchised by the demise
of the Wafd and was concerned about the effects of the increasing
role played by radical ideologies, especially the Muslim
Brotherhood. Whilst there are no statistics available of the
circulation of *Al-Manarah al-Misriyyah*, estimations of attendance of
meetings held by Sergius were high and can be seen as a reflection
on his personal popularity and ability to mobilise Coptic grassroots
opinion.[43]

**Figure 5** Macarius III on the front cover of *Al-Manarah al-Misriyyah*,
1st February 1944.

Perhaps most significant in aiding Macarius' victory, however, was the backing of the *Majlis al-Milli*. Ibrahim Fahmi al-Minyawi (1887–1958), who claimed to speak on behalf of the whole *Majlis*, issued a statement in January 1944 in which he confirmed the council's support for Macarius as patriarch. He cited the inappropriate candidates from amongst the monks as reasoning for the *Majlis*'s election of a Bishop.[44] Minyawi represented the belief of an increasing number of lay Copts who viewed the role of the *Majlis al-Milli* as a necessary institution for the administrative needs of the community.[45] This, it was argued, would enable the patriarch, clergy and ecclesiastical structures of the Church to focus on spiritual matters. For Minyawi and the *Majlis*, Macarius represented a reformist cleric willing to forego the control of *waqf* in favour of the *Majlis*. [46] It is worth noting that the composition of the *Majlis* itself had shifted since its creation in 1874; early members had been wealthy landowners who had played an important role in politics, such as Boutros Ghali Pasha. However, by the 1940s the composition of the *Majlis* was more reflective of the emergence of a professional, educated class who were the product of the educational and modernisation policies implemented by the Church and Egyptian state since the mid-nineteenth century. Ibrahim Minyawi himself was a medical physician. Eligibility rules for voting in the *Majlis* provide a useful indicator of the changing social composition of Copts within the actual council itself. All members, were to have yearly salaries that exceeded LE 120 per annum, or paid over LE 60 a year in rent of property, if a trader.[47] To put these sums in context, the average wage of an Egyptian employee in the Civil Service in 1942 was LE 100 per annum, falling short of the requirements to participate in the *Majlis*.[48] These requirements are significant since they highlight that it would be false to paint the *Majlis* as fully representative of the Coptic laity in the mid-twentieth century. Nonetheless, it also provides evidence that the new professional classes were at the forefront of communal politics replacing landowners, a reflection of wider developments within Egyptian Society.

Minyawi led the pro-Macarius *Majlis* with a number of high profile campaigns and rallies using *Misr* as his voice piece.[49] At a meeting in a school in the Fajallah district of Cairo, Minyawi declared that: 'No-one can achieve our hopes for reform and lead the people and the Church towards glory and happiness except His Holiness Anba Macarius'.[50] Similarly, speaking at the Doctors' syndicate on the anniversary of Yu'annis' death, Minyawi called for support for Macarius as the only suitable candidate for reform.[51] Rallying at professional syndicates had become commonplace after the failure of Wafd nationalist enthusiasm following 1936.[52] The syndicates represented the professionalization of certain occupations while Minyawi targeted potential Coptic voters. The call of support from other syndicates was forthcoming, with the lawyers, councillors, judges and public prosecutors all submitting comparable statements. Similarly, *Jam'iyyat al-Tawfiq* also added its support to Macarius' campaign highlighting the popular support and role of the Tawfiq Society.[53]

The nomination and campaign of the three main candidates reveals a substantial amount about the ways in which patriarchal elections had shifted. The importance surrounding the election of a new patriarch was, closely related to pledges, manifestos and agendas, thus revealing the development of contrasting opinions concerning the nature of the Church and the character of its spiritual leader. This had in part been influenced by the policies of modernisation and education implemented by previous patriarchs and the state, thus enabling more Copts to reach the electoral threshold and participate in proceedings. Similarly, the proliferation of the press, benevolent societies and the *Majlis al-Milli* increasingly filled the void that had been created in the political and religious landscape. The lack of opportunity for Copts to participate in national constitutional politics after 1936, along with the emergence of more radical ideologies which threatened the cohesiveness of the community, had resulted in a shift of focus to communal internal affairs. The electoral process of selecting the patriarch offered the perfect opportunity for the displaced fervour of participation. Yet in doing so, it revealed factionalism within the community itself, a process which was not favoured by all.

Writing an article in the popular cross-confessional *Al-Ahram*, Tawfiq Doss (1875–1950), the former Coptic minister in the Liberal Constitutionalist Party, discussed the negative aspects of the new electoral process that was taking place, representing a shift from the traditional methods that had been adopted while Doss had been in government.[54] Doss had received an invitation for an election meeting concerning one of the candidates for the patriarchy, his main concern however was that another rally could be taking place elsewhere at the same time, meaning that he could not make an informed choice. In addition to this, Doss was extremely disappointed by the practice of insulting other opposing candidates in the campaign process. This, he argued, was an attack on the dignity and integrity of the Church: 'all candidates are respectable religious men, one of whom will ultimately become the new head of the community'.[55] Doss highlighted that through this new form of publicity-led electioneering, the Coptic 'community' could become factionalised between candidates. Instead, Doss recommended avoiding personal meetings promoting individuals, insisting that public propaganda for or against any spiritual leader of the Church was quite inappropriate; the election of the patriarch should not be treated as a political campaign.[56] Doss's reaction is representative of a traditional style of politics promoted by the landowning elite and was based on personal contacts of localised networks which had by 1944 become obsolete.

The question of avoiding factionalism within the community also found resonance with those who had failed to ensure their own candidates' success. Qommus Luqa, whilst disappointed with the outcome, was satisfied that the principal support for Macarius' victory had come from within the Coptic community itself rather than the government or King, a reference to Yu'annis' bribe.[57] Macarius's victory was however, the result of the 'unscrupulous electioneering on the part of reactionary elements in the Coptic community', a reference to Ibrahim Minyawi Pasha, and thus revealing the differing attitudes within the community.[58] Luqa remained concerned with the spirituality of the Church, rather than who was to be in control of the distribution of *waqf*, and was clearly disheartened by the results of the election as suggested by a small six line article, twenty-eight pages into his March 1944 edition of *Al-Yaqazah* mentioning the new pope.[59] The same edition also included a short poem which revealed the exacerbation of Luqa and his followers. Entitled, 'Divisions…! Oh Leaders of the People an

Invitation to Unity', the impact of the factionalism on the Coptic community and Church were clearly highlighted:

Leaders of the people and fulfillers of promise/The people invite you to listen carefully to their call

Listen to the people today complaining about their illness/And kill the illness by reviving the medicine

What has happened to the fulfillers/For the love and peace has disappeared

Protect unity between you as a great monument/That stands high and tall

Treat the situation with the highest wisdom/Throw away your spite and shun animosity

Oh leaders protect our hopes/You are the example of hope

The poem, like 'Oh Fezzed Shaykh', reveals the importance of periodicals and newspapers as organs to air remonstration, representation and to reconcile rifts both within the community and externally.

Although the campaigns led to divisions, or exemplified those already there, Macarius' coronation was a celebrated occasion. Many hundreds of Copts packed into St. Mark's church, whilst thousands massed in the streets where loud speakers publicised the event.[60] Macarius was favourably compared to Abu Islah by two daily Coptic-owned newspapers *Misr* and *Al-Muqattam,* as well as the populist *Al-Manarah.* It was prophesised that after eighty years of stalemate, Macarius would re-establish the Coptic dream of a *nahda.*[61] As a result, Macarius was portrayed as a groom who was finally re-united with his bride, the Church, after an estranged prolonged engagement.[62]

## *Macarius and the Wafd Government*

Whilst no serious complaints were made of government interference in the election, some commotion was caused the day before the vote when a delay in the delivery of ballot paper caused speculation of foul play.[63] Despite this however Nahhas' Wafd government (February 1942–October 1944) were cautious of appearing to meddle in Coptic religious affairs, particularly following Makram Obeid's departure, the Black Book Affair and his subsequent imprisonment.[64] Whilst Obeid had refrained from being a sectarian leader, he had nonetheless been regarded by Nahhas and the Wafd as a representative of the Copts.[65] The only other prominent Copt in the Wafd government following Obeid's demise, was Ibrahim Farag Pasha (1903–1993), Director in the Ministry of Interior, who did not command the same respect and authority and supported Macarius in a completely personal capacity.[66]

Its worth noting that while the Wafd consciously appeared neutral during the election, Macarius was less than cautious. One of his primary acts following his election in February 1944 was to support Mustafa Nahhas, the Wafd leader, in a public capacity; the Patriarch regarded Nahhas with awe for his nationalist contribution in Egypt.[67] Macarius, who himself had been a strong enthusiast of the first generation principles of the Wafd as epitomised by Zaghlul, had ardently supported Qommus Sergius' role in 1919, and the image of Muslim-Christian unity against the anti-colonial struggle. A few days after the election, the Prime Minister called on the patriarch to congratulate him; in conversation Macarius stated that he would not call the Prime Minister, Nahhas Pasha, but Mustafa, as he was not only head of the government but *Mustafa al-ummah wa mukhtarah,* the 'chosen' or 'selected' of the nation.[68] This was a play on the Prime Minister's name 'Mustafa' which means the elect and is a term applied to the Prophet.[69] Similarly at the patriarch's coronation, he kissed Nahhas on both cheeks and greeted him as 'leader of the people'; an epithet traditionally reserved for Zaghlul, to the great annoyance of the King who only sent a representative, Ahmad Hassanin Pasha to the coronation.[70] Macarius' actions were in contrast to his previous attitude to the royalist 'Ali Mahir, of *Al-Ittihad* Party, who became Prime Minister

(August 1939–June 1940) and had visited Asyut. All Coptic notables in the community were invited to welcome the leader, but Macarius only sent a deputy to the event. When 'Ali Mahir called on Macarius to remonstrate, the patriarch replied that church duties stood in his way, but that he mentioned the government in his prayers. Macarius viewed the royalist *Al-Ittihad* Party as regressive and in complete contrast to the Wafd and their nationalist legacy.[71]

Macarius' attitude towards Nahhas and the Wafd, was not welcomed by all. Indeed, many Copts who had felt disenfranchised were against what they interpreted as a political partnership between patriarch and state; similarly, other Copts, including Minyawi, had grown against the Wafd following the 'Black Book Affair' and particularly with the party's lack of policies in light of the growing influence of radical ideologies.[72] Minyawi who had been an ardent supporter of Makram Obeid, had fully backed the disgraced minister during his imprisonment, campaigning for his release. Minyawi later supported Obeid as Minister of Finance in Ahmad Mahir's Sa'dist government (October 1944–February 1945).[73] Writing in his memoirs, historian and Copt Luwis 'Awad argued that Minyawi's position was not unique, but reflective of many Copts from a variety of ideological and political stances; they felt alienated by the Wafd's lack of direction.[74] Macarius' visible attachment to the Wafd in the 1940s, particularly at a time when the party was loosing political momentum and grassroots support, from both Copts and Muslims, is telling. Macarius and his campaign manager Qommus Sergius, believed in early Wafdist, Zaghlul led nationalism and the end of British occupation, however they had failed to grasp the importance of the emergence of new radical nationalisms and ideologies. Similarly, such a high publicity stunt in Macarius' early days as patriarch was to sow sour seeds with Minyawi and the *Majlis* who had sincerely hoped that Macarius' platform for election would be an end to the dispute concerning *waqf*.

## Reform or Fragmentation?

Calls for religious and social reform of the Coptic Church had been prevalent since the mid-nineteenth century. Abu Islah and his successors sought, with varied efforts and success, to stimulate a spiritual and communal *nahda* through the promotion of lay education, as well as the reform of ecclesiastical structures in line with the modernisation of the state. In parallel, the creation of a community lay council, or *Majlis al-Milli*, along with the emergence of a lay Coptic Benevolent Society in 1881, provided an external framework independent from the traditional ecclesiastical structures and authority of the Church. Both the *Majlis* and the Coptic Benevolent Society reflected the prevailing social and economic realities of Egypt, particularly in the twentieth century, promoting secular education and the modernisation of the Coptic community. In general, lay activities promoted closer intra-communal association through the provision of funding. This supported a host of philanthropic and charitable societies, with similar aims and objectives throughout Egypt. Most importantly however, the lay societies and the council advocated changes in the re-distribution of charity and in fundraising procedures. The process of charity, partly sponsored through the emergence of these societies, helped to raise questions concerning the distribution of Coptic *waqf*, or religious endowments.

Elected on a reforming agenda Macarius did not initially disappoint those who advocated restructuring in the management of *waqf*. The sixty-one year old controversy concerning endowments was 'settled' only eleven days after his coronation as Patriarch.[75] Two main types of *waqf* existed in the Coptic Church; general endowments such as schools, hospitals, charities and churches, and endowments belonging to monasteries, by far the richer and the source of dispute.[76] The competence of the *Majlis*, with regards to *waqf*, was originally defined in the 1883 Decree under which the *Majlis* was formally established.[77] However, the relevant provisions of the Decree had remained a dead letter owing to the opposition of the *nazirs*, the supervisors of the *waqf* appointed by the patriarch, the heads of monasteries, and the reluctance and inability on the part of the patriarch to overcome this opposition. In 1927 a law affirmed the rights of the *Majlis* to take charge of all matters related to the Coptic endowments in general.[78] The *Majlis* came to fully control all general endowments, that is schools, hospitals and charities. However, the continued opposition of the *nazirs* and heads of monasteries nullified the effects of the law in relation to the monasteries. In a final attempt in 1928, an arête was issued by the Ministry of Interior which gave legal force to a decision that a committee of the *Majlis* should control and supervise the administration of the *waqf* belonging to the monasteries and to audit their accounts.[79] At the same time however, it conferred the rights of administration of *waqf* on the heads of the monasteries and *nazirs* as long as they remained adherent to the above mentioned controls of the committee. Despite the revision of the terms in 1928, monastic endowments remained largely in the hands of the *nazirs* and heads of the monasteries.

In 1944, Macarius decided to administer *waqf* according to the relevant provisions of the 1883 Decree as amended by Law 19 of 1927. This had been set out in his pre-election manifesto in which he gave a scathing speech to bishops and heads of monasteries entitled 'Why are we so concerned with *awqaf*?', Macarius maintained that it would be better to appoint someone to look after and administer *waqf* so that clerics could make themselves more available to God and not to

> tables of food [...] We are all monks, and being that we have given our lawful inheritance to the Church. Is it right for any person to give up his share and then demand it back thereafter? It is no longer ours.[80]

This was a clear criticism towards the heads of the monasteries who purportedly mismanaged *waqf* to their own benefit whilst the majority of Coptic monks lived in miserable conditions, little better than the peasantry.[81]

In late February 1944, Macarius came to an agreement with the *Majlis* which set out the aims of the future of endowments. Monastic *waqf* would be put to the full use of the community in order to promote a *nahda*. Religious institutional structures, such as the clerical college set up in 1875, would be reorganised in order to promote the standards of education for monks and clergy, while also ensuring a separation between administrative and spiritual matters. Any surplus money would be spent on other reforms which the patriarch deemed necessary.[82] All monastic trusts, which had been exclusively within the domains of the heads of monasteries and *nazirs*, would henceforth be administered by a central office located at the patriarchate in Cairo.[83] Macarius, was to become the supreme Director of the Coptic *waqf* and supervise a committee composed of Minyawi and four other elected members of the *Majlis al-Milli* approved by the patriarch. The role of the new committee would include an immediate inventory of existing *waqf* and an investigation of the spending habits of the *nazirs*. The re-appointment or dismissal of serving *nazirs* would then be decided by the patriarch following the advice of the *Majlis* findings.[84] In this way, Macarius could ensure that the traditional ecclesiastical structures and authority of the patriarch would remain to oversee the distribution of funds, while also removing the abuses perpetrated by bishops and monks. Similarly the *Majlis al-Milli*, while assuming that they had autonomy of actions, separating the administration from the religious structures of the Church, would in fact have been subject to the restrictions and oversight of the patriarch.

This decision however provoked outcry; abbots who had been independently administering the finances of their monasteries, categorically refused to let their authority wane.[85] The dispute took on a very public flavour with numerous open letters and petitions being published in different newspapers. The first of these was submitted by a number of prominent bishops and was published in the increasingly pro-bishop, and pro-Holy Synod, *Al-Muqattam* newspaper in March 1944.[86] The undersigned included Theofolis, the bishop of Jerusalem who had competed against Macarius in the Patriarchal elections two weeks earlier.[87]   For Theofolis, the question over *waqf* was of great importance, particularly given he was accused of having mismanaged his own endowments.[88] The petition referred to the patriarch's intention of handing over *waqf* for administration to the *Majlis al-Milli*. In reference to the 1927 law, the petition stated: 'We are sure that this was not your intention [...] Such an action would be contrary to the law and the conditions of *waqf*'.[89]   The bishops claimed that they were not opposed to reform and modernisation, and would indeed receive any suggestions for improvements to the administration, including educational and cultural programs funded by the surpluses of *waqf* funds. However, this was to occur under the supervision of the *nazirs* of the monasteries and the patriarchate.[90]

To add fuel to the dispute and in act of defiance, the bishops, heads of monasteries, and the Holy Synod, which had largely sided with Bishop Theofolis during the election campaign, made further protests through the press.[91] In May 1944, the Holy Synod, following a meeting, issued a statement to the effect that the actions of the Pope were not in the interest of the Church, and that as a result he had surrendered the leadership of the Coptic Patriarchate to the lay *Majlis al-Milli*. This, they argued, was contrary to Coptic Laws which required that the patriarch act in accordance with the Holy Synod. Thus, due to the infringement, the Holy Synod agreed that the authority of the Coptic Church would default to their control. A week later, at a general meeting in the patriarchate, it was decided that the Holy Synod's declaration was unlawful; the patriarch would remain the one and only authority of the Coptic Church.[92] Whilst these developments are only briefly discussed in Coptic sources, the Holy Synod's actions serve as evidence of its abhorrence to the lay-led *Majlis al-Milli* control of monastic *waqf* and their acquiesce by the patriarch.

In response to these protests, Macarius asserted that institutionalisation of endowments through the creation of a supervisory committee represented an ideal opportunity to regulate funds in order to reform the Church. This would be solely governed by him upon the advice of the *Majlis*, and following later protests by the Holy Synod, would also include two Monks.[93] Thus there is evidence that Macarius wished to assure the Holy Synod that whilst he was altering structures, he was safeguarding the traditional rights and authorities of the institution of the Church.

## *Awqaf and Corruption in the Majlis*

Writing about the post-war years, Anglican Rev. John Watson has argued that the left wing of the Coptic community from the mid-twentieth century were those who appealed to the *Majlis* as the ultimate authority in a Church which they essentially regarded as a Church of the laity, with the clergy as the servants of the Copts. The *Majlis* was therefore expected to act as the brake on the expenses of the Holy Synod, bishop and patriarch.[94] Thus the *Majlis al-Milli* has been painted as the saviour of darkness and as a driving force of modernisation. Nonetheless, it is necessary to highlight that the opposition of bishops, heads of monasteries and the Holy Synod against the *Majlis al-Milli* also stemmed from the *Majlis'* own misconduct and failings.[95] The heads of the monasteries claimed in 1944 that the *Majlis* had, from the beginning of its administration of non-monastic endowments in 1928, proven that they were just as an incapable an administrator and just as corrupt. In the period 1928–1932, according to *Al-Muqattam*, the *Majlis* had sold property amounting to a total of LE 61,071.[96]

In the case of the *Majlis'* supervision over Coptic schools, a similar deterioration was apparent. The Great Coptic Schools of Cairo had been amongst the best schools in Egypt and had been the brainchild of Abu Islah following the Khedival policies of state modernisation. After the government arête in 1928 which placed all non-monastic endowments in the hands of the *Majlis*, the level of the grades and education in schools declined rapidly. An illustration of the results below provides evidence of the poor results achieved in examinations of 1944:

**Table 7** Results of Students at a Great Coptic School, 1944.[97]

| Subject | Candidates | Passes | Percentage of Passes |
|---------|-----------|--------|---------------------|
| Arts | 12 | 2 | 16.6 |
| Maths | 7 | 0 | 0 |
| Science | 25 | 11 | 44 |

To place the figures in context, the national Egyptian average pass rate for the subject of Arts, which included humanities, language and literature, was 50.2 per cent, thus the Great Coptic Schools fell way below average. Similarly, the Bulaq Coptic School in Cairo, was named the worst primary education facility in the city receiving an 18 per cent pass rate in examinations compared with an Egyptian national average of 54.2 per cent in 1944.[98] The ineffectiveness of the *Majlis* was blamed on an array of failings which included personal criticisms towards 'Azmi Nawar who had been appointed governor of schools by the *Majlis*. Nawar was answerable for a lack of organisation, which in one case had resulted in a class being left unsupervised when its teacher was taken sick for two and a half months.[99]

The *Majlis al-Milli* was also rebuked for their administrative failures in the patriarchal *diwan*. In October 1937, the *Majlis* established a committee to assess the operation of the patriarchal *diwan* and present, wherever possible, suggestions for reform.[100] The results however, provided some telling signs of misadministration by the *Majlis* itself. Whilst the *diwan* had failed to collect LE 33,108 in outstanding land rents from tenants in the period 1934–36, it became apparent that a third of this sum was actually owed by the *Majlis* itself. In other words, the *Majlis* had rented buildings and facilities from the patriarchate but had not paid their dues. The lay committee, upon reporting their findings in January 1938, cancelled their own debts, whilst heavily criticising the patriarchate for the outstanding LE 20,093.[101] In another case, which was also under *Majlis* supervision, the administration had failed to collect over five years worth of rent from lands in Shinbura, in the Governate of Mansura, whilst simultaneously extending the lease to the same tenants for a further three years.[102]

These examples of *Majlis* mal-administration are very significant as they challenge Coptic historiography such as Samir Seikaly, which has portrayed the *Majlis* as a 'progressive, effecient' institution against a 'reactionary' Church.[103]   Instead, Macarius' attempts in 1944 to address religious endowments opened up the forum for greater factional debate.

### A White Suit and a Red Bow-Tie

The protracted dispute between the *Majlis*, the Holy Synod and Macarius concerning the control of *waqf*, also resulted in growing hostility from Minyawi towards the patriarch. He viewed Macarius as stalling the process in favour of the monks and Holy Synod, particularly following their remonstrations in the press in March 1944. In one feature article, Minyawi vociferously articulated in *Misr*, that he had only backed Macarius' nomination to the patriarchy as there were 'no other suitable candidates'.[104] Minyawi had also attempted to use old connections with the Wafd in order to settle the stalemate in his favour. In May 1944, Minyawi had visited Prime Minister Nahhas to intervene in the dispute; the government declined. Nahhas claimed that he would not 'accept the responsibility of spilling monk's blood inside the monasteries'.[105] It was suggested that Macarius' strong personal relationship with Nahhas had rendered the Wafd unwilling to interfere in the internal dispute, whilst Minyawi's close relationship with Obeid also did not help matters.[106]

Unlike the Holy Synod in *Al-Muqattam*, or Minyawi in *Misr*, Macarius was far more cautious about adopting a direct public forum such as the press to air his grievances. In order to avoid confrontation, the patriarch indirectly spoke through his Patriarchal Secretary, as well as through Qommus Sergius. Ironically, in a statement to the press issued through his secretary, Macarius announced his regret that the dispute over endowments was being played out in such a public forum as the newspapers.[107] This regret was re-iterated by the Egyptian daily *Al-Ahram*, who refused to publish future accounts concerning the controversy and contended that other newspapers should leave all parties involved to deal with matters 'between themselves and in the interest of their community'.[108]

Qommus Sergius' personal accounts of meetings with the patriarch also offer some insightful commentaries, particularly following Macarius' announcement to relinquish *waqf* to the *Majlis*. Explaining Macarius' position, Sergius claimed that the patriarch would not forgo the Holy Synod and bishops and that he did not wish to fight the lay *Majlis*, but work with it; however, it was Minyawi who was not co-operating.[109] Sergius, described the *waqf* dispute as the 'Mummy's Curse', given that every patriarch who touched the issue was plagued by it.[110] In a conversation between Macarius and Sergius, the patriarch resisted any calls for the government to intervene; despite what Sergius called the 'virtual imprisonment' that Macarius was under, a reference to the stalemate.[111]

Finally, it is possible to identify another Coptic faction in the active discussions concerning the *waqf* dispute. Though not as vociferous as Minyawi, the *Majlis al-Milli* and the Holy Synod,

Qommus Luqa nonetheless participated in the ongoing debates. Describing himself as a 'neutral reformer' Luqa wrote guarded commentaries.[112] Following his 'Invitation to Unity' in March 1944, Luqa had completely refrained from using *Al-Yaqazah* to discuss intra-communal disputes. Instead, he dedicated his pages to religious and spiritual discussions, as well as benevolent and philanthropic activities. However, following the raucous press attacks against the patriarch, Luqa explained his position. In a piece entitled 'The Coptic Issue', Luqa divided the dispute into two camps, the heads of the monasteries, supported by the bishops and *nazirs* on the one hand, and the *Majlis al-Milli* on the other.

Luqa described the Church as a battleground for fighting and struggle; each camp attempting to score a victory against the other, destroying it through 'arrows of insults and slanders'. Luqa argued that heads of monasteries had increased their capital and doubled their income, whilst the Church did not benefit. Similarly, the *Majlis al-Milli* did not prove its capability to administer *waqf* under its supervision; the *Majlis* had 'not achieved a single achievement in the 16 years following the re-adoption of 1883'. In fact, the council had postponed projects which included the Coptic College, whilst girls and boys schools were also closed; this despite the schools having been a proud Coptic achievement. [113]

In contrast however, Luqa described 'people of true reform' as having stood neutral; the 'true reformers', which included himself and followers, had kept away to give the *Majlis* and the heads of the monasteries room to finish the dispute in peace. Luqa's statement, through *Al-Yaqazah*, was thus a clarification of the 'present struggle'; it is worth noting that Luqa commonly used the term *Al-nazal al-hadir*, which was also used in the Arabic press as a reference to the struggle against colonial occupation.[114] Luqa's position in the *waqf* dispute was clear:

> The Church has been suffering in recent years in a spiritual deficit and the solution involves much work and effort and requires in turn much money[...] All these issues require money and to achieve them we have to agree amongst ourselves that spending should come from the Church endowments. The purpose of the waqf is not to hold it

without use, but to use its income to satisfy different Church needs. The Church laws says that waqf is unrestricted for the needy.[115]

The varied factions and opinions had clearly impacted Macarius' ability to resolve the situation. In the face of ongoing criticisms led by the Holy Synod, which claimed that the patriarch had foregone the clergy, and Minyawi, who had portrayed Macarius as frail in age and weak in character, the patriarch under the pretence of ill health went into monastic retreat in the Eastern Desert Monastery of St. Anthony's.[116] The Coptic community rather than appear united, reformed and strong in the face of perceived external threats, was in fact increasingly factionalised, weak and fragmented as an entity.

In an attempt to lend support to the patriarch as the epitome of the head of the community, the government sent tacit support to Macarius' aims, thus serving to reinforce traditional government ties with the hierarchy of the Church. The new Sa'dist Party under Ahmad Mahir (October 1944–February 1945) which, had taken over from Nahhas' Wafd government, pursued a similar policy to its predecessor. In a letter, Mahir implicitly leant his government's support to Macarius who had been in self-imposed exile since August 1944:

> I know that due to your ill health you are in the monastery and that there are important issues that need your attention in the patriarchate. I am sorry that I cannot attend personally to your return, but if you could kindly return and tell us when, we will send a large delegation to meet and accompany you through the streets of Egypt.[117]

Whilst Mahir, like Nahhas and the Wafd, did not wish to appear to be directly meddling in Coptic affairs, he did nonetheless give some indication that the government supported the patriarchate in the ongoing dispute; the government would appear by Macarius' side upon his return to Cairo. In response to the Prime Minister's request, who himself was a former Wafdist and Zaghlul supporter, Macarius described how the ongoing situation had taken its toll on him, 'Whilst I have only been patriarch for half a year, it feels like half a century'. Clarifying his position, Macarius explained that through the creation of a supervisory committee, he had wished to bring the *Majlis al-Milli* under greater scrutiny. As the overseer of all endowments, Macarius had no intention of imparting the authority of the patriarchy to the *Majlis*; he had 'suffered from the *Majlis al-Milli*'s insistence of unlawful interference in Church affairs and clerical judgement.'[118] In the following extract of the letter, Macarius' physical frailty as an ailing old man, frustrated by the negotiations and the manifestation of the question of reform, is extremely apparent:

> [...] I remonstrated with Minyawi and his fellow *Majlis al-Milli* members, I begged with a broken heart and tears to Minyawi. I asked him to have mercy on me and to be kind to me and to accept my plea in such hard times. [I told him that] I cannot breathe and my stomach was burning and much more of the similar sayings. But he never responded or cared about my pain, crying and remonstration and had no mercy on me and did not return my requests. I therefore decided to go away to the monastery.[119]

By mid-1945, the stalemate and factionalism led Macarius, with the support of the Holy Synod, to pass a new resolution concerning the monastic endowments with the aim of asserting a clerical position of authority. The new reformed supervisory committee would be established controlling, checking and reporting the actions and accounts of the *nazirs* and directors. However, instead of two monks, it would be composed of twelve members including archbishops, clergy and Coptic notables, all to be appointed by the patriarch in his capacity as the Supreme overseer, *waqf*.[120] This was in contrast to the previous 1944, resolution which had called for a council to be made up of the patriarch and four lay *Majlis* members.

Safeguards to ensure that *waqf* was run efficiently were also put into place. Resolution No. 8 called for the accounts and work of the *Majlis* to be inspected by a committee appointed by the patriarch within 30 days, in default of which legal proceedings would be taken to ensure the proper control of the endowments fund.[121] The new resolutions, which were passed by the Holy

Synod, had no legal or permanent effect but merely demonstrated the frustration and factionalism that had emerged between the *Majlis al-Milli* and the clergy, while Ibrahim Luqa sat on the side lines watching the dispute that was played out in public.

In the months leading up to Macarius' death in 1945, the press was used once again as an organ to voice factionalism. Whilst Sergius attacked *Misr* as a soap box for the *Majlis*, even calling Minyawi 'Hitler', editorials in *Misr* regularly demonised Sergius as an obstructionist block to progress.[122] It was clear by mid-1945 that the endowments were no longer the central issue at stake but rather that the dispute had taken on the form of a personal vendetta between rivalling factions. This reared itself once more during Macarius' funeral in late 1945. *Ruz al-Yusuf* magazine, founded in 1926 and concerned with political and social news, reported that a 'Coptic leader' marched immediately behind the funeral procession wearing a white suit and red tie, a sign of total disrespect.[123] The Coptic leader was later identified by *Al-Wataniyyah* magazine as Ibrahim Minyawi.[124]

# 6

# A COPTIC REVOLUTION:
# *HARAKAT AL-TATHIR*
# (1952–1954)

## The Philosophy of the Revolution

Between January 1950 and July 1952, numerous demonstrations were organised against the British occupation. These included the traditional political participants, such as the Wafd and Liberal Constitutionalists, as well the newer, more radical parties like the Socialist Party, formerly known as *Misr al-Fatat*, the Muslim Brotherhood, and the Young Muslim Men's Association (YMMA).[1] The return to power of the Wafd in January 1950 brought immense hope of political and social change; the party had promised the repeal of the 1936 Anglo-Egyptian Treaty, the right for citizens to bear arms, and an amnesty for political prisoners. However, by early 1951 the Wafd was undermined once again, with accusations of corruption and collaboration with the British and the Palace. This mounting pressure led Prime Minister Nahhas' fifth ministry (1950–1952), to unilaterally repeal the 1936 Treaty in October 1951.[2] This, however, was not enough and by January 1952 the city centre of Cairo was on fire. By July 1952, when the Free Officers carried out their bloodless coup, there was an atmosphere of political and social upheaval prevalent in Egypt.

The Free Officers had formed during the Second World War and a committee was established under the leadership of Gamal 'Abd al-Nasser (1918–1970). Nasser, who became an officer the year following the Anglo-Egyptian Treaty, aimed to establish a democratic government by force, ousting the British and landed aristocratic political parties like the Wafd, which had dominated

Egypt's political scene since 1919. The army, which carried out the coup on the evening of 23rd July 1952, was 'a model of military planning and execution, the most efficient thing done in Egypt for many years'.[3] The military coup was implemented under the figure-head of General Muhammad Naguib, who, as the eldest and most high-ranking of the group, led the movement until he was deposed in late 1954 in favour of Nasser. The main aims of the revolution, as stated by Anwar al-Sadat (1918–1981), a leading Free Officer and later President of Egypt (1970–1981), were:

> [...] to get Egypt out of the middle-ages, to turn it into a modern, ordered, viable state, while at the same time respecting the customs of the people. On this last point, respecting the customs of the people does not mean chaining them down to a dead past, it means respecting the essential and invisible continuities in a nation's life. We would conserve everything that did not impede on the real progress of the community.[4]

The Free Officers did not initially build a popular revolutionary organisation but erected themselves as a vanguard. As a result, widespread participation was not implemented and, instead, the Revolutionary Command Council (RCC) was established for a transitional period, in the name of order: 'We needed order, but we found nothing but chaos. We needed unity but we found nothing but dissention. We needed work, but we found nothing behind us only indolence and sloth.'[5]

The military coup of July 1952 acted as the impetus, marking the beginning of the end for the old political order which had dominated Egypt. All political organisations and elites which had hitherto ruled, including the Wafd Party, were dissolved; King Farouk was also forced to abdicate on 26th July 1952, leaving his infant son Fu'ad II as regent.[6] Egypt officially became a republic a year later, as the monarchy was abolished, similarly, all political parties were also dissolved and many leaders of opposition groups arrested.[7]

## The Rhetoric of Tathir

Coptic reaction to the revolution, like that of the general Egyptian populace, was surprisingly slow and not forthcoming, much to the dismay of even Nasser himself:

> Before July 23rd, I had imagined that the whole nation was ready and prepared, waiting for nothing but a vanguard to lead the charge against the battlements, whereupon it would fall in behind in serried ranks, ready for the sacred advance towards the great objective. And I had imagined that our role was to be a commando vanguard. I thought that this role would not take more than a few hours [...] Then suddenly came reality after July 23rd. The Vanguard performed its task and charged the battlements of tyranny. It threw out Farouk and then paused, waiting for the series ranks to come up in their sacred advance toward the great objective [...] for a long time we waited. Crowds did eventually come, and they came in endless droves- but how different is the reality from the dream! [8]

Indeed, even newspaper coverage of the revolution in the days following was sluggish, and although the daily *Al-Ahram* reported on 24th July 1952 'The Revolution is Born', the rest of the edition was mainly dedicated to the Korean War (1950–1953), as well as a double-page spread concerning how a modern fitted kitchen could revolutionise the lifestyles of the urban Egyptian housewife.[9] Having surveyed a variety of Egyptian newspapers and magazines in the days immediately after the revolution, it is clear that responses, reactions and commentaries to events were particularly sparse, thus perhaps highlighting the perception that, given the political unrest that Egypt had undergone in the years preceding 1952, it was wise to adopt a policy of caution.

Despite this however, the concept of *harakat al-tathir*, (a purification or cleansing movement), increasingly found resonance and was repeatedly used by the press in the days following the initial shock of the revolution. This was a reference to the purges and subtractions that were taking place. For example, when discussing the forced abdication of King Farouk in July 1952, a newspaper reported that 'The army controls the situation until it purifies'.[10] This concept of cleansing or purification was portrayed, particularly in what remained of the press, as a natural process of the revolution which sought to modernise, reform and ensure the social and political progression of Egypt, in other words, to regenerate the country.

The initial cautious attitudes vis-à-vis the Free Officers was evident in the responses of various Coptic organisations to the revolution. For example, the first official Coptic group to acknowledge and congratulate the revolutionaries was *Al-Tawfiq* on 31st July 1952, almost a week after the event. Students and young professional educated laymen had dominated *Al-Tawfiq*; precisely the disenfranchised middle class which the RCC had hoped would support the revolutionaries.[11]

**Figure 6** Revolutionary Command and Church Leadership.
(Left to Right) Gamal Abd Al-Nasser, Muhammad Naguib, Pope
Yusab and Qommus Sergius, September 1952.[12]

By late September, Coptic newspapers were already appropriating the language of *tathir* which had increasingly become evident in secular national dailies. For example, an unsigned open letter was published on behalf of 'the Copts' by *Misr* to President Naguib on the two month anniversary of the revolution. This praised him for the Free Officers' actions, particularly in relation to the RCC's commitment to freedom from tyranny and the *tathir* of the old structures of the state.[13]

As a staunch supporter of the *Majlis al-Milli* and reform, *Misr* throughout August 1952 published a series of anonymous articles entitled 'Change as we want it'. These articles took advantage of the opportunity of the revolution and appropriated its language through demands for reform, change and *tathir* throughout the structures of the Coptic Church in an attempt to mirror wider events in Egypt.[14] For example, one article, published in August 1952, discussed the role of ecclesiasts within the Church, making a direct comparison between Muhammad Naguib and the Coptic patriarch. The article encouraged Pope Yusab II to use the weapon of reform, or *islah*, to provide moral guidance for a disenchanted community.[15] *Misr* also enthusiastically returned to the question of reforming *waqf* an issue which had been at an impasse since Pope Macarius' attempts to solve the issue in the mid-1940s.

Similarly, the Free Officers were also enthusiastic to promote a number of issues in relation to the Copts which, while related to national unity, also had an underlying reformist agenda: the possibility of *tathir* within Coptic ecclesiastical structures if co-operation was not forthcoming. In an attempt to solidify a narrative of national unity, the Free Officers, and particularly General Muhammad Naguib, also endeavoured to rally the support of the Coptic community.[16] This was regarded as particularly important given sectarian conflict had increased in the months preceding the 1952 coup. In January 1952, a church in the city of Suez was burnt following riots between Copts and Muslims.[17] Five Copts had been killed after supporters of the Muslim Brotherhood had believed that the Copts were acting as spies for the British.[18] The event caused Pope Yusab II to make noisy remonstrations to Prime Minister Nahhas and the Wafd government, whilst Ibrahim Farag Pasha, a Copt in Nahhas's government, was called upon to resign by the Church in protest. Protests and petitions in a number of newspapers were published as evidence of Coptic remonstrations at the events.[19] Historian Mustafa Al-Feki argues that had Obeid, the former Party Secretary of the Wafd who was forced to resign in

1942, been in the current Nahhas cabinet, the backlash against the Suez church burnings would have been more confined.[20]

As a result of Suez, Naguib actively sought to bolster a Coptic-Muslim image of national unity reminiscent of 1919. In a speech given at the Coptic Youth Society in Alexandria in September 1952, Naguib announced that the basis of an Egyptian *nahda* was the unity between Copts and Muslims; he had invited Coptic lay and religious-led organisations, including the Coptic Benevolent Society and *Al-Tawfiq*, to follow his lead throughout the country and cleanse the old administrative machines.[21] Thus Naguib was not only negotiating a place for Copts in post-revolutionary Egypt, but also actively lobbying reformist Coptic organisations with similar agendas to encourage *tathir*, modernisation and reform. The impact of these calls was clear: the language of the philosophy of the revolution was adopted by many of the benevolent societies which increasingly operated as pressure groups to address the shortcomings of the patriarchy. *Al-Tawfiq*, the Coptic Benevolent Society, and many professional middle class men linked the failings of the patriarchy with that of King Farouk and the *ancien régime* of the Wafd.[22] In the immediate aftermath of the revolution, hundreds of telegrams arrived from Copts making vocal demands on the RCC: 'As you have purged the country, purge our patriarchate' and that 'the Copts are an indivisible part of the nation; and your purging movement must embrace them'.[23]

Importantly, Naguib courted those sharing these opinions, and accepted an invitation at a patriotic ceremony organised by Qommus Sergius at his Church in Qulqali in September 1952.[24] Sergius, who had immediately been able to establish close links with the RCC due to his nationalist credentials in 1919, had popular Coptic backing and used the same rhetoric as the revolution to lend credence and legitimacy to his demands. In the presence of General Naguib, Sergius issued a statement reminding the Patriarch that the King of Egypt had to abdicate due to the will of the people, and that the new Revolutionary Command required purification everywhere. The threat was directed against Pope Yusab's handling of the question of *waqf*, along with the actions of his personal servant Malak Girgis who, was accused of simony. Malak, who was originally a peasant, and whose own personal salary did not exceed

LE 10 a month had, by 1952, amassed six properties and was running a saloon car; Malak was said to preside over the choice of bishops, the promotion of priests and the distribution of all property.[25] Indeed, Qommus Luqa, whilst *wakil* of the Church, personally witnessed attempts to sell ecclesiastical positions, including priesthoods and deaconaries. Similar rumours had also spread concerning payments and bribery for the promotion of high ecclesiastical offices, including bishoprics:[26]

> I witnessed an event that confirmed this [simony] to me. An overly ambitious man personally offered me, or to my Church projects in Heliopolis, LE 5,000 in return for a Bishopric in a diocese [...] I also discovered the [Papal] courtiers had hands in transferring the priests of Cairo, in spite of the fact that this was within the scope of my job as wakil. This however, was being manipulated by someone else.[27]

Qommus Sergius, in General Naguib's presence, declared that fifteen days were given to the patriarch to operate administrative reforms otherwise Sergius would direct a march on the patriarchate.[28] By associating himself with Naguib, Sergius was able to mobilise enough support to remove the corrupt patriarchal servant, who was replaced by his brother. *Misr* depicted the whole episode as part of the *harakat al-tathir* initiated by the revolution; Naguib and the RCC required a cleansing of all institutional and religious structures.[29] Indeed, an audit committee addressing characters of 'disrepute' was also forced upon the structures of the Al-Azhar in the early months of the revolution.[30]

*Misr* reported in August 1952 that "cleansing" had finally, thanks to Naguib and the revolution, begun within the Church.[31] The momentum of cleansing within Church structures spread so considerably after the activities of September 1952, that calls were made by prominent writers in a number of non-Coptic newspapers and magazines to extend the purification movement into the monasteries.[32] Indeed, five Copts who were accused of corruption, having worked in close association with Malak, were also subjected to the purge. 'Abdu, the head deacon, 'Adli, the Pope's chauffeur, Ayyub, the porter, Qommus Girgis, overseer of the Red Mountain

Monastery, and Qommus Mikhail, the overseer of Ayra Monastery were all removed from their positions.[33]

Whilst the process of *tathir* in the Church excited many voices who had been opposed to the servant Malak and his tyranny, there were also casualties. At a meeting in late September 1952, a deal was struck between the *Majlis al-Milli* and the patriarch, resulting in the excommunication of Qommus Sergius and the severance of all his ecclesiastical dignities.[34] Having lost Malak, the patriarch was determined to see the vocal Sergius also gone. It was reported that Sergius' continuous attempts to raise publicity and highlight his own agenda had become detrimental to the Church and increasingly caused embarrassment. Similarly, the *Majlis al-Milli*, and in particular Ibrahim al-Minyawi, who had an intense personal rivalry with Qommus Sergius, supported his dismissal.[35] Sergius's previous contributions to the Egyptian nationalist movement in 1919 were sidelined in favour of a temporary alliance between former enemies. Similarly, the RCC which had been prepared to use Qommus Sergius's nationalist credentials to promote their own agenda of national unity earlier that month also remained silent.[36]

### Negotiating a Place in Post-Revolutionary Egypt

The impetus of the revolution was also adopted by a series of political associations and groups in the months following July 1952. Mainly comprised of young, educated, male Copts, loosely affiliated to the activities of the philanthropic societies, these organisations attempted to assert political and constitutional Coptic rights. In particular, calls were made by *Misr*, representing a reformist Coptic voice, supporter of the revolution and generous benefactor to Coptic benevolent and philanthropic societies, that it was time for the RCC to correct the 'traditions which have been established over the last few decades which have resulted in the removal of Copts from specific jobs'. Calls were also made to the RCC to change television and radio broadcasting laws, which only permitted Copts to transmit on special religious occasions.[37]

Similarly, other political demands were raised by a small fringe Coptic organisation which had political aspirations. *Al-Hizb al-Democrati al-Misihi* (HDM), had been formed in the late-1940s as a reaction to the political disenfranchisement and ideological threats of the extreme right-wing paramilitary and religious parties.[38] The HDM, though not an official political party, had many of the structures of a political pressure group. Led by the prominent Coptic lawyer Ramsis Gabrawi, who had been a strong Wafdist supporter prior to Makram Obeid's departure in 1942, the group sought to mobilise popular Coptic opinion following the demise of the Wafd. The HDM has been described by the prominent Egyptian Marxist, Abu-Sayf Yusuf, writing in the 1980s, as a reaction amongst the middle and upper-classes to the failure to obtain independence, a reference to not only Egyptian political independence from British occupation, but also Coptic political rights within a constitutional democratic political system.[39]

In the immediate aftermath of the revolution, the HDM, which had been in operation for several years, attempted to gather the support of the new regime and appropriate its nationalist rhetoric by changing its own name to *Al-Hizb al-Democrati al-Qawmi* (HDQ), or the National Democratic Party, in an attempt to secure their demands.[40] A declaration of requests which, had nationalist overtones but, were clearly focussed on Coptic concerns were published in *Misr* in the hope that they would curry favour with the RCC. These included calls for the separation of religion from state, proportional representation in parliament, and the removal of building restrictions on churches. Similarly, calls were also made for the re-distribution of land and improvement of the conditions of peasants, highlighting a social reformist agenda and a total commitment to human rights.[41] Unlike Qommus Sergius, who had demanded administrative and clerical reforms within the religious framework of the Church in September 1952, the HDQ sought to rally the support of the RCC by couching their demands in secular terms.

Whilst the HDQ included mainly professional and educated middle-aged Copts, the period immediately prior to and after the revolution also witnessed the rise of a number of active Coptic youth organisations. Their concerns, like those of the HDQ, were varied in character, although in large part greatly reflective of political, religious and social concerns prevalent within Coptic society. Immediately prior to the revolution, universities in particular, became fertile ground for student discontent; both

Muslim and Coptic students played a crucial role in the rallying of nationalist and student interests which were largely, although not exclusively, split between support for the Muslim Brotherhood, the Wafd and the left.[42] This intense atmosphere of student politics also gave impetus to the rise of a group of Coptic youths who were based at Fu'ad I University and who had substantial links with the Great Benevolent Society and in particular *Al-Tawfiq*.[43] In November 1951, the group of mainly male Copts decided to put an end to the corruption of the Church and to 'save her honour' by favouring the takeover of *waqf* by the *Majlis al-Milli*. It was hoped that following this the Church and the *Majlis al-Milli* would be free to pursue the political and representational concerns of the Coptic community in Egyptian politics.[44]

A youth conference, which was planned by the group to coincide with a patriarchal meeting, was scheduled although this was subsequently prevented by the Ministry of Interior under instructions from the Patriarchal servant Malak.[45] While the actions of the Coptic youths of Fu'ad I University are little known, they are significant as they serve to reveal the role of youth movements. These were closely linked to Coptic non-religious benevolent societies in addressing long-standing intra-communal factionalism, and the impact that this had on national representation of Copts in political mobilisation in the immediate period prior to the revolution.

Following the revolution however, the most notable example of a Coptic youth movement, was that of *Jama'at al-Ummah al-Qibtiyyah*, (JUQ), (The Coptic Nation Society), established by the young lawyer Ibrahim Fahmi Hilal. With their Head-Office in downtown Cairo, and commanding a following, according to Hilal, of 92,000 members, the JUQ were closely associated with the HDQ, and participated in a number of joint activities.[46] In 1953, the JUQ attempted to register with the Ministry of Social Affairs as an official religious society, as all political parties had been banned in January that year.[47] While the JUQ asserted that they were a religiously motivated society in their registration application, thus bringing them in line with other Coptic-led benevolent societies, a number of Egyptian and primarily Coptic historians, have questioned the reasons behind the emergence of *Jama'at al-Ummah al-Qibtiyyah*. Their interpretation of the movement has been largely influenced by the political climate in which they themselves were writing during the 1970s, which was characterised by strong Muslim-Christian sectarian tensions. Coptic historian Samira Bahr has argued that the organisation emerged as a religious movement, a reaction to the Muslim Brotherhood.[48] As stated by Bahr: 'The creation of *Jama'at al-Ummah al-Qibtiyyah* was for the promotion of a revival [*Ihya*] of Coptic Nationalism as a result of the drowning effects towards Islamic religiosity that was promoted by the Muslim Brotherhood'.[49] The second school of analysts, writing almost a decade after Bahr, have viewed the JUQ differently. Free of the inter-communal Muslim-Christian factionalism that had dominated the late Sadat era, Abu Sayf Yusuf, a prominent left-wing writer, takes on a more Marxist interpretation of the events. Whilst he regarded the JUQ as a religious organisation, in his view their motivation was not a reaction to the Brotherhood but rather the result of long-term economic and political failings following the downfall of the Wafd.[50] Historian Rafiq Habib, has also viewed the creation of the organisation as a middle-class reaction to the political void following the Wafd's negotiation of the 1936 Treaty.[51]

Bahr is correct to argue that there was an element of religious fervour which influenced the JUQ. Indeed, in late 1953, over a year after the revolution, the JUQ issued a ten-point manifesto, or covenant, which reveals a marked resemblance to the Muslim Brotherhood's *Al-Wasayah al-'ashirah* (The Ten Commandments).[52] The JUQ Manifesto included demands for the attachment to the Holy Bible, and attention by Coptic youths to spiritual and moral issues, thereby serving as some indication of the influence of the Muslim Brotherhood.[53] Bahr's interpretation however, does not take into account the role of other religious youth associations, including *Shabaab Muhammad* (Muhammad's Youths), who undoubtedly also had an effect on the JUQ. For example, numerous calls were made in the period immediately before the revolution to create a counter society to *Shabaab Muhammad,* and name it the Coptic Youth Society.[54] Similarly, Bahr's interpretation fails to take into account the influence of Pharaonic nationalism, other radical ideologies and most importantly the impact of the 1952 Free Officers revolution on the formation of the JUQ.

Beginning with the Pharaonic connotations of the group, the main symbolic logo for the JUQ was the 'Key of the Nile' or Pharaonic 'Ang' cross, which, whilst an expression of Egypt's Pharaonic identity, also had Coptic connotations. Secondly, the JUQ also displayed features of a paramilitary organisation, echoing the activities of *Misr al-Fatat* which later became the Socialist Party and the Wafd's *Fariq al-Shabaab*. This included the establishment of a boy-scout group, with a special uniform to be worn on presentation occasions; Hilal himself also acknowledged the influence of *Misr al-Fatat* in a letter published in 1953.[55]

Thirdly and most importantly, Bahr does not take into consideration the impact of the 1952 revolution, reforms implemented by the new junta or the policy of *tathir* which followed on the growth and ideology of the JUQ. In a speech published as an open letter, Ibrahim Hilal articulated his position which attempted to negotiate a political place for the Copts in post-revolutionary Egypt.[56] The speech, which was addressed to the committee in charge of drafting a new constitution in order to replace the 1923 text, is significant. Hilal, while clearly airing his approval for the Free Officers and their fight against British imperialism, called for a national *nahda* in more than one direction.[57] Despite the conscious effort asserted by the Free Officers to promote 'the image of the cross with the crescent; the publication of the pictures of the church with the mosque; and the presence of the priest with the shaykh on many public occasions', the revolution had failed in one vital regard: removing the constraints that had been set by the 1923 constitution.[58] Hilal argued that the 1923 constitution had planted the roots of sectarian hate through the representation of the state as a religion itself; in doing this, Hilal argued, the nation took upon itself the religion of the majority, Islam became the embodiment of the Egyptian state, and, consequently, the Copts 'were wronged, persecuted and discriminated'. [59]

Hilal was particularly worried about the way in which Egyptian identity was defined in both the 1923 constitution and the new draft. He argued that, whilst the British occupiers promoted a policy of divide and rule, there could be no case, or excuse, for the drafters of the new constitution to follow their lead. Hilal contended that the wording of the new constitution led by the RCC discriminated against the Copts, identifying Egyptian identity as Islamic and Muslim:

> It was decided that it was necessary that the President of the state should be Egyptian, Muslim, and that his father and grandfather were also Egyptian etc. [...] The incredible thing about this is that any person who entered Egypt can become (as long as they are Muslim, and their father and grandfather declared they were Egyptian) the president of the country. And the Copt, who is the original Egyptian who knows about his nation from the dawn of history, is forbidden from taking part in the governance of his country or even attaining a position that is open to other people.[60]

Hilal was therefore attempting to claim a political share for the Copts in the post-revolutionary Egyptian nation by ensuring the inclusion of the Copts in the national narrative. The publication of the speech and open letter received much praise and backing from a number of influential Muslim and Coptic political and religious leaders throughout Egypt. Indeed in a letter issued from the patriarchate itself, and co-signed with Pope Yusab II's insignia ring, there was hearty approval for the work of the JUQ in asserting that the Copts were an integral part of post-revolutionary Egypt.[61] The letter was also passed on to the leading Islamic law professor, 'Abd al-Razziq al-Sanhuri (1895–1971), who had previously worked closely with Makram Obeid in the mid-1930s to promote student political activity on university campuses.[62] Al-Sanhuri argued that the JUQ's case was 'worthy of study by those drafting the constitution. I congratulate the writers for their national pride, courage and love for the great Egypt'.[63] Whilst the JUQ demonstrated their intention to work within the state apparatus through their requests for constitutional rights, the JUQ also sought to address intra-communal failings within the Church which they regarded as having rendered the institutional structure of the Church as obsolete.

## *Al-Tathir* of the Church

By January 1953, less than five months after Malak's removal from the patriarchate, the fervour of *tathir* that had initially gripped the Church in the wake of the revolution in Egypt had waned.[64] Malak, who had been allowed to return, continued his personal administration of funds and selling of religious offices. Despite this however, calls for modern, efficient administrative channels for the control of *waqf* did gain the outspoken support of Guindi 'Abd al-Malek, Minister of Supply, who as the only Coptic Minister in Nasser's Cabinet bore governmental responsibility for Coptic affairs and would play an important role in events to follow.[65]

## *The Abduction of Pope Yusab II*

In the early hours of 26th July 1954, eighty-seven JUQ members attacked the Orthodox Coptic patriarchate in Cairo. Their aim was to abduct the patriarch following a demonstration concerning the continued mal-administration of Church structures.[66] Twelve JUQ members formed the core constituents of the premeditated abduction. Led by the 24 year old lawyer Ibrahim Hilal, the main vanguard was university educated and included six mid-to-high ranking civil servants. The joint General Secretary's of the organisation, Wagee Tawfiq Bulus and Thabet Girgis Gabriel, both held degrees in commerce and had became allies while at university through their association with the Coptic Benevolent Society.[67] The timing of the event was crucial, it marked the two-year anniversary of the abdication of King Farouk and the instigation of the RCC-led *tathir*. It also served to reveal the radicalisation of the political actions of the JUQ as inspired by the revolution.[68]

The main protagonists of the JUQ, including Hilal himself, approached the patriarchate compound before sunrise and informed the doorkeeper, Dawoud, that Bishop Yuhanna of Giza had been 'shredded in a train accident', and that it was of the utmost urgency that they spoke to the patriarch. Initial reports suggested that one of the youths was dressed as a priest, although this was later discredited.[69] Once inside, the only two soldiers present were attacked and their weapons removed; the group were also confronted by two elderly Ethiopian servants in the bishops' quarters, who were subsequently tied up. Yusab, upon hearing the noise, opened the door of his quarters to his would be abductors.[70]

In his only full published interview, over fifteen years later in 1970, Hilal recalled to historian Malak Luqa how Yusab was 'torn between astonishment and disbelief, staring at us for over five minutes before uttering a word'.[71] It is at this juncture, the meeting with the patriarch, that there are two conflicting accounts of what followed. According to Hilal's interview with Luqa, he immediately presented the patriarch with a series of documents. These included the unconditional abdication of the pope from the See of St. Mark along with the patriarch's exile to the St George Monastery in Old Cairo, thus mirroring the abdication of King Farouk precisely two years earlier. Hilal also demanded the reorganisation of Coptic Church structures, including a union between the religious Holy Synod and the *Majlis al-Milli*. The aim here was, according to Hilal, to force closer co-operation between the two fragmented units of the Church. Similarly, and perhaps most importantly, new elections were also to be held for all Coptic institutions including the papacy based on universal franchise.[72] This had been at the forefront of debates since the 1928 electoral changes which only permitted those with incomes higher than LE 120 to vote, thus serving to exclude the vast majority of Copts. The existing system also ensured that questions of accountability regarding the administration of the Church were left to the control of a small, unrepresentative clique.

An alternative account, recalled in *Misr* on 31st July 1954, and entitled 'The Whole Story', describes the incident of the abduction and dialogue between the pope and abductors using a variety of police investigative sources and reports, as well as brief commentaries and statements made by some of the abductors, including those issued to the police by Hilal himself at the time of his arrest.[73] This account is important as, unlike the interview with Malak Luqa taken fifteen years after the incident, it is not subject to criticisms of reflection and consideration. Instead, the document released by *Misr* was based on immediate eye-witness accounts and testimonials. However, the agenda of the pro-*Majlis*, pro-RCC *Misr* newspaper is also questionable, and one could conversely argue that Hilial's account in 1970 was subject to less sensitivity given that existing political and religious leaderships had changed.[74] It is perhaps worth noting that non-Coptic newspapers only paid lip-service to the abduction: *Al-Ahram,* for example, treated the issue as an intra-communal affair, instigated by some unruly youths, and made short reference in a side inset box on the front page.[75]

*Misr,* unlike *Al-Manarah al-Misriyyah* and other Coptic papers, was one of the few newspapers that continued to be published in the aftermath of the revolution and thus serves as a useful tool.[76] *Misr* reported that, upon entering the patriarch's quarters, an extensive dialogue took place between Yusab and his abductors. Below is a small translated extract of the exchange:

Pope: What do you want my sons?

Hilal: We are *Jama'at al-Ummah al-Qibtiyyah,* sent by the government to let you know that the Prime Minister ['Abd al-Nasser] would like you to abdicate from the Church in favour of the Bishop of Minya as a temporary measure until we can elect another pope. In an attempt to keep your honour and dignity, we have come to transfer you to any place you want before the government does so themselves.

Pope: The Church has a constitution my son and the government cannot interfere in that. The resignation of the patriarch has particular conditions and the only one who can agree to this is the Holy Synod.[77]

The dialogue's structure, fluidity and civility are telling: Yusab's response to Hilal's request is co-ordinated and lucid, particularly given that the former had been abruptly woken. While the dialogue may have been embellished somewhat by *Misr,* there are nonetheless questions concerning the motivations for the actions of the JUQ. On the one hand, it is possible to interpret the JUQ as having carried out their actions with the approval of the Egyptian government, the implicit suggestion being, that the JUQ were merely pawns in the national policy of *tathir.* Indeed, Pope Yusab himself later recalled, according to *Misr,* that the JUQ had answered that the abdication was the wish of all Copts and a 'big character

outside the Church', perhaps insinuating Nasser himself.[78] Prime
Minister Nasser was increasingly gaining strength and would shortly
replace Muhammad Naguib as the *de-facto* leader of the
revolutionary command. Naguib, like Pope Yusab, Qommus
Sergius and King Farouk, would also become a victim of the
revolutionary *tathir*.[79] This argument would also lend itself to the
fact that student and youth activities following the revolution
increasingly came under regime-initiated and controlled bodies, and
were no longer motivated by anti-government aspirations.
However, given the way in which various Coptic organisations,
groups and newspapers, such as *Al-Tawfiq*, HDQ and *Misr*,
appropriated the language of the revolution to meet their own
communal and political goals in the period between 1952–1954, it
is also possible to view the actions of the JUQ as self-initiated,
particularly as students and youths were proclaimed by the new
establishment as the pioneers of the revolutionary future.[80]

Yusab, having signed the abdication documents in favour of the
bishop of Minya, was driven away in a taxi, with the Egyptian
security forces in hot pursuit while several shots were allegedly
fired.[81] Much of the account, by both Hilal in Luqa's interview and
in *Misr*, has Hollywood-esque overtones, leading one to perhaps
question the use of artistic licence in relaying the actual events.
Yusab was driven to the St. George Monastery in Old Cairo, where
one of the youths informed Deaconess Mary that the Pope had
arrived and was waiting outside in a taxi. Highlighting the ad-hoc
nature of the whole scenario, it took over an hour for the
Deaconess to allow Pope Yusab into the monastery fearing that he
was in fact an impostor.[82]

Meanwhile, the remaining JUQ members, under siege from the
Egyptian security forces at the patriarchate, demanded that the
Holy Synod call an immediate session and decide on the abdication
of Yusab.[83] By dawn on 26th July most of the churches in Cairo and
Alexandria, as well as the principle governates and press agencies,
had received a declaration signed by the JUQ announcing the
pope's abdication and condemning the corruption that was
rampant in the Church under his rule.[84] By late afternoon, all
abductors and protesters were apprehended by state security forces
and taken to the citadel prison.[85]

## Consequences of Reform

While the events of July 1954 have been effectively confined to an anecdote, the actions of the JUQ had wider repercussions, highlighting more serious long-term failings in the Coptic Church which other historians and commentators have failed to recognise. The JUQ were able to carry out the abduction of the patriarch and receive relatively little admonishment following the incident by either the community or the government, precisely because their actions were the expressions of long-held Coptic grievances. Although, the lay *Majlis al-Milli* issued a condemnation of the actions carried out by the JUQ in August 1954, it also cited the need for reform and governmental assistance to cleanse the Church and help it to achieve a *nahda*; 'All this will prevent the youth from using the excuse of reform in any actions that they may subsequently take'.[86] For the *Majlis*, the youths' actions could be used to secure new legislation which would implement *waqf* changes. Furthermore, calls were made by the *Majlis al-Milli* to amend the Papal electoral constitution. Regarding non-administrative issues, the *Majlis al-Milli* would also take the opportunity to raise on-going concerns over Coptic rights with the RCC.[87]

While reproaching the JUQ, the clergy and particularly the Holy Synod, were also similarly careful not to condemn them. At a meeting held in September, the Holy Synod, as the highest authority in the Church after the pope, agreed that it should take important steps to define the authority of the patriarch in order to stop corruption. It also agreed to promote the *tathir* of the courtiers.[88] Bishop Michael of Asyut, leading the discussion, argued that:

We should not play down the actions of *Jama'at al-Ummah al-Qibtiyyah* by arguing that they were either unemployed or workers. If the patriarchal chair continues in this method, then the Church will continually shake [...] I declare that Church issues and matters are now in the hands of the servant Malak.[89]

Thus the Holy Synod clearly recognised that the JUQ had legitimate qualms and, unlike British Foreign Office descriptions, were not merely an 'extremist youth group'.[90] The Bishops who had invited Yusab to attend their meeting, requested that the pope withdraw his legal case against the accused JUQ members and release an official statement of forgiveness. The bishops also requested that the pope officially stop his courtiers from continuing in their roles.[91]

Yusab, however, vehemently criticised the Holy Synod for its sentiments, announcing: 'I said there was a conspiracy in the Holy Synod'. This was a reference to the fact that having failed to reconcile the Holy Synod, bishops and heads of the monasteries with the *Majlis*, it appeared to Yusab that they had all formed a counter alliance against the constitutional head of the community. The Synod's requests were followed by the voluntary withdrawal of sixteen bishops to hermitage in the St. Anthony's monastery until their demands were met. In support for the Holy Synod's strong line, the Coptic Association, a lay-led society based in Alexandria, also issued a statement recognising the authority of the Holy Synod as the highest Coptic power.[92] Priests in Cairo and in the Harit al-Rum area also issued statements of support, while *Misr* commented that the Holy Synod's actions were a 'revolutionary movement against the ocean of corruption in Coptic society'.[93]

In the months that followed the abduction of Yusab, several crucial amendments to the structures of the Church, in the name of 'modernisation' and *tathir*, occurred. Malak was once again dismissed and, more importantly, a three-man committee to aid Yusab was to be created.[94] These bishops would be responsible for the administration of patriarchal issues.[95] Regarding the JUQ, Yusab was coerced into sending a letter to the Egyptian Public Prosecutor:

It is our intention to have peace and content for all Coptic Children as God has appointed us protector over them. It is our duty according to God's law that we should bear the weakness of the weak, as we are sure that the actions of our young men of that day were forced by their Hamas [enthusiasm and passion]. For this reason, I have decided to forgive them to the fullest extent of forgiveness according to God's law and worrying for their future. I wish you to take my words and to stop their court case and leave them free and wish them all the best of luck and intentions.[96]

All 86 JUQ men involved were eventually acquitted, and released without charge.[97] Between 1954 and Yusab's death in 1956, a supervisory committee of bishops assumed shared duties with the patriarch. [98] The Holy Synod's triumph was short-lived, however, as the committee soon stopped functioning, and Malak returned. Internal quarrels continued, and in June 1955 the RCC finally intervened decisively by suspending elections of the *Majlis al-Milli* and publishing a list of twenty-four distinguished laymen who were to assume the old functions of the *Majlis*, as well as removing Malak.[99]

Early in September 1955 there was one more battle between the reforming bishops and patriarch. Following an attempt by Yusab to remove a particularly 'offensive bishop' from the monastery, twelve other bishops demanded, in the name of the Holy Synod, that the patriarch should himself be abstracted and forbidden to live in Cairo or Alexandria and that a council of three bishops should assume his functions. The *Majlis al-Milli* endorsed this request and, despite the patriarch's protests, Nasser's government accepted their position on 21st September.[100] From the end of the initial stabilisation of the new regime in 1954, the RCC was increasingly able to consolidate its control over student movements, trade unions and political opposition which included the pope and the Church: the RCC assumed control and encouraged the patriarch to retire to a monastery in Asyut where he remained until his death in 1956.[101]

# EPILOGUE

The death of Yusab in 1956 left the Coptic community hopelessly divided over the issue of a successor and reform. A Presidential Decree in November 1957 attempted to regulate the election of the Coptic Orthodox Patriarch, highlighting the increasingly pertinent link between affairs of the community and the post-revolutionary Egyptian state.[1] In 1959 Kyrillos VI, a former monk was elected to head the See of St. Mark. Despite criticisms for his overtly pious nature, strenuous efforts were made by the new pope to put the community into 'order'.[2]

The embarrassing episodes of open disputes between members of the *Majlis*, Holy Synod and lay Copts, particularly youths, led Kyrillos to the conclusion that new bishoprics dedicated to communal advancement should be created. At the forefront of this were a number of young educated Copts, who were placed in positions of influence. This new generation of clergy had their roots in the reformist traditions and focussed closely on the educational reforms of the priesthood as well as the wider community. They were also dedicated to the elimination of some of the worst administrative abuses of the past. Amongst the first new reforms, a 1960 Decree stated that no priest could be ordained unless he was a graduate of the newly founded Coptic seminary. Efforts were also implemented to preserve and revive the Coptic language and culture.[3]

Despite these reforming measures however, friction continually manifested itself within the community. First, the relationship between Kyrillos and the newly appointed bishops revealed tensions. The new appointments, which were not confined to a geographical diocese but related to furthering reform in the church, included the bishopric of public relations and social services. In 1962, Father Antonius was ordained Shenouda, Bishop of ecclesiastical education and president of the Coptic theological seminary.[4] Shenouda had played an important role in furthering the aims of religious societies throughout Cairo during the 1940s, and was the first editor-in-chief of the magazine *Madaris al-Ahad* which was launched in 1947. Having worked closely with Coptic educated youths, Shenouda proved to be an extremely keen, enthusiastic and often vocal edition to the higher echelons of the Church. From the outset Shenouda asserted his strong will, bringing him into direct confrontation with Professor Sami Gabra who had headed the Coptic Institute. The institute was a largely autonomous and secular body and the dispute led to Professor Gabra's resignation; Shenouda had proved to be in favour of a centralisation of power. Moreover, Shenouda's Friday gatherings, which attracted a significant number of youths, began to have political undertones leading the bishop and the pope into direct altercation with one another.[5] As in the case of pre-revolutionary Egypt, factional outlooks differed: 'Shenouda's generation looked on the Church as an all-embracing institution, which was there to deal with issues of temporal as well as spiritual, whereas Pope Cyril's [Kyrillos] generation preferred to see the Church as solely a spiritual body'.[6] Up to Kyrillos's death in 1971, friction between the pope and a number of high ranking young bishops continuously reared itself, although it was largely checked with the tacit support of the government.

A second source of intra-communal tension was the relationship between the patriarch and the lay Coptic community. Kyrillos was continually criticised for his dedication to prayer which, it was claimed, he undertook at the expense of papal duties.[7] In 1967, after ongoing disputes between the rivalling factions, the *Majlis* declared that it was unable to undertake costs for running the papal headquarters. It also claimed that due to Kyrillos's frivolity in establishing a new monastery near Alexandria, it was unable to pay the salaries of priests and employees of the Church and resorted to *Al-Tawfiq* society for funds. The state owned newspaper *Al-Ahram*, reported later that month, that the Patriarchate was in financial difficulties and that it was LE 31,000 in debt.[8] In response to this slur, Kyrillos refused to receive any callers during the Easter celebration. However, following a personal meeting between him and President Nasser, the dispute was settled. The Egyptian state would cover the deficit in funds while Nasser ordered the immediate dissolution of the *Majlis*.[9]

These episodes serve to highlight that Coptic factionalism and claims of corruption and mismanagement continued well into the post-revolutionary period. Nasser was however, determined not to let internal dissention within the Coptic community weaken the wider fabric of the new Egyptian state. It is therefore not entirely surprising that he intervened without being over scrupulous about the observances of traditional procedures in suppressing dissention among various factions of Copts. Nasser's policies served to re-establish a hierarchical structure within the Coptic Church; total religious guidance and authority would be through the figure of the patriarch, while the state and president would serve political needs.

**Figure 7** Opening of a Cathedral in Cairo. (Left to Right) Anwar Sadat, Emperor Selassie, President Nasser and Pope Kyrillos.

A close and personal relationship was forged between Nasser and Kyrillos during the 1960s. This is noteworthy as it helped to create an image of a united Egypt in battle against external imperial forces but resolutely solidified in its Egyptian, pan-Arab and, to a lesser extent, its pan-African agenda. Indeed, the autocephaly of Ethiopia from the Coptic Church in 1959 under Kyrillos, helped assert and further relations between Nasser and Emperor Haile Selassie.[10]

Moreover, domestically the 'Coptic tool' proved useful in helping to forge a united Egyptian demonstration of grief following the spectacularly poignant defeat of 1967 at the hands of Israel. The apparition of the Virgin Mary the following year in the district of Zeitoun, was heralded by Muslims and Copts alike as a demonstration of faith in the face of adversity.[11]

Despite this picture of national unity advanced and perpetuated by the state, Coptic concerns towards state practice and policies remained consistent with those prior the revolution. For instance, repeated debates concerning the subject of religious instruction in schools took place: 'For Nasser, religious instruction and the appeal to Islam in general were largely a matter of political convenience and an instrument for appeasing radical Muslims.'[12] Other problems that continued and were exacerbated under Nasser's regime included the prohibition of regular Coptic broadcasts on the television and radio as well as the contentious question of Church building permits.[13] Some efforts were made to promote greater representation of Copts in the cabinet and parliament, although these were largely cosmetic measures. Nasser had initially implemented a policy which insured the presence of at least one Copt in the Cabinet, and after 1956 he institutionalised a system by which ten members would be directly appointed to parliament. This policy continued until until the 2011 uprising and was aimed to ensure, albeit in a rudimentary manner, the representation of Copts and women in parliament.

While it is hoped that this work has contributed to understanding some of the dynamics of various factions within the Coptic community during the nineteenth and twentieth century, greater analysis is needed of Coptic participation from a variety of classes, coalitions and parties, on both the constitutional and communal level. It is only with expanding the remit of analysis beyond the boundaries of national history and persecution discourses, that a more nuanced understanding can be achieved of Copts in Egypt and their contribution to the historical and political discourse.

# APPENDIX 1
## Notes on Church Structure

In the period discussed, the patriarch was the head of the entire Coptic Church with the archbishops, bishops and priests under his ecclesiastical authority. Originally in the third century, the head of the Church was always the bishop of Alexandria, who was also known as pope; consequently, the two terms, pope and patriarch, became interchangeably used to describe the head of the Coptic Church.[1] Whilst the Coptic pope usually resides in Cairo, he is styled as the patriarch of Alexandria.[2]

The Holy Synod is the highest ecclesiastical body in the Church and is responsible for the Church's spiritual, clerical, structural, organisational and economic affairs. From the fourth century, the leading episcopates, made up the Holy Synod and were obliged to attend all important ecumenical councils and meetings.[3]

The bishops, in Coptic *Episkopos* and in Arabic *Usquf*, are more commonly referred to as *Anba*.[4] The bishop is considered to be a clergyman of the highest order in the Coptic Church, and is senior to priests and deacons. From a historical point of view, the Coptic Church regards bishops as successors of the apostles. The role of the bishop includes ordaining priests and deacons in accordance to the needs of his diocese. He is also responsible for providing for the needs of the clergy and the deacons, as well as the poor, the widows and the orphans of the diocese; this is affiliated to the bishops role as manager of his own diocese' funds.

Priests, are usually chosen from among the pious deacons in the Church and are known as *Qasis*. When a person is chosen as a candidate, a document is submitted testifying the candidate's aptitude and good character; a priest must be married in order to qualify to hear the confessions of women and make family visits. The ranks of priesthood vary and include *Qommus*, or canon, who would usually be a highly educated priest that had been raised to this status by a bishop.[5]

The deacon, or *Shammas*, is the lowest ecclesiastical rank in the hierarchy of the Coptic Church, and is subordinate to bishop. The minimum age for a deacon at ordination was set at twenty-five years old and like a priest, the deacon is subject to the same rules regarding marriage. Deacons are first and foremost subordinate assistants to priests and bishops, and are not entitled to perform any of the sacramental services that are the prerogative of the clergy. A deacon may be recommended for the promotion to archdeacon, and later ordained a priest with the approval of his congregation.[6]

# APPENDIX 2
## Coptic Patriarchs

| Dates | Patriarch |
|---|---|
| 1810–1852 | Boutros VII |
| 1852–1854 | Vacant |
| 1854–1861 | Kyrillos IV (*Abu Islah*) |
| 1862–1870 | Demetrius II |
| 1870–1874 | Vacant |
| 1874–1927 | Kyrillos V |
| 1928–1942 | Yu'annis XIX |
| 1942–1944 | Macarius III |
| 1944–1946 | Vacant |
| 1946–1956 | Yusab II |
| 1956–1959 | Vacant |
| 1959–1971 | Kyrillos VI |
| 1971–2012 | Shenouda III |
| 2012–Present | Tawadros II |

# APPENDIX 3
## Non-Muslims in Government

| Head of Cabinet | Cabinet Term | No. in Cabinet | Copt | Name of Copt and Ministry |
|---|---|---|---|---|
| Mustafa Fahmi | 17/1/1892–15/1/ 1893 | 6 | 1 | Takran Pasha (Foreign Affairs) |
| Hussein Fakhri | 15 /1/1893–18/1/1893 | 6 | 2 | Takran Pasha (Foreign Affairs) Boutros Ghali (Finance) |
| Mustafa Riyad | 19/1/1893–15/4/1894 | 6 | 2 | Takran (Foreign Affairs) Boutros Ghali (Finance) |
| Nubar Pasha | 15/4/1894–12/11/1895 | 5 | 2 | Nubar Pasha (Internal and Prime Minister) Boutros Ghali (Foreign Affairs) |
| Mustafa Fahmi | 12/11/1895–11/11/1908 | 6 | 1 | Boutros Ghali (Foreign Affairs) |
| Boutros Ghali | 12/11/1908–21/2/1910 | 6 | 1 | Boutros Ghali (Prime Minister and Foreign Affairs) |

Continued

| | | | | |
|---|---|---|---|---|
| Muhammad Said | 23/2/1910– 5/4/1914 | 6 | 1 | Yusuf Saba (Finance) |
| Hussein Rushdi | 5/4/1914– 19/12/1914 | 8 | 1 | Yusuf Wahbi (Finance) |
| Hussein Rushdi | 19/12/1914– 9/10/1917 | 7 | 1 | Yusuf Wahbi (Finance) |
| Hussein Rushdi | 10/10/1917– 9/4/1919 | 7 | 1 | Yusuf Wahbi (Finance) |
| Hussein Rushdi | 9/4/1919– 22/4/1919 | 7 | 1 | Yusuf Wahbi (Finance) |
| Muhammad Said | 20/5/1919– 21/11/1919 | 7 | 1 | Yusuf Wahbi (Finance) |
| Yusuf Wahbi | 20/11/1919– 21/5/1920 | 8 | 1 | Yusuf Wahbi (Prime Minister and Finance) |
| Muhammad Tawfiq Nasim | 21/5/1920– 16/3/1921 | 8 | 1 | Yusuf Soliman (Finance) |
| Adli Yakan | 16/3/1921– 24/12/1921 | 9 | 1 | Naguib Boutros (Agriculture) |
| Abd al-Khaliq Tharwat | 1/3/1922– 29/11/1922 | 10 | 1 | Wasif Semeika (Transport) |
| Muhammad Tawfiq Nasim | 30/11/1922– 9/2/1923 | 10 | 1 | Yusuf Soliman (Finance) |
| Yahya Ibrahim | 15/3/1923– 27/1/1924 | 10 | 1 | Fawzi al-Muti' (Agriculture) |
| Sa'd Zaghloul | 28/1/1924– 24/11/1924 | 10 | 2 | Murqus Hanna (Public Works) Wasif Boutros Ghali (Foreign Affairs) |
| Ahmad Zawir | 24/11/1924– 13/3/1925 | 9 | 2 | Yusuf Qattawi (Finance) Nakhla al-Muti' (Transport) |

Continued

| | | | | |
|---|---|---|---|---|
| Ahmad Zawir | 13/3/1925–7/6/1926 | 10 | 2 | Yusuf Qattawi (Transport) Tawfiq Doss (Agriculture) |
| Adli Yakan | 7/6/1926–21/4/1927 | 10 | 1 | Murqus Hanna (Finance) |
| Abd al-Khaliq Tharwat | 25/4/1927–16/3/1928 | 10 | 1 | Murqus Hanna (Foreign Affairs) |
| Mustafa Nahhas | 16/3/1928–25/6/1928 | 10 | 2 | Wasif Boutros Ghali (Foreign Affairs) Makram Obeid (Transport) |
| Muhammad Mahmoud | 25/6/1928–2/10/1929 | 9 | 1 | Nakhla al-Muti' (Agriculture) |
| Adli Yakin | 3/10/1929–1/1/1930 | 10 | 1 | Wasif Seimeika (Agriculture) |
| Mustafa Nahhas | 1/1/1930–19/6/1930 | 10 | 2 | Wasif Boutros Ghali (Foreign Affairs) Makram Obeid (Finance) |
| Ismail Sidqi | 19/6/1930–4/1/1933 | 9 | 1 | Tawfiq Doss (Transport) |
| Ismail Sidqi | 4/1/1933–27/9/1933 | 10 | 1 | Nakhla al-Muti' (Foreign Affairs) |
| Abd al-Fattah Yahya Ibrahin | 27/9/1933–14/11/1934 | 10 | 1 | Saliib Sami (War and Maritime) |
| Muhammad Tawfiq Nasim | 14/11/1934–30/1/1936 | 8 | 1 | Kamil Ibrahim (Foreign Affairs and Agriculture) |

Continued

| 'Ali Mahir | 30/1/1936–9/5/1936 | 9 | 1 | Sadiq Wahba (Agriculture) |
|---|---|---|---|---|
| Mustafa Nahhas | 9/5/1936–31/7/1937 | 12 | 2 | Wasif Boutros Ghali (Foreign Affairs) Makram Obeid (Finance) |
| Mustafa Nahhas | 1/8/1937–30/12/1937 | 11 | 2 | Wasif Boutros Ghali (Foreign Affairs) Makram Obeid (Finance) |
| Muhammad Mahmoud | 30/12/1937–27/4/1938 | 16 | 1 | Murad Wahba (Agriculture) |
| Muhammad Mahmoud | 27/4/1938–24/6/1938 | 13 | 1 | Murad Wahba (Trade and Industry) |
| Muhammad Mahmoud | 24/6/1938–18/8/1939 | 12 | 1 | Saba Habashi (Trade and Industry) |
| 'Ali Mahir | 18/8/1939–27/6/1940 | 15 | 1 | Saba Habashi (Trade and Industry) |
| Hassan Sabri | 27/6/1940–14/11/1940 | 16 | 1 | Saliib Sami (Supplies) |
| Hussein Sirri | 15/11/1940–31/7/1941 | 13 | 1 | Saliib Sami (Trade and Industry) |
| Hussein Sirri | 31/7/1941 – 4/2/1942 | 15 | 1 | Saliib Sami (Foreign Affairs) |
| Mustafa Nahhas | 4/2/1942–26/5/1942 | 12 | 2 | Makram Obeid (Finance) Kamil Sidqi (Trade and Industry) |
| Mustafa Nahhas | 26/5/1942–8/10/1944 | 15 | 1 | Kamil Sidqi (Finance) |

Continued

| | | | | |
|---|---|---|---|---|
| Ahmad Mahir | 8/10/1944–15/1/1945 | 13 | 2 | Makram Obeid (Finance) Raghib Hanna (Trade and Industry) |
| Ahmad Mahir | 15/1/1945–24/2/1945 | 15 | 2 | Makram Obeid (Finance) Raghib Hanna (Without Portfolio) |
| Mahmoud Fahmi Nuqrashi | 24/2/1945–15/2/1946 | 15 | 2 | Makram Obeid (Finance) Raghib Hanna (Without Portfolio) |
| Ismail Sidqi | 16/2/1946–9/12/1946 | 13 | 1 | Saba Habashi (Trade and Industry) |
| Mahmoud Fahmi Nuqrashi | 9/12/1946–28/12/1948 | 13 | 1 | Naguib Iskandar (General Health) |
| Ibrahim 'Abd al-Hadi | 28/12/1948–25/7/1949 | 17 | 1 | Naguib Iskandar (General Health) |
| Hussein Sirri | 25/7/1949–3/11/1949 | 20 | 1 | Naguib Iskandar (General Health) |
| Hussein Sirri | 3/11/1949–1/1/1950 | 15 | 1 | Saliib Sami (Trade and Industry) |
| Mustafa Nahhas | 12/1/1950–27/1/1952 | 17 | 1 | Ibrahim Farag (Regional Affairs) |
| 'Ali Mahir | 27/1/1952–1/3/1952 | 12 | 1 | Saliib Sami (Agriculture) |

Continued

| Ahmad Naguib al-Hilali | 1/3/1952–2/7/1952 | 13 | 2 | Saliib Sami (Trade and Industry) Naguib Ibrahim (Public Works) |
|---|---|---|---|---|
| Hussein Sirri | 2/7/1952–22/7/1952 | 14 | 1 | Naguib Ibrahim (Public Works and Finance and Economics) |
| Ahmad Naguib al-Hilali | 22/7/1952–24/7/1952 | 15 | 2 | Yusuf Sa'd (Public Works) Mirrit Ghali (Regional Affairs) |
| 'Ali Mahir | 24/7/1952–7/9/1952 | 13 | 1 | Alfonis Grees (Agriculture) |
| Muhammad Naguib | 7/9/1952–18/6/1953 | 16 | 1 | Farid Antoun (Supplies) |
| Muhammad Naguib | 18/6/1953–25/2/1954 | 14 | 1 | William Salim Hanna (Regional Affairs) |
| Gamal 'Abd al-Nasser | 25/2/1954–27/2/1954 | 18 | 1 | William Salim Hanna (Regional Affairs) |
| Muhammad Naguib | 8/3/1954 –17/4/1954 | 18 | 1 | William Salim Hanna (Regional Affairs) |

# NOTES

## Introduction

[1] See statements issued in conjunction with the Coptic Assembly of America, http://www.copticassembly.org/ Date accessed, 20 January 2010.

[2] Quoted in *Masry al-Youm*, 20 January 2010.

[3] Saad Hagras talking on 'Wijhit Nazar' (Point of View), on *Al-Masriyya* Channel, 11 January 2010.

[4] 'Egypt Police Arrest Christmas Murder Suspects', *The Guardian*, 8th January 2010.

[5] Quoted in *Masry al-Youm*, 20 January 2010.

[6] 'Letters accusing armed Coptic Militia of Naga Hammadi's incident' in http://www.ikhwanweb.com/article.php?id=22572 Date accessed, 11th January 2010.

[7] For example see, David Zeidan, 'The Copts-Equal, Protected or Persecuted? The Impact of Islamization on Muslim-Christian Relations in Modern Egypt', *Islam and Christian-Muslim Relations*, Vol. 10, No. 1. (1999) pp. 53–69.

[8] Kyriakos Mikhail, *Copts and Moslems under British Control : A Collection of Facts and a Résumé of Authoritative Opinions on the Coptic Question*, (London: Smith, Elder, 1911).

[9] Mikhail, *Copts and Moslems under British Control*, p. viii.

[10] See, C. A. Bayly, 'Representing Copts and Muhammadans: Empire, Nation and Community in Egypt and India, 1880–1914', in *Modernity and Culture: From the Mediterranean to the Indian Ocean*, ed. Leila Fawaz, and C. A. Bayly, (Columbia: Columbia University Press, 2002).

[11] Bajilo Basili, *Hal rahab al-Aqbat bi-fath al-'Arab?* (No Publisher, no date) Chapters 1–4.

[12] Meinardus, *Two thousand years,* p. 38.

[13] Otto Meinardus, *Coptic Saints and Pilgrimages,* (Cairo: American University of Cairo Press, 2002) p. 26.

[14] Saphinaz Amal Naguib, 'The Era of Martyrs: Texts and Contexts of Religious Memory', in *Between Desert and City : the Coptic Orthodox Church Today,* ed. Nelly van Doorn-Harder, and Kari Vogt, p. 124 (Oslo: Novis Forlag, 1997).

[15] Naguib, 'The Era of Martyrs', p. 123.

[16] Muhammad Hassanein Heikal, *Autumn of Fury : The Assassination of Sadat,* (London: Deutsch, 1983) pp. 55–90; John Waterbury, 'The 'Soft State' and the Open Door; Egypt's experience with Economic Liberalisation, 1974–1984' in *Comparative Politics,* Vol. 18, No. 1. (1985), pp. 65–83.

[17] See, Mona El-Ghobashy, 'Unsettling the Authorities: Constitutional reform in Egypt', in Middle East Report, No. 226 (2003), pp. 28–34.

[18] For examples see, John Eibner, *Christians in Egypt: Church under Seige,* (Washington: Institute for Religious Minorities in the Islamic World, 1993); Shawky Karas, *The Copts since the Arab invasion : strangers in their land,* (Jersey City: American, Canadian and Australian C. Coptic Associations, 1986); Edward Wakin, *A lonely Minority: The Modern story of Egypt's Copts,* (New York: William Morrow & Co., 1963).

[19] Milad Hanna, *Na'am...Aqbat, lakin...Misriyun,* (Cairo: Maktabat Madbuli, 1980).

[20] Milad Hanna, *The Seven Pillars of the Egyptian Identity,* (Cairo: General Egyptian Book Organization, 1994) p. 13.

[21] Hanna, *Na'am...Aqbat* pp. 23–29; See also, William Sulaiman, 'Tayyarat al-fikr al-Masihi fi'l waqi' al-Misri' in *Al-Mas'ala at-ta'ifiyya fi Misr,* (Beirut, 1980) pp. 177–180.

[22] Tariq al-Bishri, *Al-Muslimun wa-al-aqbat fi itar al-Jama'ah al-Wataniyah,* (Beirut, 1982) pp. 391–395.

[23] See Hani Labib, *Al-Muwatanah wa-l-'awlamah: Al-Aqbat fi Mujtama' Mutaghayir,* (Cairo: Dar al-Shuruq, 2004).

[24] Paul Sedra, 'Class Cleavages and Ethnic Conflict: Coptic Christian Communities in Modern Egyptian Politics' in *Islam and Christian-Muslim Relations,* Vol. 10, No. 2. (1999) pp. 220–221.

[25] For instance, there are no references, bibliography or appendices in Milad Hanna's, *Na'am...Aqbat.*

[26] For example see Barbara Lynn Carter, *The Copts in Egyptian Politics,* (London: Croom Helm, 1986).

[27] Sample of collections viewed include, *Bourse Egyptienne,* (Cairo), 1945–1956; *The Daily Telegraph* (London), 1908; *The Egyptian Gazette,* (Cairo),

1910, 1947–1948, 1954; *The Egyptian Mail*, (Cairo), 1943–45; 1952; *The Times* (London), 1911.

[28] An original application was made in September 2004 followed by subsequent attempts in May 2005 and February 2007.

[29] The following are a small sample: *Al-'A'ilah al-Qibtiyyah* (Alexandria), 1909–1910; *Al-Fata al-Qibtiyyah* (Cairo), 1905–1910; *Al-Iman* (Cairo), 1905–1908, 1941–1942.

[30] *Al-Majallah al-Qibtiyyah* (Cairo), 1907–1930.

[31] Qommus Sergius' Magazine, *Al-Manarah al-Misriyyah* 1935–1953 ; Qommus Ibrahim Luqa's Magazine, *Al-Yaqazah* 1927–1928, 1943–1948.

[32] *Al-Watan* (Cairo); *Misr* (Cairo), 1944–1954 ; *Al-Muqattam* (Cairo), 1944; *Al-Ahram* (Cairo), 1952–1954; *Al-Misri* (Cairo), 1944, 1953–54; *Al-Wataniyyah* (Cairo), 1911–1953.

[33] For example, Ahmad 'Urabi, *Mudhakkirat al-Za'im Ahmad 'Urabi : Kashf al-sitar 'an sirr al-asrar fi-l-nahdah al-Misriyah al-mashhurah bi-l-Thawrah al-'Urabiyah,* (Cairo: Matba'at Dar al-Kutub wa-al-Watha'iq al-Qawmiyah bi-l-Qahirah, 2005) Vol. I–III.

[34] Fredrick Cooper, *Colonialism in Question: Theory, History and Knowledge,* (Berkeley: University of California Press, 2005) p. 65.

## Chapter 1

[1] See Afaf Lutfi al-Sayyid Marsot, *Egypt in the Reign of Muhammad Ali,* (Cambridge: Cambridge University Press, 1984); P. J. Vatikiotis, *The History of Modern Egypt: From Muhammad Ali to Mubarak,* (London: Fourth Edition, 1991); F.H. Lawson, *The Social Origins of Egyptian Expansion during the Muhammad Ali Period,* (New York: Columbia University Press, 1992).

[2] See entry in Al-Jabarti, 15th May 1800, *'Aja'ib al-athar fi al-tarajim wa-al-akhbar,* Vol. III. 183.

[3] Ehud Toledano, 'Social and Economic Change in the Long Nineteenth Century' in *The Cambridge History of Egypt,* ed. M. W. Daly, (Cambridge: Cambridge University Press, 1998) Vol. II. 259.

[4] Toledano, 'Social and Economic Change in the Long Nineteenth Century', 259–263.

[5] Lane, *An Account of the Manners and Customs,* 23.

[6] Lane argues that the remainders were probably Arabs, North Africans, Nubians, Mamluks and Franks. Although it should be noted that Lane, by his own admission, consults few Copts. See Lane, *An Account of the Manners and Customs,* 24.

[7] For more on Muhammad 'Ali see Khaled Fahmy, *All the Pasha's Men: Mehmed Ali, his Army and the Making of Modern Egypt,* (Cambridge: Cambridge University Press, 1997); Toledano, 'Social and Economic Change in the Long Nineteenth Century', 264.

[8] Malcolm Yapp, *The Making of the Modern Near East 1792–1923*, (London: Longman, Eighth Edition, 1996) 146.

[9] Ira Lapidus, *A History of Islamic Societies*, (Cambridge: Cambridge University Press, Second Edition, 2002) 515.

[10] 'Abd al-Rahman Al-Jabarti, *Tarikh Muddat al-Faransis bi Misr: Napoleon in Egypt: Al-Jabarti's chronicle of the French occupation 1798*, (Princeton, New Jersey: Markus Wiener Publishers, 2004) and *'Adja'ib al-Athar: Fil-Taradjim wal-akhbar*, (Cairo: Dar al-Kutub, 1997–1998) Vol. I–IV.

[11] Al-Jabarti, *'Aja'ib al-athar fi al-tarajim wa-al-akhbar* Vol. IV. 63–4.

[12] Malak Luqa, *Al-Aqbat, al-nashaah wa-al-sira'a: min al-qarn al-awwal ila al-qarn al-'ishrin*, (Cairo: Maktabat Anjilus, 2001) 530.

[13] Luqa, *Al-Aqbat, al-nashaah wa-al-sira'a*, 521.

[14] 'Abdin Palace Archives: Mahfuzat 'Abdin Khedival Diwan 1819 taken from Luqa, *Al-Aqbat, al-nashaah wa-al-sira'a*, 521.

[15] J. Tajer, *Aqbat wa Muslimun munthu al-fath al-Arabi ila 'Aam 1922*, (Cairo: 1951) 232.

[16] Magdi Sami Zaki, *Historire des Coptes d'Egypte*, (Paris, 2005) 773.

[17] Antuni, *Wataniyat al-Kanisah*, Vol. I. 351; Lane, *An Account of the Manners and Customs*, 538.

[18] Lane, *An Account of the Manners and Customs*, 537.

[19] Al-Jabarti, *'Aja'ib al-athar fi al-tarajim wa-al-akhbar*, Vol. IV. p. 447.

[20] Lane, *An Account of the Manners and Customs*, 548.

[21] Zaki, *Histoire des Coptes d'Egypte*, 773.

[22] See Robert Hunter, *Egypt under the Khedives 1805–1879: From Household Government to Modern Bureaucracy*, (Pittsburgh: University of Pittsburgh Press, 1984).

[23] Lapidus, *A History of Islamic Societies*, 513.

[24] Kenneth Cuno, *The Pasha's Peasants : Land, Society, and Economy in Lower Egypt, 1740–1858*, (Cambridge: Cambridge University Press, 1992) 86–88.

[25] Fahmy, *All the Pasha's Men.*, p. 97; Yapp, *The Making of the Modern Near East*, 146.

[26] Yapp, *The Making of the Modern Near East*, p. 146; Tolendano, 'Social and Economic Change in the Long Nineteenth Century', 263.

[27] Benjamin Braude, 'Foundation Myths of the *Millat* System' in *Christians and Jews in the Ottoman Empire: The Functioning of a Plural Society, Volume I: The Central Lands*, ed. Braude and Lewis, (Holmes and Meier, 1987) 69; Kepal Karpat, 'The Ottoman and Ethnic Confessional Legacy in the Middle East', in *Ethnicity, Pluralism and the state in the Middle East*, 40.

[28] Lane, *An Account of the Manners and Customs*, 548.

[29] P. Hardy, 'Djizya' in *Encyclopaedia of Islam*.

[30] Lane, *An Account of the Manners and Customs*, 548.

[31] The Ministry of Interior (1857), Public Works (1864), Justice (1872), Agriculture (1975) were later added the original six ministries.

[32] Yapp, *The Making of the Modern Near East*, 148; Tolendano, 'Social and Economic Change in the Long Nineteenth Century', 256–7.

[33] M. Berger, *Bureaucracy and Society in Modern Egypt: A Study of Higher Civil Service*, (Princeton: Princeton University Press, 1957) 22 cites Jean Deny who catalogued and de-classified Turkish Archives in Cairo.

[34] Lapidus, *A History of Islamic Societies*, 513.

[35] Yapp, *The Making of the Modern Near East*, 149.

[36] Lapidus, *A History of Islamic Societies*, 13–14.

[37] Yapp, *The Making of the Modern Near East*, 150.

[38] Lane, *An Account of the Manners and Customs*, 525.

[39] James Heyworth-Dunn, *An Introduction to the History of Education in Modern Egypt*, (London: 1938) 87.

[40] Heyworth-Dunn, *An Introduction to the History of Education*, 146.

[41] Lane, *An Account of the Manners and Customs*, 553.

[42] Al-Antuni, *Al-Aqbat, al-nashaah wa-al-sira'a*, Vol. I. 350.

[43] Ramzi Tadrous, *Al-Aqbat fi al-qarn al-'ishrin*, (Cairo, 1911) 42–48.

[44] G. Baer, *A History of Landownership in Modern Egypt, 1800–1950*, (London: Oxford University Press, 1962) 63; For more on Coptic notables and bureaucrats in nineteenth century Egypt see Magdi Guirguis' article 'Restructuring Egyptian Society' in *Al-Ahram Weekly*, 15–21 September 2005.

[45] Yapp, *The Making of the Modern Near East*, 147.

[46] Fifty primary schools that were set to be established went unheeded. See Yapp, *The Making of the Modern Near East*, 148.

[47] Yapp, *The Making of the Modern Near East*, 148.

[48] Vatikiotis, *The History of Modern Egypt*, 102.

[49] Lane, *An Account of the Manners and Customs*, 548.

[50] Tajor, *Aqbat wa Muslimun*, 238.

[51] R. H. Davison, 'Turkish attitudes concerning Christian-Muslim equality in the nineteenth century' in *The Modern Middle East: A Reader*, ed. Hourani, Khoury and Wilson, (London: I. B. Tauris, 2004) 61–81.

[52] Meinardus, *Two Thousand Years*, 69.

[53] Cooper, *Colonialism in Question*, 75.

[54] Samir Seikaly, 'Coptic Communal reform: 1860–1914' in *Middle Eastern Studies*, Vol. 6, No. 1, (1970) 270; For example 'Abd al-Sayyid discusses *Zaman al-Islah* in *Hafl al-dhikra al-mi'awiyya al-'ula li-abi al-islah*, (Cairo: 1960).

[55] For our purposes and henceforth, Kyrillos IV will be referred to as Abu Islah in order to avoid confusion with subsequent patriarchs with the same name.

[56] See, Yacoub Nakhla Rufila, (1847–1905) *Tarikh al-ummah al-qibtiyyah*, (1898); Mikhail Sharubim (1853–1912) wrote the extensive four volume work *Al-Kafi*, dedicating a whole volume to Abu Islah.

[57] 'Abd al-Sayyid, *Hafl al-dhikra.*

[58] Seikaly, 'Coptic Communal reform: 1860–1914', 248.

[59] Quoted by Heyworth-Dunn from C. N. S Sonnini *Travels in Upper and Lower Egypt,* (London: 1799) Vol. II. 162.

[60] 'Abd al-Sayyid, *Hafl al-dhikra,* 46.

[61] Lane, *An Account of the Manners and Customs,* 553.

[62] 'Kyrillos al Raba' in *Al-Hilal* 1892, 339, although Samir Seikaly is correct to report that this has not appeared anywhere else. Seikaly, 'Coptic Communal reform: 1860–1914', 270.

[63] Seikaly, 'Coptic Communal reform: 1860–1914', 249.

[64] For Kyrillos' early career as Monk Daud in the St Anthony's monastery see, Luqa, *Al-Aqbat, al-nashaah wa-al-sira'a,* 527–528.

[65] Luqa, *Al-Aqbat, al-nashaah wa-al-sira'a,* 528.

[66] Seikaly, 'Coptic Communal reform: 1860–1914', 248.

[67] It is claimed that the very same printing press was later used by Mikh'ail 'Abd al-Sayyid to found the Coptic *Al-Watan* newspaper. See Anba Mattewos, *Tarikh Babawat al-Qursi al-Askandriyyah,* (Cairo: Harmony, Second Edition, 2002) 48; Luqa, *Al-Aqbat, al-nashaah wa-al-sira'a,* 529.

[68] Transcript of speech given by Abba Seraphim, Metropolitan of Glastonbury, 'The renewal of Coptic Orthodoxy in the Twentieth Century', 30th May 1995, in *The Glastonbury Bulletin,* No. 92, March 1996.

[69] Sulayman Nasim, 'Education, Coptic' in *Coptic Encyclopaedia,* 931–933.

[70] Seikaly, 'Coptic Communal reform: 1860–1914', 249.

[71] Meinardus, *Two Thousand Years,* 70.

[72] Butcher, *The Story of the Church in Egypt,* p. 399; Mattewos, *Tarikh Babawat,* 46–7.

[73] Butcher, *The Story of the Church in Egypt,* 399.

[74] J. M. Landau, 'Kuttab' in *Encyclopaedia of Islam.*

[75] Quoted from Heyworth-Dunn, *An Introduction to the History of Education,* 85.

[76] Mattewos, *Tarikh Babawat,* 44–45.

[77] Vatikiotis, *The History of Modern Egypt,* 102.

[78] Khedive Ismail in 1863 added a further 500 feddans of land in the same area to be used by the Church. Luqa, *Al-Aqbat, al-nashaah wa-al-sira'a,* 71.

[79] Paul Sedra, 'Ecclesiastical Warfare: Patriarch, Presbyterian and Peasant in Nineteenth Century Egypt', (Working Paper, New York University, 2005) 306; Luqa, *al-Aqbat, al-nashaah wa-al-sira'a,* 528; Mattewos, *Tarikh Babawat,* 45.

[80] Nasim, 'Education, Coptic' in *Coptic Encyclopaedia,* 931–933.

81 Heyworth-Dunn, *An Introduction to the History of Education*, 338.

82 The school remains active until today under the name of al-Malik Gabrel School; See also Severus al-Muqaffa', *Tarikh Misr: min Bidayat al-qarn al-awwal al-Miladi .hatta nihayat al-qarn al-'ishrin: min khilal makhtutat Tarikh al-batarikah*, (Cairo: Maktabat Madbuli, 2006) Vol. IV. Part II. 1373; Seikaly, 'Coptic Communal Reform: 1860–1914' 249; Mattewos, *Tarikh Babawat*, 45.

83 Nasim, 'Education, Coptic' in *Coptic Encyclopaedia*, 931–933.

84 See Seikaly, 'Coptic Communal reform: 1860–1914', 270.

85 Mustafa Al-Feki, *Copts in Egyptian Politics*, (Egypt: General Egyptian Book Organisation, 1991) 30.

86 Nasim, 'Education, Coptic' in *Coptic Encyclopaedia*, 931–933.

87 It was claimed that through the education of women, the community was cultivating good mothers, See Al-Misri, *Qissat al-Kanisah al-Qibtiyyah*, Vol. IV. 320; Sedra, 'Ecclesiastical Warfare', 306; Luqa, *Al-Aqbat, al-nashaah wa-al-sira'a*, 528–9; Mattewos, *Tarikh Babawat.*, 45–6.

88 See Heyworth-Dunn for exact statistics and gender base of school, *An Introduction to the History of Education*, 420–421.

89 'The New Society and its Early Struggles', in *Yes Magazine*, CMS Quarterly, April–June 1999; Also see, Eugene Stock, *The History of the Church Missionary Society: its Environment, its Men and its Work*, (London: Church Missionary Society, 1899–1916) Vol. I–IV.

90 For more on the activities and achievements of the CMS in Africa, see parts 1–2 in Gordon Hewitt, *The Problems of Success: A History of the Church Missionary Society 1910–1942*, Vol. I. (London: published for Church Missionary Society by SCM Press, 1971).

91 Kenneth Cragg, 'Being Made Disciples: The Middle East' in *The Church Mission Society and World Christianity 1799–1999*, ed. K. Ward & B. Stanley, (UK: Curzon Press, 2000) 121.

92 Cragg, 'Being Made Disciples: The Middle East', 123.

93 Fowler, *Christian Egypt*, 250.

94 Fowler, *Christian Egypt*, 250.

95 All five men sent were German and from the Basle Seminary: Samuel Gobat (1799–1879) later to become Bishop in Jerusalem (1846–1879), J. R. T. Leider, Theodore Mueller, William Kruse and Christian Krugler. Soon after their arrival in Alexandria, Gobat and Krugler went to Abyssinia to continue with missionary activity there. See, 'The First Missionaries to be sent from the New Society', in *Yes Magazine*, April–June 1999; Watson, *In the Valley of the Nile*, 120; For destinations of missionaries see, Church Missionary Society, *Register of Missionaries (Clerical, Lay & Female) and Native Clergy from 1804 to 1904. In Two Parts.* (No publisher, 19–?).

[96] Hewitt, *The Problems of Success*, 303.

[97] Hewitt, *The Problems of Success*, 306.

[98] CMS minutes of an interview with the Coptic Patriarch Boutros, 30th December 1839 taken from Seikaly, 'Coptic Communal reform: 1860–1914', 247.

[99] Watson, *In the Valley of the Nile*, 122–123.

[100] Watson, *In the Valley of the Nile*, 125.

[101] Watson, *In the Valley of the Nile*, 127.

[102] Quoted in Watson, *In the Valley of the Nile*, 130–131.

[103] Gurminder Bhambra, *Rethinking Modernity*, (New York: Palgrave, 2007) 3.

[104] Butcher, *The Story of the Church in Egypt*, Vol. II. 397; See also Seikaly, 'Coptic Communal reform: 1860–1914', 248; Hewitt, *The Problems of Success*, 306; 'Abd al–Sayyid, *Hafl al-dhikra*, 89–92.

[105] Tawfiq Iskarus, *Nawabigh al-Aqbat wa-mashahiruhum fi al-qarn al-tasi' 'ashar*, (Egypt: al-Tawfiq Publishers 1910–1913) 182–183.

[106] Watson, *In the Valley of the Nile*, 133.

[107] Fowler, *Christian Egypt*, 274.

[108] Watson, *In the Valley of the Nile*, 135.

[109] *Presbyterian 1863 Annual Report*, quoted in Sedra, 'Ecclesiastical Warfare', 299.

[110] Watson, *In the Valley of the Nile*, 147.

[111] Taken from the *Presbyterian Egyptian Missionary Association Minutes*, No. 130 quoted in Sedra, 'Ecclesiastical Warfare', 299.

[112] Sedra, 'Ecclesiastical Warfare', 300; Also see Omnia Shakry, 'Schooled Mothers and Structured play: Child rearing in turn of the century Egypt', in *Remaking Women: Feminism and Modernity in the Middle East*, ed. Lila Abu-Lughod, (Princeton University Press, 1998).

[113] Mirrit Boutros Ghali, 'Tadrus Shinudah Al-Manqabadi' in *Coptic Encyclopaedia*, 2197.

[114] Luqa, *Al-Aqbat, al-nashaah wa-al-sira'a*, 531.

[115] *Presbyterian Egyptian Missionary Association Minutes*, No. 129 quoted in Sedra, 'Ecclesiastical Warfare', 307.

[116] Watson, *In the Valley of the Nile*, 150.

[117] Watson, *In the Valley of the Nile*, 151.

[118] Watson, *In the Valley of the Nile*, 152.

[119] Seikaly, 'Coptic Communal reform: 1860–1914', 250.

[120] For the text of the Humayun decree see, M. S. Anderson, *The Great powers and the Near East, 1774–1923* (London: Edward Arnold, 1970) 63–5.

[121] Adel Azer Bestawros, 'Community Council, Coptic' in *Coptic Encyclopaedia*, 581.

[122] Al-Misri, *Qissat al-Kanisah al-Qibtiyyah*, Vol. V. 24.

123 Seikaly, 'Coptic Communal reform: 1860–1914', 251.

124 Barsum Girgis Bey, Yaqub Nakhla Rufila Bey, See, *Qammus al-tarajim al-Qibtiyyah*, (Alexandria: St Mina Educational Services, 1995) 277.

125 Bishop Mattewos, suggests that Murqus created the *Majlis al-Milli* in an attempt to retain the Patriarchal seat in a more permanent capacity. See, *Wataniyat al-Kanisah*, 76.

126 Girgis Filuthawus 'Awad, *Tarikh al-Ighumanus Filitha'us*, (Cairo: 1905) 114–115.

127 Kedourie 'Ethnicity, Majority, and Minority in the Middle East', 26–28.

128 Al-Misri, *Qissat al-Kanisah al-Qibtiyyah*, Vol. V. 25.

129 '1874 *Majlis al-Milli* constitution' reprinted in full in *Al-Manarah al-Misriyyah*, 14th March 1944.

130 Adel Azer Bestawros, 'Community Council', in *Coptic Encyclopaedia*, 581–582.

131 '1874 *Majlis al-Milli* constitution' reprinted in full in *Al-Manarah al-Misriyyah*, 14th March 1944.

132 Bestawros, 'Community Council', 581–582.

133 Seikaly, 'Coptic Communal reform: 1860–1914', 251.

134 Al-Muqaffa', *Tarikh Misr*, Vol. IV. Part II. 1504.

135 Seikaly cites the prominent clergyman, Girgis Filuthawus 'Awad, as evidence of Kyrillos' promise. See also, *Tarikh al-Ighumanus Filitha'us*, 138–139.

136 Al-Muqaffa', *Tarikh Misr*, Vol. IV. Part II. 1507.

137 'Awad, *Tarikh al-Ighumanus*, 142–3; Seikaly, 'Coptic Communal reform: 1860–1914', 252.

138 Al-Muqaffa', *Tarikh Misr*, Vol. IV. Part II. 1505.

139 Butcher, *The Story of the Church in Egypt*, 403; E. Abrahamian, 'Oriental Despotism: the Case of Qajar Iran', in *International Journal of Middle East Studies* Vol. 5, (1974), 3–31.

140 Butcher, *The Story of the Church in Egypt*, 403.

141 Al-Misri, *Qissat al-Kanisah al-Qibtiyyah*,, Vol. V. 27.

142 Father Mathew Attia, *The Theological School of Alexandria*, Accessed: 05/03/2007 http://www.coptic.org.au/modules/resources_literature/article.php?articleid=106; Al-Misri, *Qissat al-Kanisah al-Qibtiyyah*, Vol. V. 27; Seikaly, 'Coptic Communal reform: 1860–1914', 252.

143 Al-Misri, *Qissat al-Kanisah al-Qibtiyyah*, Vol. V. 27; Seikaly, 'Coptic Communal reform: 1860–1914', 251.

144 'Abd al-Sayyid, *Hafl al-dhikra*, 32.

145 Bestawros, 'Community Council, Coptic', 581.

## Chapter 2

1 'Urabi, *Mudhakkirat al-Za'im Ahmad 'Urabi*, Vol. II. 700.

2 For more on British motives behind the occupation of Egypt see: John Galbraith, and Afaf Lutfi al-Sayyid-Marsot, 'The British Occupation of Egypt: Another View' in *International Journal of Middle Eastern Studies*, Vol. 9. No. 4, (1978) 471–488.

3 For further discussion on British intentions regarding the longevity of occupation see: Ronald Robinson and John Gallagher, *Africa and the Victorians: The Climax of Imperialism in the Dark Continent*, (New York: 1961) 121–59, and A. G. Hopkins, 'The Victorians and Africa: A Reconsideration of the Occupation of Egypt 1882' in *The Journal of African History*, Vol. 27, (1986) 363–391.

4 Robert L. Tignor, 'The 'Indianization' of the Egyptian Administration under British Rule' in *The American Historical Review*, Vol. 68. No.3. (1963) 637.

5 Tignor, 'Indianization' p. 650; Lord Kitchner who fought in the Boer War 1899–1902 and followed a scorched earth policy, later became Commander-in-Chief in India (1902–1909) and British Governor General of Egypt and the Sudan (1911–1914), See Brigadier General Colin Robert Ballard, *Kitchener* (London: Faber and Faber, 1930); Also Reginald Wingate who became Governor General of Sudan and High Commissioner of Egypt, See Sir Ronald Wingate, *Wingate of the Sudan : The Life and Times of General Sir Reginald Wingate, Maker of the Anglo-Egyptian Sudan*, (London: J. Murray, 1955).

6 Tignor, 'Indianization' 650; For more on officers in the Egyptian Army, see E. Be'eri, *Army Officers in Arab Politics and Society*, (Prager, 1970) 305–325.

7 Al-Rafi'i , 'Abd al-Rahman *'Asr Isma'il*, (Cairo: 1932) Vol. I. 106.

8 British Documents on Foreign Affairs, Doc 30, Vol. XVIII: 'Library Memorandum on the Caisse de la Dette Publique'; Afaf Lutfi al-Sayyid-Marsot 'The British Occupation of Egypt from 1882' in *The Oxford History of the British Empire. The Nineteenth Century*, Andrew Porter, ed. (Oxford: Oxford University Press, 2001) 653.

9 For exact statistics of debt repayment see, Al-Rafi'i, *'Asr Isma'il*, 29–51; Tignor, 'Indianization' 637.

10 Tignor, 'Indianization' 638; Al-Rafi'i, *'Asr Isma'il*, 29–51.

11 Al-Sayyid-Marsot, 'The British Occupation of Egypt from 1882', 653.

12 See Joseph Szyliowicz, 'Education and Political Development in Turkey, Egypt and Iran', *Comparative Education Review*, Vol. 13 (1969), 150–166; See also Girguis Salama, *Athar al-Ihtalal al-Britani fi al-Ta'lim al-Qawmi fi Misr 1882–1922* (Cairo: 1966).

[13] Cromer, *Modern Egypt*, Vol. II. 538.

[14] The three R's (as in the letter 'R') is a phrase sometimes used to describe the foundations of a basic skills oriented education program within schools: reading, writing and arithmetic. TNA: PRO, FO 633/VIII, Cromer to A. G. Freemantle, 17th December 1896; Cromer, *Modern Egypt*, Vol. II., 533.

[15] Donald Reid, 'Educational and Career choices of Egyptian Students, 1882–1922' in *International Journal of Middle East Studies*, Vol. 8. No. 3. (1977) 356; Also *Statistique Scolaire d'Egypte 1912–1912* (Cairo: 1913).

[16] Cromer, *Modern Egypt*, Vol. II. 527.

[17] Cromer, *Modern Egypt*, Vol. II. 528.

[18] These figures do not however reflect the special credits that were also introduced for the construction and maintenance of school buildings. For more details see Cromer, *Modern Egypt*, Vol. II. 525–542.

[19] Tignor, 'Indianization', p.659; Reid, 'Educational', 359.

[20] Reid, 'Educational', 359.

[21] Ibrahim, *The Copts*, 12.

[22] Sana Hasan, *Christians versus Muslims in Modern Egypt: The Century-Long Struggle for Coptic Equality*, (Oxford: Oxford University Press, 2003) 35.

[23] Tadrous, *Al-Aqbat fi al-qarn al-'ishrin*, 12.

[24] Cromer, *Modern Egypt*, Vol. II. 210.

[25] Cromer, *Modern Egypt*, Vol. II. 202.

[26] Cromer, *Modern Egypt*, Vol. II. 206.

[27] Cromer, *Modern Egypt*, Vol. II. 203.

[28] See opinions by 'W', 'Copts and Moslems in Egypt' in *Blackwoord's Magazine*, August 1919, quoted in Bayly, 'Representing Copts and Muhammadans', 170.

[29] Cromer, *Modern Egypt*, Vol. II. 210; Doris Abouseif, 'The Political Situation of the Copts, 1799–1923', in *Christians and Jews in the Ottoman Empire: The Functioning of a Plural Society, Volume II: The Arab Speaking Lands*, ed. Braude and Lewis (Holmes and Meier, 1987) 194.

[30] Cromer, *Modern Egypt*, Vol. II. 207–208; Al-Feki, *Copts in Egyptian Politics*, 31.

[31] Cromer, *Modern Egypt*, Vol. II. 208.

[32] Cromer, *Modern Egypt*, Vol. II. 211–212.

[33] *Al-Tawfiq*, 11th October 1907.

[34] Christian includes Coptic, Catholic and Protestant Schools. Statistics taken from, *Al-Tawfiq*, 16th July 1903.

[35] In 1907, the total population of Egypt stood at 11,189,978, Christians (including foreigners) comprised 881,693, thus making up 7.6 per cent of the total population, See 'Percentage of Christians in Census years 1917–1976' in *Arab Republic of Egypt, Central Agency for Public Mobilisation and*

*Statistics: The General Population and Housing Census, 1976* (Cairo: 1977); Reid, 'Educational', 362.

[36] Tajer, *Aqbat wa Muslimun*, 248.

[37] 'Percentage of Christians in Census years 1917–1976' in *Arab Republic of Egypt, Central Agency for Public Mobilisation and Statistics: The General Population and Housing Census, 1976.*

[38] *The Times*, 27th April 1911; Yapp, *The Making of the Modern Near East*, 230; Luqa, *Al-Aqbat, al-nashaah wa-al-sira'a*, 767.

[39] Luqa, *Al-Aqbat, al-nashaah wa-al-sira'a*, 767.

[40] Mikhail, *Copts and Moslems*; For summary of Sir Eldon Gorst's opinion of the 'Coptic Question' see amended report TNA: PRO, FO 371/111, Sir Gorst to Sir Grey, 18th March 1911.

[41] *Qammus al-tarajim al-Qibtiyyah*, 182–183.

[42] Mikhail, *Copts and Moslems*, 66.

[43] *The Times*, 27th April 1911; Mikhail, *Copts and Moslems*, 66.

[44] Statement by Sir Gorst published in *The Times*, 2nd February 1911.

[45] For Sir Gorst's visit to Upper Egypt see *The Times*, 26th January 1911.

[46] Kyriakos Mikhail, *The Freedom of the Press in Egypt: An Appeal to the Friends of Liberty by Kyriakos Mikhail*, (London: Third Edition, 1914) 107, 121.

[47] For Original telegrams see TNA: PRO, FO 371/1111, 16th February 1911.

[48] TNA: PRO, FO 371/1111, Telegram sent by Coptic representatives to Sir Grey, Sir Bigger (Buckingham Palace) and Members of the House of Commons, 16th February 1911.

[49] TNA: PRO, FO 371/1111, Miscellaneous notes, 22nd February and 25th February 1911.

[50] TNA: PRO, FO 371/1111, Copy of Parliamentary Questions from Tory politician Sir William Bull to Foreign Secretary Sir Grey, 24th February 1911.

[51] TNA: PRO, FO 371/1111, Sir Gorst to Sir Grey, 11th March 1911.

[52] TNA: PRO, FO 371/1111, Report: Foreign Missionary activity and support for Copts, May 1911.

[53] Mikhail, *The Freedom of the Press in Egypt* p. 121; For Coptic expectations and British 'impartiality' towards the Copts and Muslims, see Cromer, *Modern Egypt*, Vol. II. 209.

[54] Mikhail, *Copts and Moslems*, Introduction written by A. J. Butler, p. xii.

[55] Mikhail, *Copts and Moslems*, Introduction written by A. J. Butler, p. xii.

[56] For example see letter to *The Times*, 20th September 1910; Bayly, 'Representing Copts and Muhammadans', 180; see also chapter 1 for more details.

[57] Bayly, 'Representing Copts and Muhammadans', 180–3.

[58] Justin McCarthy, *The Ottoman Turks: An Introductory History in 1923*, (Longman, 1997) 222.

[59] Yapp, *The Making of the Modern Near East*, 220–221.

[60] Yapp, *The Making of the Modern Near East*, 221.

[61] 1 Feddan = 24 Kirat = 4200 Square meters = 1.038 Acres.

[62] Seikaly, 'Coptic Communal Reform', 268.

[63] Al-Feki, *Copts in Egyptian Politics*, 34; Luqa, *Al-Aqbat, al-nashaah wa-al-sira'a*, 533.

[64] Robert Tignor, 'Bank Misr and Foreign Capitalism', in *International Journal in Middle Eastern Studies*, Vol 8. No. 2. (1977) 161–181; Anouar Abdel-Malek, *Egypt, Military Society : The Army Regime, the Left, and Social change under Nasser*, (New York: Randon House, 1968) 251–252; Muhammad Tal'at Harb, *'Ilaj Misr al-iqtisadi wa-mashru' bank al-Misriyin wa bank al-Ummah*, (Cairo: Dar al-Kutub wa-al-Watha'iq al-Qawmiyah, 2002).

[65] Adel A. Beshai, 'The Place and the Present Role of the Copts in the Egyptian Economy: Traditions and Specializations' in *Christian Communities in the Arab Middle East*, ed. Andrea Pacini, (Oxford: Oxford University Press, 1998) 192.

[66] For further discussion on the role of Lay communal leaders see discussion in Chapter 4.

[67] Meinardus, *Two Thousand Years*, 85–92.

[68] Ami Ayalon, *The Press in the Arab Middle East: A History*, (New York: Oxford University Press, 1995) 42.

[69] Ali Fahmy Muhammad, *The Future of Egypt*, (Cairo: Hilal Publishers, 1911) 64.

[70] Al-Antuni, *Wataniyat al-Kanisah al-Qibtiyah*, Vol. I. 386; *Qammus al-tarajim al-Qibtiyyah*, 233.

[71] *Al-Watan* Newspaper, 22nd May 1908.

[72] For the activities of Mustapha Kamil in the establishment of *Hizb al-Watani*, see, 'Abd al-Rahman Rafi'i, *Mustafa Kamil ba'ith al-harakah al-wataniyah*, (Cairo: al-Sharq, 1939) 262–272.

[73] See Carter, *The Copts in Egyptian Politics*, 10.

[74] Rafi'i, *Mustafa Kamil*, 301; *Qammus al-tarajim al-Qibtiyyah*, 212–3.

[75] *Qammus al-tarajim al-Qibtiyyah*, 126–7.

[76] Rafi'i, *'Asr Ismail*, Vol. II. 270.

[77] See Gamal Badawi's article on Wisa Wasif in *Wafd* Newspaper 1986; *Qammus al-tarajim al-Qibtiyyah* 272–3.

[78] Al-Antuni, *Wataniyat al-Kanisah al-Qibtiyah*, Vol. II. 386.

[79] Rafi'i, *'Asr Ismail*, Vol. II. 420.

[80] Abouseif, 'The Political Situation of the Copts' 195.

[81] Yunan Labib Rizq, 'Nation's Party', in *Coptic Encyclopaedia*, 1987.

[82] For later advocates of this approach see Taha Husayn, *Mustaqbal al-thaqafah fi Misr*, (Cairo: Matba'at al-Ma'arif, 1938).

[83] *Qammus al-tarajim al-Qibtiyyah*,168.

[84] *Al-Fata al-Qibti*, April 1908.

[85] *Al-Firu'an*, 1910–11 and October 1913.

[86] Carter, *The Copts in Egyptian Politics*, 11.

[87] *Al-Fata al-Qibti*, April 1908.

[88] For example see *Al-Firu'an*, October 1913; Tawfq Habib began his early career with the Coptic *Al-Watan* gaining himself a reputation as a talented journalist regularly writing in *Al-Ahram*. *Qammus al-tarajim al-Qibtiyyah*, 56–57.

[89] Article penned by Fanous and published in *The Daily Telegraph*, 8th September 1908.

[90] Rafi'i, *Mustafa Kamil*, 143–146; Ayalon, *The Press in the Arab Middle East*, 59.

[91] Shawky Karas, a conservative Copt who had immigrated to the US in the 1960s founding of the American Coptic Association wrote a book with a similar title in which he accused Islam of usurping Coptic rights, *Copts Strangers in their own Land* (Jersey City: American, Canadian and Australian C. Coptic Associations, 1986).

[92] *Qammus al-tarajim al-Qibtiyyah*, 49–50.

[93] Abouseif, 'The Political Situation of the Copts', 197.

[94] Malak Badrawi, *Political Violence in Egypt, 1910–1925: Secret Societies, Plots and Assassinations*, (Surrey: Curzon, 2000) 22.

[95] See Mikhail in *The Times*, 27 April 1911; Vatikiotis, *The History of Modern Egypt*, 208.

[96] Al-Antuni, *Wataniyat al-Kanisah al-Qibtiyah*, Vol. II. 386.

[97] Al-Antuni, *Wataniyat al-Kanisah al-Qibtiyah*, Vol. II. 387.

[98] For Egyptian public opinion on the Dinshawi incident, see, Rafi'i, *Mustafa Kamil*, 207–218.

[99] Donald Reid, 'Political Assassination in Egypt 1910–1954' in *International Journal of African Studies*, Vol. 15. No. 4. (1982) 627.

[100] For details of incident and trial see Rafi'i, *Mustafa Kamil*, 208–212; Vatikiotis, *The History of Modern Egypt*, 206.

[101] Vatikiotis, *The History of Modern Egypt*, 211.

[102] Al-Rafi'i, *'Asr Ismail*, 238.

[103] TNA: PRO, FO 371/1111, Memorandum: Contrast between British official declarations and British Policy, April, 1911.

[104] 'Crime 120 'Abdin 1910: Testimony of Ibrahim al-Wardani' quoted in Badrawi, *Political Violence in Egypt*, 22.

[105] Vatikiotis, *The History of Modern Egypt*, 207–210.

[106] *Egyptian Gazette*, 26th April 1910.

[107] *Egyptian Gazette*, 26th April 1910; Badrawi, *Political Violence in Egypt*, 33.

[108] Badrawi, *Political Violence in Egypt*, 33–34.

[109] Maitre Tawfiq Doss, 'The Question of Government Posts' in *The Coptic Congress, held in Assiout on March 6, 7 and 8, 1911: The Speeches*, (No publisher) 19–32.

[110] TNA: PRO, FO 371/1111, Sir Gorst to Sir Grey, 18th March 1911.

[111] *Al-Mu'ayyad*, 4th March 1911.

[112] *Al-Mu'ayyad*, 6th March 1911.

[113] *Al-Ahli*, 7th and 8th March 1911.

[114] *Al-Mu'ayyad*, 7th March 1911.

[115] *Al-Liwa*, 6th March and 18th March 1911.

[116] *Al-'Alam*, 26th March 1911.

[117] *The Times*, 1st May 1911.

[118] Muhammad, *The Future of Egypt*, 67.

[119] Ayalon, *The Press in the Arab Middle East*, 52.

[120] For creation of Wafd see, Sa'd Zaghlul, *Mudhakkirat Sa'd Zaghlul*, (Cairo: al-Hayah al-Misriyah al-'Ammah lil-Kitab, 1990–1998,) Vol. VIII. and IX.; Albert Hourani, *Arabic thought in the Liberal Age 1798–1939*, (Cambridge: Cambridge University Press, 1983) 211.

[121] Lloyd E Ambrosius, *Wilsonian Statecraft: Theory and Practice of Liberal Internationalism during World War I* , (Wilmington: SR Books, 1991).

[122] The two other Wafd delegates were Ali Pasha Sha'rawi, a member of the Legislative Assembly and 'Abd al-Aziz Bey Fahmy, a lawyer and member of the Legislative Assembly. See, British Documents on Foreign Affairs, Doc. 74, Vol. I, Telegram Sir Wingate to Lord Balfour, 17th November 1918.

[123] British Documents on Foreign Affairs, Doc. 216 Vol. I, Sir Allenby to Curzon, 6th April 1919.

[124] British Documents on Foreign Affairs, Doc 183, Vol. I, Sir Allenby to Curzon, 1st April 1919.

[125] British Documents on Foreign Affairs, Doc 139, Vol. I, Sir Cheetham to Curzon, 10th March 1919.

[126] British Documents on Foreign Affairs, Doc 186, Vol. I, Sir Allenby to Curzon, 4th April 1919.

[127] British Documents on Foreign Affairs, Doc 147, Vol. I, Sir Cheetham to Curzon, 10⁵ʰ March 1919.

[128] See M. W. Daly, *The Sirdar: Sir Reginald Wingate and the British Empire in the Middle East*, (Philadelphia: American Philosophical Society, 1997) and Matthews Hughs, *Allenby and British Strategy in the Middle East 1917–1919*, (London: Frank Cass, 1999); See also, British Documents on Foreign Affairs, Doc 158, Vol. I, Memorandum, Allenby Appointed, 21st March 1919.

[129] Hourani, *Arabic Thought*, 212.

[130] Al-Bishri, *Al-Muslimun wa-al-Aqbat*, 133–163.

[131] Hanna, *Na'am... Aqbat*, 77.

[132] See Al-Feki, *Copts in Egyptian Politics*, front cover.

[133] G.Civimini in *Corriere della Serra*, 30th December 1919,taken from Lothrop Stoddard, *The New World of Islam*, (Scribner Press, 1921) 213.

[134] Huda Sha'rawi, *Harem Years: The Memoirs of an Egyptian Feminist (1879–1924)*, (London: Virago, 1986) 84.

[135] Beth Baron, *Egypt as a woman: Nationalism, Gender and Poltics*, (Unoversity of Claiforbia Press, 2005) 125.

[136] For the best example of an exception to this approach see, Beinin, and Lockman., '1919: Labour Upsurge and National Revolution', in *The Modern Middle East: A Reader*, ed. Hourani, Khoury and Wilson, (London: I. B. Tauris, 1993) 395–428, who discuss the role of labour and union movements during 1919.

[137] Janice Terry, *The Wafd 1919–1952: Cornerstone of Egyptian Political Power*, (London: Third World Centre for Research and Publishing, 1982); James Whidden, *The Egyptian Revolution : Politics and the Egyptian Nation 1919–1926*, Thesis (PhD) – SOAS, University of London, 1998.

[138] *Al-Manarah al-Misriyyah*, 30th November 1949.

[139] Dar al-Watha'iq al-Qawmi (Egyptian National Archives): Mahafiz 'Abdin 541, Letter from Pope Kyrillos V to Sultan Fuad, 27th April 1919, Reprinted in Muhammad Afifi, *Al-Din w-al-siyassah fi-Misr al-Mu'asar: Qommus Sergius*, (Cairo: Dar al-Sharouk, 2001) 118.

[140] Qommus Basili Bulus, *Dhikrayati fi nisf qarn*, (No Publisher, 1991 141.

[141] See interview with Sergius in *al-Muswar*, 16th April 1954.

[142] Sergius went on to father five sons and five daughters, for more on his family life see, *al-Watani* Newspaper, 6th September 1964.

[143] *Al-Firu'an*, October 1913, p.7; Ibrahim Hilal, 'Sarjiyus, Malti', in *Coptic Encyclopeadia*, 2096–2097.

[144] *Al-Firu'an*, October 1913; Bulus, *Dhikrayati fi nisf qarn*, 145.

[145] *Al-Firu'an*, October 1913; al-Antuni, *Wataniyat al-Kanisah al-Qibtiyah*, Vol. I. 427.

[146] *Al-Firu'an*, October 1913; Hilal, ' Sarjiyus, Malti', 2096–2097; The Egyptian edition of *Al-Manarah al-Murqusiyah* was founded in 1928 and ran to 1935 when it changed its name to *Al-Manarah al-Misriyyah*, running for a further eighteen years. For more, see discussion in Chapter 3 concerning the Coptic Press and its uses.

[147] *Al-Firu'an*, October 1913.

[148] *Al-Firu'an*, October 1913; *Qammus al-tarajim al-Qibtiyyah*, 113.

[149] *Al-Musawar*, Interview with Sergius, 16th April 1954; Antuni, *Wataniyat al-Kanisah al-Qibtiyah*, Vol. I. 427.

150 *Qammus al-tarajim al-Qibtiyyah*, 113.

151 TNA: PRO, FO 141/480/20, Transcript of meeting with Ibrahim Bey al-Guindi (Editor of *al-Watan*), 26th October 1920.

152 *Al-Mansurah*, Fifty year anniversary of 1919 revolution special edition, 7th March 1969.

153 See, *al-Manarah al-Misriyyah*, 31st August 1944.

154 *Akhir Sa'a*, Reprint of original Sergius interview with Farag Gabron, 20th August 1944.

155 'Abd al-Rahman Rafi'i, *Thawrat sanat 1919: tarikh Misr al-qawmi min sanat 1914 ila sanat 1921*, (Cairo: Maktabat al-Nahdah, 1946) Vol. I. 152.

156 *Akhir Sa'a*, Reprint of original Sergius interview with Farag Gabron, 20th August 1944; in British Documents on Foreign Affairs, Doc 163, Vol. I, Sir Cheetham to Curzon, 22nd March 1919.

157 *Akhir Sa'a*, Reprint of Sergius interview with Farag Gabron, 20th August 1944; *al-Manarah al-Misriyyah*, 31st August 1944; Lami al-Muti'i, *Mawsu'at hadha al-rajul min Misr*, (Cairo: Dar al-Sharuq, 1997) 426.

158 Antuni *Wataniyat al-Kanisah al-Qibtiyah*, Vol. I. 428.

159 *Al-Manarah al-Misriyyah*, 30th November 1949.

160 'Afifi, *Al-Din wa-l Siyassah fi Misr*, 19; For more on Egypt as a woman see, Beth Baron, *Egypt as a Woman: Nationalism, Gender and Politics*, (California: University of California Press, 2005).

161 British Documents on Foreign Affairs, Doc 185, Vol. I, Sir Allenby to Curzon, 3rd April 1919.

162 *Al-Musawar*, Interview with Sergius, 16th April 1954; *Akhir Sa'a*, Reprint of Sergius interview with Farag Gabron, 20th August 1944.

163 For more on British attitudes see: TNA: PRO, FO 141/480/20, Transcript of meeting with Ibrahim Bey al-Guindi (Editor of *al-Watan*), 26th October 1920.

164 *Akhir Sa'a*, Reprint of Sergius interview with Farag Gabron, 20th August 1944; *Al-Manarah al-Misriyyah*, 17th April 1936 and 31st August 1944.

165 Dar al-Watha'iq al-Qawmi (Egyptian National Archives): Mahafiz 'Abdin 541: Letter from Pope Kyrillos V to Sultan Fuad, 27th April 1919, Reprinted in full in Afifi, *Al-Din wa-l Siyassah*, 118.

166 Dar al-Watha'iq al-Qawmi (Egyptian National Archives): Mahafiz 'Abdin 541: Letter from Pope Kyrillos V to Sultan Fuad, 27th April 1919, Reprinted in Afifi, *Al-Din wa-l Siyassah*, 118.

167 Muhammad, *The Future of Egypt*, 64.

168 Al-Rafi'i, *'Asr Ismail*, Vol. II, 123; Al-Muti'i, *Mawsu'at hadha al-rajul min Misr*, 425; Wilfred Blunt, *Secret History of the English Occupation of Egypt : Being a Personal Narrative of Events* (London : T. Fisher Unwin, 1907) 153.

169 Rafi'i, *Thawrat sanat 1919*, Vol. II. 35.

[170] Basili, *Dhikrayati fi nisf qarn*, 149.

[171] *Akhir Sa'a*, Reprint of Sergius interview with Farag Gabron,    20th August 1944.

[172] *Al-Manarah al-Misriyyah*, 31st August 1944.

## Chapter 3

[1] TNA: PRO, FO 141/516/7, Promulgation of Electoral Law.

[2] TNA: PRO, FO 141/516, Memorandum, 18th April 1922; Hourani, *Arabic Thought*, p. 213.

[3] TNA: PRO, FO 141/452/5, 'The Third reserve in the Declaration of February 28th 1922 for the Protection of Religious Minorities', 9th January 1924.

[4] See, Zaghlul, *Mudhakkirat Sa`d Zaghlul*, Vol. VIII and IX.

[5] Selma Botman, *Egypt: From Independence to Revolution 1919–1952*, (Syracuse: Syracuse University Press, 1991) p. 55.

[6] For more on the 'liberal period' of Egyptian party politics see, Afaf Lutfi al-Sayyid-Marsot, *Egypt's Liberal Experiment, 1922–1936*, (Berkeley: University of California Press, 1977); El-Mountacer, *The Dilemma of Liberalism in the Middle East : A Reading of the Liberal Experiment in Egypt, 1920s–1930s*, Thesis (PhD)–Princeton University, 1991.

[7] Marius Deeb, *Party Politics in Egypt: The Wafd and its rivals, 1919–1952*, (London: Ithaca Press, 1979) p. 311.

[8] *Qammus al-tarajim al-Qibtiyyah*, p. 126.

[9] Deeb, *Party Politics in Egypt*, p. 245.

[10] British Documents on Foreign Affairs, Doc. 20, Vol. VI,   New Zaghlul Ministry, 28th January 1924; *Qammus al-tarajim al-Qibtiyyah*, pp. 372–373; Abouseif, 'The Political Situation of the Copts', p. 200; Meinardus, *Two Thousand Years*,  p. 90.

[11] Terry, *The Wafd 1919–1952*, p. 208.

[12] Haggai Erlich, *Students and University in Twentieth Century Egyptian Politics*, (London: Cass, 1989) p. 95.

[13] Deeb, *Party Politics in Egypt*, p. 317.

[14] Israel Gershoni & James Jankowski, *Redefining the Egyptian Nation 1930–1945*, (Cambridge: Cambridge University Press, 1995) p. 147.

[15] Israel Gershoni, 'The Reader– 'Another Production'': The Reception of Haykal's biography of Muhammad and the Shift of Egyptian Intellectuals to Islamic Subjects in the 1930s' in *Poetics Today*, Vol. 15. No. 2. (1994) p. 242; Muhammad Husayn Haykal, *Hayat Muhammad*, (Cairo: Misr Publishers, 1933); See also,  Nadav Safran, *Egypt in Search of a Political Community: An Analysis of the Intellectual Political and Intellectual Evolution of Egypt, 1804–1952*, (London: Harvard University Press, 1961) pp. 165–180.

[16] Gershoni, 'The Reader– 'Another Production', p. 243.

[17] Hourani, *Arabic Thought*, p. 213; Deeb, *Party Politics in Egypt*, p. 245.

[18] British Documents on Foreign Affairs, Doc. 8, Vol. XX, Lampson to Viscount Halifax, January 1939.

[19] British Documents on Foreign Affairs, Doc. 111, Vol. XVI, Anglo-Egyptian Treaty 1936; Botman, *Egypt from Independence to Revolution*, p. 57.

[20] Botman, *Egypt from Independence to Revolution*, p. 60.

[21] British Documents on Foreign Affairs, Doc. 14, Vol. XVIII, Lampson to Eden, 19th March 1937.

[22] TNA: PRO, FO 371/31572, Report of Cost of living in Egypt compiled by the Shell Company in Egypt Ltd., February 1942.

[23] TNA: PRO, FO 141/452, Protection of Religious Minorities, 26th February 1922.

[24] Abouseif 'The Political Situation of the Copts', p. 200; Total Population was 12,7171,864, whilst Christians (including foreign) in 1917 were 1,025,853, See Ministry of Finance; Statistics and Census Dept. *Population of Egypt*, Government Press, Bulaq, Cairo.

[25] *Al-Ahram* , 16th May 1922.

[26] Tawfiq Doss (1875–1950), A graduate from Law School, Doss had gained himself a reputation as defender of citizens in political cases. He was a representative on the 1923 Constitution committee and a supporter of the Constitutional Liberal Party, See, *Qammus al-tarajim al-Qibtiyyah* p. 57.

[27] Hasan, *Christians versus Muslims*, pp. 39–40.

[28] See Murqus Hanna Pasha's comments in *Al-Ahram*, 16th May 1922.

[29] *Al-Ahram*, 16th May 1922.

[30] Kedourie, 'Ethnicity, Majority, and Minority in the Middle East', p. 29.

[31] Salama Musa (1887–1957) A popular member of the association of Christian Youth which was open to Muslim and Jewish youth and was founded in 1922.

[32] *Al-Ahram*, 16th May 1922.

[33] Abouseif, 'The Political Situation of the Copts', p. 200.

[34] Hassan, *Christians versus Muslims*, p. 40.

[35] TNA: PRO, FO 141/772/8, Number and costs of Foreign Nationals in Egyptian Civil Service, 10th August 1936.

[36] Beshai, 'The Place and the Present Role of the Copts', p. 193.

[37] Beshai, 'The Place and the Present Role of the Copts, p. 193.

[38] TNA: PRO, FO 141/498/5, Report Copts in Government: Hugh Jones, 19th May 1932.

[39] TNA: PRO, FO 141/755/11, Memorandum by Ronald Campbell Acting High Commissioner, 7th October 1933.

[40] Cromer, *Modern Egypt*, Vol. II, p. 525.

[41] TNA: PRO, FO 141/772/8, Number and costs of Foreign Nationals in Egyptian Civil Service, 10th August 1936.

[42] TNA: PRO, FO 141/489/5, Report: Copts in Government Service by Hugh Jones, 19th May 1932.

[43] 44.2 per cent of all employees in the Finance department (1922–1952) were Coptic owing to the Copts traditional expertise in monetary affairs. TNA: PRO, FO 141/498/5, Report: Copts in Government Service by Hugh Jones, 19th May 1932.

[44] Percy Loraine, British High Commissioner to Egypt 1928–1934. See Gordon Waterfield, *Professional Diplomat: Percy Loraine of Kirkland,, 1880–1961*, (London: J Murray, 1973).

[45]TNA: PRO, FO 141/749/5 Despatch to the Foreign Office, 24th July 1933.

[46]TNA: PRO, FO 141/749/5 Despatch to the Foreign Office, 24th July 1933.

[47]TNA: PRO, FO 141/489/5 Report: Copts in Government Service by Acting Financial Advisor Llewelyn Hugh Jones, 19 May 1932.

[48]TNA: PRO, FO 141/755/11 Memorandum by Ronald Campbell Acting High Commissioner, 7th October 1933.

[49] In 1967, the Church was unable to pay the salaries of 300 priests due to financial difficulties. Nasser provided LE 31,000 from the public fund. TNA: PRO, FCO 51/32, Memorandum, 19th May 1967.

[50] TNA: PRO, FO 141/749/5 Despatch to the Foreign Office, 24th July 1933.

[51] TNA: PRO. FO 141/557/5, Christian religious instruction in Egyptian elementary schools, 16th May 1935.

[52] TNA: PRO. FO 141/557/5, Christian religious instruction in Egyptian elementary schools, 16th May 1935.

[53]TNA: PRO. FO 141/557/5, Christian religious instruction in Egyptian elementary schools, 16th May 1935.

[54] TNA: PRO, FO 141/452, Protection of Religious Minorities, 26th February 1922.

[55] Meinardus, *Two Thousand Years,* pp. 86–87.

[56] For more on Obeid and Zaghlul's relationship see, TNA: FO 141/505/3 Police and Intelligence reports on the activities of Professor Makram Obeid, 1921–1929.

[57] TNA: FO 141/505/3 Police and Intelligence reports on the activities of Professor Makram Obeid, 1921–1929.

[58] Muhammad Husayn Haykal, *Mudhakirat fi al-Siyasa al-Misriyyah, 'Ahd Faruq 1937–1952,* (Cairo: 1952) Vol. II, p. 264.

[59] Obeid, *Muhadarat Ma'ali al-Ustath Makram Obeid Pasha fi-al-Jami'a al-Misriyha,* (Cairo, November 1936).

60 Al-Feki, *Copts in Egyptian Politics,* p. 107.

61 James Jankowski, *Egypt's Young Rebels: 'Young Egypt' 1933–1952,* (Stanford: Hoover Institution Publications, 1975) pp. 9–10.

62 British Documents on Foreign Affairs, Doc. 161, Vol. XVII, Memorandum respecting the Blue-shirt Movement; For more details see also Jankowski, *Egypt's young rebels* pp. 24–26; pp. 34–7.

63 British Documents on Foreign Affairs, Doc. 161, Vol. XVII, Memorandum respecting the Blue-shirt Movement.

64 British Documents on Foreign Affairs, Doc. 161, Vol. XVII, Memorandum respecting the Blue-shirt Movement; Deeb, *Party Politics in Egypt,* p. 353.

65 British Documents on Foreign Affairs, Doc. 161, Vol. XVII, Memorandum respecting the Blue-shirt Movement.

66 British Documents on Foreign Affairs, Doc. 160, Vol. XVII, Lampson to Eden, 9th January 1937.

67 Luwis 'Awad, *Al-Huriyya wa naqd al-huriyyah,* (Cairo: 1971) p. 20.

68 Jankowski, *Egypt's Young Rebels,* p. 57.

69 Jankowski, *Egypt's Young Rebels,* p. 58.

70 'Abd al-Rahman Rafi'i, *Fi a'qab al-Thawrah al-Misriyah,* (Cairo: 1950) Vol. III. p. 120.

71 Haykal, *Mudhakkirat,* Vol. II. p. 264; Malak Badrawi, 'Financial Cerberus? The Egyptian Parliament 1924–1952' in *Re-envisioning Egypt 1919–1952,* ed. Goldschmidt and Salmoni., (Cairo: American University Press, c.2005) p. 111.

72 William Stadiem, *Mamlaka fi-sabeel Imra'a,* (Cairo: Dar al-Huda, 1993) p. 242.

73 Al-Feki, *Copts in Egyptian Politics,* p. 157.

74 Rafi'i, *Fi a'qab al-thawrah,* Vol. III. p. 120.

75 Haykal, *Mudhakirat,* Vol II. pp. 285–6.

76 Al-Feki, *Copts in Egyptian Politics,* p. 169.

77 Al-Feki, *Copts in Egyptian Politics,* p. 177.

78 Bishri, *Al-Muslimun wa-l-Aqbat,* p. 580.

79 Ayalon, *The Press in the Arab Middle East,* p. 61.

80 For example the Suez Church burnings in 1952; See, *Al-Ahram,* 5th January 1952; *Misr,* 5th January 1952; *Al-Watan,* 6th January 1952.

81 Richard Mitchell, *The Society of the Muslim Brothers,* (Oxford: Oxford University Press, 1993) p. 9.

82 Mitchell, *The Society of the Muslim Brothers,* p. 5; Deeb, *Party Politics in Egypt,* p. 379.

83 Deeb, *Party Politics in Egypt,* p. 379.

84 Robert Landen, 'The Rise of Mass Doctrinal Parties: The Program of Hassan al-Banna and the Muslim Brotherhood, 1936' in *The Modern Middle*

*East: A Source Book for History,* (ed.) B. Fortna, et. al. (Oxford: Oxford University Press, 2007) p. 68.

[85] Hasan Al-Banna, *Nahw al-Nur* , (Cairo: Jam'iyyat al-Ikhwan al-Muslimin, 1936); Landen, 'The Rise of Mass Doctrinal parties', p. 68.

[86] Article II. 7, p. 70.

[87] Article I. 2, p. 69.

[88] It is beyond the scope of this discussion to discuss the wealth of literature available on the Muslim Brotherhood, however for ideology, policies and the emergence see, Zakariya Sulayman Bayyumi, *al-Ikhwan al-Muslimun wa-al-Jama'at al-Islamiyah fi al-hayat al-siyasiyah al-Misriyah, 1928– 1948*, (Cairo: Maktabat Wahbah, 1979); Yusuf al-Qaradawi, *al-Ikhwan al-muslimun : 70 'aman fi al-da'wah wa-al-tarbiyah wa-al-jihad,* (Cairo: Maktabat Wahbah, 1999); Brynjar Lia, *The Society of the Muslim Brothers in Egypt : The Rise of an Islamic Mass Movement 1928–1942,* (Reading: Garnet, 1998) p. 249.

[89] Vernon Egger, *A Fabian in Egypt: Salama Musa and the Rise of the Professional classes in Egypt 1909–1939,* (London: University Press of America, 1986) p. 176.

[90] See: Salama Musa, *Misr asl al-hadara,* (Cairo: Al-'Asriyah Publishers, 1935) and *al-Balagha al-asriyyah wa-l-lugha al-'arabiyyah* (Cairo: Al-'Asriyyah Publishers, 1945).

[91] Salama Musa, *Tarbiyat Salama Musa,* (Cairo: Al-kitab al-Misri publishers, 1947) p. 125; *Misr,* 14th May 1946.

[92] *Misr,* 24th April 1946, Article by Salama Musa; Also see, TNA: PRO FO 141/1086, Dispatch to Foreign Office London, 16 May 1946.

[93] *Misr,* 20th April 1946.

[94] *Misr,* 30th April 1946.

[95] *Misr,* 30th April 1946.

[96] *Misr,* 20th April 1946, Article by Salama Musa.

[97] *Misr,* 23rd April 1946.

[98] *Misr,* 13th May 1946.

[99] *Misr,* 11th May 1946.

[100] *Misr,* 11th May 1946.

[101] *Misr,* 24th April 1946.

[102] Musa, *Tarbiyat Salama Musa,* p. 126; *Misr* Newspaper, 1st May 1946, Article by Salama Musa.

[103] Musa, *Tarbiyat Salama Musa,* p. 126; Egger, *A Fabian in Egypt,* p. 176.

[104] Mitchell, *The Society of the Muslim Brothers,* p. 27.

[105] *Misr,* 1st May 1946; Mitchell, *The Society of the Muslim Brothers,* pp. 26–7.

[106] TNA: PRO FO 141/1086, Dispatch to Foreign Office London, 16th May 1946.

[107] Zaki, *Histoire des Coptes d'Egypte,* p. 899.

[108] Ibrahim, *The Copts,* p. 14.

[109] Landen, 'The Rise of Mass Doctrinal parties', p. 68.

[110] *Misr*, 15th May 1946.

[111] *Misr*, 18th May 1946.

[112] *Misr*, 10th May 1946; Heyworth-Dunn, *Trends, Op. Cit.*, p. 11; Lia, *The Society of the Muslim Brothers*, p. 249.

[113] *Al-Aqaleem* , 28th January 1938.

[114] For example, the Young Men's Muslim Association (YMMA) founded in 1927 and modelled on the structure of the YMCA, with the support of Hassan al-Banna; For more on the role played by the YMCA and their links with missionaries in Egypt, See; Clarence Shedd, *History of the World's Alliance of Young Men's Christian Associations*, (London : SPCK, 1955) pp. 667–670.

[115] *Al-Yaqazah*, October 1943.

[116] Although adopting the same name, the Egyptian version of *Al-Manarah al-Misriyyah* was different in format and content to the early version of the magazine published in Khartoum.

[117] *Al-Manarah al-Misriyyah*, 12th October 1944.

[118] *Al-Manarah al-Misriyyah*, 31st May–23rd August 1946.

[119] *Al-Manarah al-Misriyyah*, 24th May 1947.

[120] See Articles entitled 'Donkey for Imperialists', 'Banna the Moth' and 'Banna the Wolf', *Al-Manarah al-Misriyyah*, May to October 1947.

[121] Ayalon, *The Press in the Arab Middle East*, p. 79.

[122] For example, the blind Shaykh Imam and colloquial poet Ahmad Fouad al-Negm, famously criticised the 1967 defeat: 'How nice to watch our soldiers come back empty-handed from the line of fire the battlefields of Abdel Gabbar, he will ruin everything'. The song placed blame directly at President Nasser's door who, was portrayed as Abdel Gabbar. This was seen an insult to the entire military institution and a subversive power irreconcilable with the regime's need to improve its image and contain the anger and disillusionment of the masses, resulting in their imprisonment. See, Ahmad Fouad al-Negm, *Bayan hamm: shi'r*, (Beirut: Dar al-Farabi, 1976).

[123] *Al-Manarah al-Misriyyah*, 5th July 1947.

[124] Lucie Ryzova, 'Egyptianizing Modernity through the 'New Effendiya': Social and Cultural Constructions of the Middle Class in Egypt under the Monarchy', in *Re-envisioning Egypt 1919–1952*, ed. Goldschmidt, et.al, (Cairo: American University Press, c.200) p. 129.

[125] Ryzova, 'Egyptianizing Modernity through the 'New Effendiya', p. 140.

[126] Ryzova, 'Egyptianizing Modernity through the 'New Effendiya', p. 129.

[127] Ryzova, 'Egyptianizing Modernity through the 'New Effendiya', p. 130.

[128] *Misr,* 13th May 1946. (n. 127)
[129] *Misr,* 13th May 1946. (n. 128)

## Chapter 4

[1] See, Ahmad Hilmi Shalabi, *Fusul min tarikh harakat al-islah al-ijtimai fi Misr,* (Cairo: al-Hay'ah al-Misriyah al-'Ammah lil-Kitab, 1988) p. 19.

[2] Baron, 'Islam, Philanthropy and Political culture in inter-war Egypt: The Activism of Labiba Ahmad' in *Poverty and Charity in Middle Eastern Contexts,* ed. Bonner, et al., (Albany: State University of New York Press, 2003) p. 239.

[3] Mine Ener, *Managing Egypt's Poor and the Politics of Benevolence 1800–1952,* (New Jersey: Princeton University Press, 2003) p. 100.

[4] Mine Ener, 'The Charity of the Khedive' in *Poverty and Charity in Middle Eastern Contexts,* p. 190.

[5] Ener, 'The Charity of the Khedive' p. 191.

[6] See Mark Cohen, 'The Foreign Jewish Poor in Egypt', in *Poverty and Charity in Middle Eastern Contexts.*

[7] For more on 'Abduh's philosophy on religion and human progress see his book, *Risalat al-tawhid,* Cairo, 1918.

[8] Nabeel A Khoury, *Islam and Modernization in the Middle East : Muhammad Abduh, an ideology of Development,* Thesis (Ph.D.) State University of New York at Albany, 1976, pp. 35–6.

[9] *Qammus al-tarajim al-Qibtiyyah,* p. 169; 'Aziz 'Atiya, 'Literature, Copto-Arabic' in *Coptic Encyclopaedia,* p. 1465.

[10] Shalabi., *Fusul min tarikh,* p. 20.

[11] Bonner, Ener, Singer (ed.) *Poverty and Charity in Middle Eastern contexts,* (Albany: State University of New York Press, 2003) p. 2.

[12] Ingrid Mattson, 'Status Based Definitions of Need in Early Islamic Zakat and Maintenance Laws' in *Poverty and Charity in Middle Eastern contexts,* p. 31.

[13] For example, al-Tahtawi advocated state welfare and private philanthropy for those who were poor because of disability. For more see, Juan Cole, *Colonialism and Revolution in the Middle East: social and cultural origins of Egypt's 'Urabi movement,* (Cairo: American University in Cairo Press, 1999) pp. 43–44.

[14] See discussion below; also, Mariam Hoexter, *Endowments, Rulers and Community: Waqf al-Haramayn in Ottoman Algiers,* (Leiden: Brill, 1998) p. 144; Ron Shaham, 'Christian and Jewish Waqf in Palestine during the late Ottoman Period' in *Bulletin of the School of Oriental and African Studies, University of London,* Vol. 54, No. 3., 1991, pp. 460–472.

[15] Ener, 'The Charity of the Khedive', p. 150.

[16] Shaham, 'Christian and Jewish Waqf', p. 462.

[17] Mariam Hoexter, 'Charity, the Poor and Distribution of Alms in Ottoman Algiers', in *Poverty and Charity in Middle Eastern Contexts*, p. 150.

[18] Indeed there is also some suggestion that the Coptic Benevolent Society, was actually the brainchild of the Muslim journalist 'Abdullah al-Nadim who in 1879 had created the Muslim Charitable Society in Alexandria and attended the opening session of the Coptic Benevolent Society. See, Ener, *Managing Egypt's Poor*, p. 102; al-Muqaffa', *Tarikh Misr*, Vol. IV. Part II. p. 1496.

[19] Lambeth Palace Archives: Coptic Church of Egypt- General Correspondence 1930–1959 A.O.C File 57, Report by Boutros Effendi Simaan on 'The Great Benevolent Coptic Society', May 1949.

[20] *Diamond Jubilee of al-Tawfiq Society Report*, (Cairo: 1967).

[21] Ener, *Managing Egypt's Poor*, p. 104.

[22] *Great Coptic Benevolent Society Report*, (Cairo: 1922).

[23] Hewitt, *The Problems of Success*, p. 306.

[24] Fowler, *Christian Egypt*, p. 251.

[25] Hewitt, *The Problems of Success*, p. 306.

[26] Watson, *In the Valley of the Nile*, p. 181.

[27] Fowler, *Christian Egypt*, p. 278.

[28] Basilios Butros remained the President of the FHBS until his death in 1921, Nasim, Sulayman., 'Friends of the Bible' in *Coptic Encyclopaedia*, p. 1124.

[29] *Qammus al-tarajim al-Qibtiyyah*, p. 43.

[30] See *Al-Rabta al-Masihiyyah*, March 1909 and April 1909.

[31] Lambeth Palace Archives: Coptic Church of Egypt- General Correspondence 1930–1959 A.O.C File 57, Report by Boutros Effendi Simaan on 'The Friends of the Bible Society', March 1949.

[32] Hewitt, *The Problems of Success*, p. 306.

[33] Lambeth Palace Archives: Coptic Church of Egypt- General Correspondence 1930–1959 A.O.C File 57, Report by Boutros Effendi Simaan on 'The Friends of the Bible Society', March 1949.

[34] Temple Gairdner (1873–1928) had been an active member of the CMS and well respected in Egypt for his knowledge of the region and colloquial Arabic. See biography written by his colleague in the Egyptian mission, Constance Evelyn Padwick, *Temple Gairdner of Cairo*, (London : SPCK, 1929).

[35] Lambeth Palace Archives: Coptic Church of Egypt- General Correspondence 1930–1959 A.O.C File 57, Report by Boutros Effendi Simaan on 'The Friends of the Bible Society', March 1949.

[36] Lambeth Palace Archives: Coptic Church of Egypt- General Correspondence 1930–1959 A.O.C File 57, Report by Boutros Effendi Simaan on 'The Friends of the Bible Society', March 1949.

[37] For more on the role played by the YMCA in Egypt, See, Shedd, *History of the World's Alliance*, pp. 667–670.

[38] Lambeth Palace Archives: Coptic Church of Egypt- General Correspondence 1930–1959 A.O.C File 57, Report by Boutros Effendi Simaan on 'The Friends of the Bible Society', March 1949.

[39] Ladislaus van Zeelest, 'Franciscans in Egypt' in *Coptic Encyclopaedia*, p. 1124.

[40] Luqa, *Al-aqbat, al-Nashaah wa-al-sira'a*, p. 598.

[41] *Risalat al-Hayat*, Obituary written by Iskander Ibrahim, 21st December 1950.

[42] *Risalat al-Hayat*, Obituary written by Girgis Filathowas 'Awad, 21st December 1950.

[43] TNA: PRO, FO 141/650/7, Minutes, 7th December 1930.

[44] *Al-Yaqazah*, first published in 1924 edited by Qommus Ibrahim Luqa.

[45] *Al-Yaqazah*, 9th May 1928.

[46] *Al-Yaqazah*, October 1943.

[47] *Al-Yaqazah*, April 1944.

[48] *Al-Yaqazah*, October 1943.

[49] For more on activity of society, see special '9 Year Anniversary of the Central Iman Society' edition, *Al-Fata al-Qibti* , January 1908; The Iman Benevolent Society published *Al-Fata al-Qibti* , or 'The Coptic Youth' monthly magazine between 1905–1910 in Cairo and later from 1941 *Al-Iman* , of 'The Faith' monthly magazine in collaboration with Girgis Boutros and the infamous Coptic preacher Ghattas Bishara.

[50] Iman Benevolent Society Manifesto in *Al-Fata al-Qibti*, March 1908.

[51] *Al-Fata al-Qibti*, March 1908.

[52] *Al-Fata al-Qibti*, April 1908.

[53] *Al-Fata al-Qibti*, March 1909.

[54] *Al-Fata al-Qibti*, March 1908.

[55] *Al-'Ailah al-Qibtiyah*, 1st April 1909.

[56] *Al-Rabta al-Masihiyyah*, March 1909.

[57] See, *Al-'Ailah al-Qibtiyah*, 1st April 1909; *Al-Fata al-Qibti* magazine, February 1908 and March 1908.

[58] *Al-Firu'an*, October 1913.

[59] *Al-Firu'an*, October 1913.

[60] *Al-Yaqazah*, October 1944.

[61] Hilmi Ahmad Shalabi, *Al-Aqbat wa-al-islah al-ijtimai fi Misr : dawr Jamiyat al-Tawfiq, 1891–1952* (Cairo: Maktabat al-Anjlu al-Misriyah, 1992?) p. 33.

[62] Report of *Jamiyyat al-Tawfiq*: November 1891–April 1892, taken from Shalabi, *Al-Aqbat*, p. 33

[63] Shalabi, *Al-Aqbat*, p. 33.

[64] See *Al-Tawfiq*, December 1904 for details of magazine publication.

[65]For example the Tawfiq society's Christmas donation fund for 1903 was LE 16; see *Al-Tawfiq*, January 1903.

[66] Lambeth Palace Archives: Coptic Church of Egypt- General Correspondence 1930–1959 A.O.C File 57, Report by Boutros Effendi Simaan on 'The Tawfiq Society', November 1949.

[67] 415 Children paid fees, 97 attended for free; see, 'School educational statistics in Egypt', in *Al-Tawfiq*, 11th October 1907.

[68] 'Finances of the Tawfiq Society' in *Al-Tawfiq*, 5th February 1903.

[69] *Al-Tawfiq*, February 1903.

[70] Lambeth Palace Archives: Coptic Church of Egypt- General Correspondence 1930–1959 A.O.C File 57, Report by Boutros Effendi Simaan on 'The Tewfiq Society', November 1949.

[71] Shalabi, *Al-Aqbat*, p. 118.

[72] Shalabi, *Al-Aqbat*, p. 117.

[73] Shalabi, *Al-Aqbat*, p. 118.

[74] '1883 *Majlis al-Milli* constitution' reprinted in full in *Al-Manarah al-Misriyyah*, 14th March 1944.

[75] '1883 *Majlis al-Milli* constitution' reprinted in full in *Al-Manarah al-Misriyyah*, 14th March 1944.

[76] Previously under the control of the patriarchate, the old printing press bought by Abu Islah had become obsolete and a new one had been ordered which was subsequently to come under *Majlis al-Milli* control. Articles 11 and 12, '1883 *Majlis al-Milli* constitution' reprinted in full in *Al-Manarah al-Misriyyah*, 14th March 1944.

[77] Bonner et. al, *Poverty and Charity in Middle Eastern contexts*, p. 2.

[78] Seikaly, 'Coptic Communal Reform', p. 261.

[79] Al-Misri, *Qissat al-Kanisah al-Qibtiyyah*, Vol. V. pp. 27–8.

[80] Al-Misri, *Qissat al-Kanisah al-Qibtiyyah*, Vol. V. p. 29.

[81] Butcher, *The Story of the Church*, p. 405.

[82] Mattewos, *Tarikh Babwat*, p.81; Al-Misri, *Qissat al-Kanisah al-Qibtiyyah*, Vol. V. p. 28.

[83] Leeder, *Modern Sons of the Pharaohs*, p. 258.

[84]See articles 1 and 5 of 1892 *Majlis al-Milli* constitution '1892 *Majlis al-Milli* constitution' reprinted in full in *Al-Manarah al-Misriyyah* , 14th March 1944.

[85] See article 7 of 1892 *Majlis al-Milli* constitution '1892 *Majlis al-Milli* constitution' reprinted in full in *Al-Manarah al-Misriyyah* , 14th March 1944.

[86] See 1892 *Majlis al-Milli* constitution '1892 *Majlis al-Milli* constitution' reprinted in full in *Al-Manarah al-Misriyyah* , 14th March 1944; Seikaly, 'Coptic Communal Reform', p. 255.

[87] For official Khedival decree, see *Al-Watan* newspaper, 18th November 1892.

[88] Al-Misri, *Qissat al-Kanisah al-Qibtiyyah*, Vol. V p. 31.

[89] Leeder, *Modern Sons of the Pharaohs*, p. 259.

[90] Later be Pope Yu'annis 1927–1942; Al-Misri, *Qissat al-Kanisah al-Qibtiyyah*, p. 35; Leeder, *Modern Sons of the Pharaohs*, p. 259.

[91] Al-Muqaffa`, *Tarikh Misr*, Vol. IV. Part. II. p.1516; Al-Misri, *Qissat al-Kanisah al-Qibtiyyah*, p. 42; Mattewos, *Tarikh Babawat*, p. 83.

[92] Riyad Pasha (1836–1911), also known as Riaz Pasha, served as Prime Minister three times, 1879–1881; 1888–1891; 1893–1894; Riyad in opposition to 'Urabi and his men in 1882, believed in benevolent autocracy and that Egyptians were not fitted for self-government and must be treated like children.

[93] Leeder, *Modern Sons of the Pharaohs*, p. 266.

[94] Butcher, *The Story of the Church*, p. 407.

[95] Butcher, *The Story of the Church*, p. 407; al-Muqaffa`, *Tarikh Misr*, Vol. IV. Part II. p. 1517.

[96] Al-Motei, *Mawsu'at hadha al-Rajul*, p. 420.

[97] See the discussion of events taken from Ibrahim Filathowas 'Awad's account reprinted in *Al-Yaqazah* , 1st January 1944.

[98] Al-Muqaffa', Severus, *Tarikh Misr*, Vol. IV. Part II. p. 1512.

[99] Mattewos, *Tarikh Babawat*, pp. 83–84.

[100] Al-Misri, *Qissat al-Kanisah al-Qibtiyyah*, Vol V pp. 27–8.

[101] Bishoy al-Antuni, *Egypt: A Historical Analysis of Public Personnel Policies in Relation to the Social System, 1883–1967*, Thesis (PhD.), (Nothwest Graduate School, Seattle, 2003) p. 26 .

[102] Leeder, *Modern Sons of the Pharaohs*, p. 261.

[103] Amendments to the *Majlis al-Milli* constitution in 1908, 1912, 1927, see reprints of each *Majlis al-Milli* constitution in *Al-Manarah al-Misriyyah*, 14th March 1944.

[104] See the agreements of 17th November 1893, Reprint of 1892 *Majlis al-Milli* constitution and its consequences in *Al-Manarah al-Misriyyah*, 14th March 1944.

[105] Transcript of speech given by Abba Seraphim, Metropolitan of Glastonbury, 'The renewal of Coptic Orthodoxy in the Twentieth Century', 30th May 1995, in *The Glastonbury Bulletin*, No. 92, March 1996.

[106] *Al-Manarah al-Misriyyah*, 14th March 1944.

[107] Anba Basilious, Metropolitan of Abu Tig, speaking in 1920 quoted in Ibrahim 'Abd al-Sayyid, *Amwal al-Kanisah al-Qibtiyah : man yadfau!? wa-man yaqbidu!?*, (Cairo: Dar al-diwan, 1997) p. 25; Leeder, *Modern Sons of the Pharaohs*, p. 251.

[108] Leeder, *Modern Sons of the Pharaohs*, p. 245.

[109] Leeder, *Modern Sons of the Pharaohs*, p. 248.

[110] Mattewos, *Tarikh Babawat*, p. 79.

111 *Al-Tawfiq,* 9th January 1908.
112 Mattewos, *Tarikh Babawat,* p. 79.
113 *Al-Tawfiq,* 26th February 1903.
114 *Al-Tawfiq,* 9th January 1908.
115 *Al- Firu'an,* 12th December 1912.
116 *Al- Firu'an,* 12th December 1912.
117 Anba Basilious, Metropolitan of Abu Tig, speaking in 1920, quoted in 'Abd al-Sayyid, *Amwal al-Kanisah,* pp. 22–23.
118 *Al-Tawfiq,* March 1908; Leeder, *Modern Sons of the Pharaohs,* p. 248.
119 *Al-Tawfiq,* March 1908.
120 *Al-Watan,* 29th October 1912 and *Misr,* 30th September 1912.
121 *Egyptian Gazette,* November 1913.
122 *Al-Watan,* 29th October 1912.
123 *Al-Firu'an,* 15th November 1913.
124 For statement see, *Al-Watan* and *Misr,* 31st October 1912.
125 *Al-Firu'an,* 15th November 1913.
126 *Al-Firu'an,* 15th November 1913.
127 *Misr,* 30th September 1912.
128 *Al-Tawfiq,* March 1908.
129 *Al-Tawfiq,* March 1908.

## Chapter 5
1 It is worth noting that even secular Copts like Salama Musa, identified with the religious institution of the Coptic Church as a valid representation of his communal identity.
2 *Al-Yaqazah,* October 1943.
3 *Al-Manarah al-Misriyyah,* 22nd January 1944.
4 *Al-Yaqazah,* October 1943.
5 TNA: PRO FO 141/968, Memorandum on Pope Yusab, December 1942.
6 For more on Yu'annis and relationship with *Majlis al-Milli,* see following files; TNA: PRO, FO 141/650/7; TNA: PRO, FO 141/749/5; TNA: PRO FO 141/755/11; TNA: PRO, FO 141/758/5.
7 This was also applicable to the rector and vice-rector of Al-Azhar and the Coptic Patriarch (decree No. 49, 15th November 1930), See 1923 Constitution and amendments incorporated in 1930 Constitution. TNA: PRO FO 141/560, Extensions of the King's prerogatives under new Constitution and uses made thereof; TNA: PRO FO 141/650/7 Minutes, 7 December 1930.
8 TNA: PRO FO 141/650/7 Handwritten Minute Smart; Transcript of speech given by Abba Seraphim, Metropolitan of Glastonbury, 'The renewal of Coptic Orthodoxy in the Twentieth Century', 30th May 1995, in

*The Glastonbury Bulletin,* No. 92 March 1996; Walter G. Smart, Oriental Secretary in Cairo. Sir Percy Loraine comments that he was 'wise, sardonic and an expert in Persian and Arabic languages and cultures' see Waterfield, *Professional Diplomat,* pp. 167–8.

[9] Lambeth Palace, AOC File 57 General Correspondence 1930–1959: Notes by Bishop Gwynne on an interview with Sir Robert van Sittart at the Foreign Office, 12th September 1930.

[10] John H. Watson, *Among the Copts,* (Brighton: Sussex Academic Press, 2002) p. 44.

[11] Al-Misri, *Qissat al-Kanisah al-Qibtiyyah,* Vol. VI. A p.119; *Al-Yaqazah,* October and December 1943.

[12] Signed Declaration of Patriarchal Election Law, 18th July 1928, reprinted in full in *Al-Yaqazah,* August 1928.

[13] Amongst the eleven bishops that signed, the Declaration in 1928, four were nominated to papacy in 1944: Bishop Macarius of Asyut, Bishop Theofolis of Jerusalem and Sharqiyyah, Bishop Yusab of Girga and Bishop Abram of Giza and Qalubiyyah. See, signed Declaration of Patriarchal Election Law, 18th July 1928, in *Al-Yaqazah,* August 1928.

[14] *Al-Yaqazah,* January 1944.

[15] Letter signed by five bishops, reprinted in Al-Misri, *Qissat al-Kanisah al-Qibtiyyah,* Vol. VI. A pp. 122–5.

[16] See *Misr,* 10th January 1944.

[17] TNA: PRO, FO 141/650/7, Memorandum by Saba Habashi, 15th December 1930.

[18] *Al-Manarah al-Misriyyah,* 22nd January 1944.

[19] *Majlis al-Milli* members: Kamel Sidqi Pasha, Dr Ibrahim Tekhla Bey, Merit Butros Ghali, Ragheb Iskander Bey and Dr. Guindi Wasif. Bishops in attendance: Bishop Yusab (Girga), Bishop Isaac, Bishop Demetrius, Bishop Thomas and Bishop Basilios.

[20] 4056 voters registered their names, 476 votes did not meet requirements, leaving 3580 voters eligible, *Al-Muqattam,* 4th February 1944; *Egyptian Gazette,* 4th February 1944.

[21] For more on Egyptian political campaigning see, Sarah Ben Nefissa, *Al-Intikhabat wa-zaba'iniyah al-siyasiyah fi Misr : tajdid al-wusta' wa-`awdat al-nakhib,* (Cairo: Markaz al-Qahirah li-dirasat huquq al-insan, 2005) and Gema Martin Munoz, *Política y elecciones en el Egipto contemporáneo (1922–1990),* (Madrid: Agencia Española de Cooperacion Internacional, Instituto de Cooperacion con el Mundo Arabe, 1992).

[22] 'L'amba Makarious évêque d'Assiout est élu Patriarche Copte', in *Le Progress Egyptien* Newspaper, 5th February 1944; Mounir Shoucri, 'Iryan Jirjis Muftah' in *Coptic Encyclopaedia,* pp. 1302–3.

[23] *Misr*, 22nd January 1944; TNA: PRO, FO 141/968 Memorandum on the Coptic Patriarchal elections, 7th February 1944.

[24] *Misr*, 22nd January 1944; TNA: PRO, FO 141/968 Memorandum on the Coptic Patriarchal elections, 7th February 1944.

[25] *Al-Muqattam* and *al-Misri* , 5th February 1944.

[26] Lambeth Palace Archives; Council on Foreign Relations Documents A.O.C 1–100: 'Note on the Present question of the Coptic Orthodox Church', 1946; *Egyptian Gazette*, 4th February 1944.

[27] *Al-Muqattam*, 'Anba Theofolis is the man of the hour', 2nd February 1944.

[28] Lambeth Palace Archives; Council on Foreign Relations Documents A.O.C 1–100: 'Note on the Present question of the Coptic Orthodox Church', 1946.

[29] *Al-Muqattam*, 2nd February and 3rd February 1944.

[30] *Al-Muqattam* and *Al-Misri*, 5th February 1944; *Egyptian Gazette*, 4th February 1944.

[31] *Al-Yaqazah*, February 1944.

[32] See copy of the letter by local Greek leader in Alexandria, Mr Apustolo, in *Al-Yaqazah*, February 1944.

[33] *Al-Yaqazah*, February 1944.

[34] *Al-Muqattam*, 2nd February 1944; *Al-Yaqazah*, February 1944.

[35] *Al-Yaqazah*, October 1943.

[36] See, *Al-Muqattam*, and *Al-Misri*, 5th February 1944.

[37] *Al-Manarah al-Misriyyah*, 1st February 1944.

[38] Shoucri, 'Macarius', p. 1489; *Al-Manarah al-Misriyyah*, 1st February 1944.

[39] *Al-Manarah al-Misriyyah*, 1st February 1944.

[40] For example of rallies, see *Al-Manarah al-Misriyyah*, January–February 1944 which included a public appearance from Qommus Sergius in Fajallah district of Cairo the day before the elections; *Al-Ahram* , 9th January 1944.

[41] *Al-Firu'an*, October 1913.

[42] *Al-Manarah al-Misriyyah* , 1st February 1944.

[43] *Al-Ahram*, 9th January 1944; *Al-Manarah al-Misriyyah*, January and February 1944 .

[44] Statement to the Coptic People by the delegates of the *Majlis al-Milli* concerning Patriarchal elections, Cairo 14th January 1944, see *Misr*, 15th January 1944 and *Al-Manarah al-Misriyyah* , 22nd January 1944.

[45] Statement to the Coptic People by the delegates of the *Majlis al-Milli* concerning Patriarchal elections, Cairo 14th January 1944, see *Misr*, 15th January 1944 and *Al-Manarah al-Misriyyah* , 22nd January 1944.

[46] Statement to the Coptic People by the delegates of the *Majlis al-Milli* concerning Patriarchal elections, Cairo 14th January 1944, see *Misr*, 15th January.

[47] *Misr*, 6th November 1943.

[48] TNA: PRO, FO 371/31572, Cost of Living, 1942.

[49] It is worth noting that *Misr* ran a similar front page to *Al-Manarah al-Misriyyah* with Macarius on the front cover, See *Misr*, 5th February 1944.

[50] Transcript of speech given by Dr Minyawi, 8th January 1944, in *Al-Manarah al-Misriyyah*, 22nd January 1944.

[51] *Misr*, 24th January 1944.

[52] Donald Reid, 'The Rise of Professions and Professional Organisations in Modern Egypt', in *Comparative Studies in Society and History*, Vol. 16, No. 1, (1974) p. 24.

[53] *Al-Manarah al-Misriyyah*, 22nd January 1944; *Misr*, 24th January 1944; *Misr*, 1st February 1944.

[54] *Al-Ahram*, 9th January 1944.

[55] *Al-Ahram*, 9th January 1944.

[56] *Al-Ahram*, 9th January 1944.

[57] TNA: PRO, FO 141/650/7, Handwritten Memorandum by W. Smart.

[58] TNA: PRO, FO 141/968, Memorandum on the Reform Party position, 9th February 1944.

[59] *Al-Yaqazah*, March 1944.

[60] *The Egyptian Gazette*, 14th February 1944.

[61] *Al-Manarah al-Misriyyah*, 15th February 1944, *Misr* and *Al-Muqattam*, 14th February 1944.

[62] *Al-Manarah al-Misriyyah*, 15th February 1944.

[63] TNA: PRO, FO 141/650/7 Handwritten Memorandum by W. Smart; *Al-Muqattam*, 3rd February 1944.

[64] Haykal, *Mudhakirat*. Vol. II, pp. 285–6.

[65] Al-Feki, *Copts in Egyptian Politics*, pp. 176–77.

[66] TNA: PRO, FO 141/968 Memorandum on Coptic Patriarch, 18th February 1944.

[67] See *Al-Misri*, and *Al-Muqattam* and *Misr* , 7th February 1944.

[68] See *Al-Misri*, and *Al-Muqattam* and *Misr* , 7th February 1944.

[69] TNA: PRO, FO 141/968, Memorandum on the Coptic Patriarchate, 18th February 1944.

[70] *Al-Muqattam*, 14th February 1944; TNA: PRO, FO 141/968, Memorandum on the Coptic Patriarchate, 18th February 1944.

[71] TNA: PRO, FO 141/968 Memorandum: The Coptic Patriarchal Election, 7th February 1944.

[72] TNA: PRO, FO 141/968 Memorandum on the Coptic Patriarchate, 18th February 1944.

[73] Ahmad Mahir, had split form the Wafd party and formed the Sa'dists. He was assasintaed in 1945. See *New York Times*, 25th February 1945. *Time Magazine*, March 1945; TNA: PRO, FO 141/968 Memorandum on the Reform Party position, 9th February 1944.

[74] 'Awad, *Al-Huriyya wa naqd al-huriyya*, p. 20.

[75] *Egyptian Gazette*, *Al-Muqattam* and *Misr*, 24th February 1944.

[76] *Al-Manarah al-Misriyyah*, 14th March 1944.

[77] '1883 *Majlis al-Milli* constitution' reprinted in full in *Al-Manarah al-Misriyyah*, 14th March 1944.

[78] '1927 Ammendment to *al-Majlis al-Milli* constitution' Reprinted in full in *Al-Manarah al-Misriyyah*, 14th March 1944.

[79] TNA: PRO, 141/650/7, Memorandum on Endowments, December 1930.

[80] Transcript of speech given by Macarius, 29th January 1944, in *Al-Manarah al-Misriyyah*, 1st February 1944.

[81] TNA: PRO 141/ 968, Record of conversation between Smart and Ibrahim Takhla of the *Majlis al-Milli*, March 1944.

[82] *The Egyptian Gazette*, 24th February 1944.

[83] 'Article 1 of Agreement concerning *Awqaf*, 23rd February 1944', reprinted in full in *Al-Manarah al-Misriyyah*, 28th March 1944.

[84] Article 3of Agreement concerning *Awqaf*, 23rd February 1944', re-printed in full in *Al-Manarah al-Misriyyah*, 28th March 1944; *The Egyptian Gazette*, *Al-Muqattam* and *Misr*, 24th February 1944.

[85] *The Egyptian Gazette*, 5th March 1944.

[86] For more on *Al-Muqattam* see, Taysir Abu Arjah, *Al-Muqattam: Jaridat al-Ihtilal al-Baritani fil-Misr*, (Cairo: al-Hay'ah al-Misriyah al-'Ammah lil-Kitab, 1997); Ayalon, *The Press in the Arab Middle East*, p. 76.

[87] The signatories included: Aghabios, Bishop of Deirut and Nazir of al-Muharak Monastery; Ibrahim, Bishop of Giza and Qalubiyyah; Canon Misac al-Anba Boli, Head and Nazir of the Abba Boli Monastery; Canon Faltaos, Nazir and head of the Virgin at Siryan monastery; Canon Bernaba Ghobryal, Nazir and head of the Sayedat Bermus monastery; Canon Bakhoum, Nazir and head of the Monastery of St. Macarius; Canon Barhoum, head of the monastery of Anba Bashwi; Basilios, Bishop of Esna and Luxor.; See, *Al-Muqattam Newspaper*, 4th March 1944.

[88] *Misr*, 4th March 1944.

[89] *Al-Muqattam*, 4th March 1944.

[90] *Al-Muqattam*, 4th March 1944.

[91] *Al-Muqattam*, 11th March 1944.

[92] *Al-Manarah al-Misriyyah*, 8th June 1944.

[93] Nasim, 'Education, Coptic', pp. 931–933.

[94] Watson, *Among the Copts*, p. 47.

[95] Lambeth Palace Archives; Council on Foreign Relations Documents A.O.C 1–100: 'Note on the Present question of the Coptic Orthodox Church', 1946; *Al-Muqattam*, 2nd February and 3rd February 1944.

[96] *Al-Muqattam*, 4th March 1944.

[97] Statistics taken from, *Al-Manarah al-Misriyyah*, 18th August 1945.

[98] *Al-Manarah al-Misriyyah*, 18th August 1945.

[99] *Al-Manarah al-Misriyyah*, 18th August 1945.

[100] *'Majlis al-Milli* committee findings of Patriarchal Diwan, 22nd January 1938', Re-printed in full in *Al-Manarah al-Misriyyah*, 13th April 1944.

[101] *'Majlis al-Milli* committee findings of Patriarchal Diwan, 22nd January 1938', Re-printed in full in *Al-Manarah al-Misriyyah*, 13th April 1944.

[102] *Al-Manarah al-Misriyyah* , 11th May 1944.

[103] See for example, Seikaly, 'Coptic Communal Reform'.

[104] *Misr*, 19th June 1944.

[105] *Al-Manarah al-Misriyyah*, 11th May 1944.

[106] *Al-Manarah al-Misriyyah*, 11th May 1944.

[107] *Al-Misri*, 8th March 1944.

[108] *Al-Ahram*, 12th March 1944.

[109] Minutes of meeting held 17th March 1944 reprinted in *Al-Manarah al-Misriyyah*, 28th March 1944; *Misr* , 21st March 1944.

[110] *Al-Manarah al-Misriyyah*, 14th March 1944.

[111] *Al-Manarah al-Misriyyah*, 28th March 1944.

[112] *Al-Yaqazah*, September–October 1944.

[113] *Al-Yaqazah*, September 1944.

[114] *Al-Yaqazah*, September 1944.

[115] *Al-Yaqazah*, March 1944.

[116] Mounir., 'Macarius III', p. 1489; TNA: PRO, FO 141/1027, Memorandum, June 1945.

[117] Letter from Prime Minister Ahmad Mahir to Pope Macarius, 18th November 1944, reprinted and published in *Al-Manarah al-Misriyyah*, 21st April 1945.

[118] Reply from Pope Macarius, to Prime Minister Ahmad Mahir, 19th November 1944, reprinted and published in *Al-Manarah al-Misriyyah*, 21st April 1945.

[119] Reply from Pope Macarius, to Prime Minister Ahmad Mahir, 19th November 1944, reprinted and published in *Al-Manarah al-Misriyyah*, 21st April 1945.

[120] Article 1, Resolutions passed by Holy Synod, 21st May 1945: See, *Al-Muqattam*, 25th May 1945, *Al-Manarah al-Misriyyah*, 2nd June 1945.

[121] Article 8, Resolutions passed by Holy Synod, 21st May 1945: See, *Al-Muqattam*, 25th May 1945, *Al-Manarah al-Misriyyah*, 2nd June 1945; TNA: PRO, FO 141/1027, Memorandum: 'Copts', 1st June 1945.

[122] *Al-Manarah al-Misriyyah*, 6th July 1944; *Al-Manarah al-Misriyyah*, 12th April 1945; *Misr*, 18th August 1945.

[123]Set up in 1926, the magazine had a circulation of 20,000 in 1947; *Ruz al-Yusuf*, 12th September 1945

[124] *Al-Wataniyyah*, 3rd October 1945.

## Chapter 6

[1] Anne-Claire Kerboeuf, 'The Cairo Fire of 26th January 1952 and the Interpretations of History', in *Re-envisioning Egypt 1919–1952*, p. 196.

[2] Kerboeuf, 'The Cairo Fire' p. 197.

[3] Yapp, *The Making of the Modern Near East*, p. 67.

[4] Anwar Al-Sadat, *Revolt on the Nile*, (London: Allen Wingate, 1957) p. 53.

[5] Gamal 'Abd al-Nasser, *Falsafat al-Thawrah*, (Cairo: Dar al-Ma'rif, 1953) p. 27.

[6] *Al-Ahram*, 27th July 1952.

[7] For example see, 'The Egyptian Kingdom becomes a Republic and Naguib its first President' in *Al-Misri*, 19th June 1953.

[8] 'Abd al-Nasser, *Falsafat al-Thawrah*, pp. 20–21.

[9] *Al-Ahram*, 24th July 1952.

[10] *Misr*, 28th July 1952.

[11] *Misr*, 31st July.

[12] It is perhaps worth noting that a similar picture was taken with Naguib and Shaykh al-Azhar on 28th July 1952 only two days after the coup.

[13] Open Letter published in *Misr*, 23rd September 1952.

[14] See *Misr*, 18th–21st August 1952.

[15] *Misr*, 19th August 1952.

[16] General Muhammad Naguib, *Egypt's Destiny: A Personal Statement*, (New York; Doubleday and Co. 1955) p. 172.

[17] *Al-Ahram*, 5th January 1952; *Misr*, 5th January 1952; *Al-Watan*, 6th January 1952.

[18] Al-Feki, *Copts in Egyptian Politics*, p. 182.

[19] *Misr*, 11th January 1952; *Al-Watan* , 17th January 1952.

[20] Al-Feki, *Copts in Egyptian Politics*, p. 183.

[21] *Misr*, 15th September 1952; *Proche Orient Chretien*, July–September 1952.

[22] See commentaries in *Misr* throughout August 1952.

[23] Lambeth Palace Archives LEC 87: Crisis in the Coptic Patriarchate, September 1952.

[24] Naguib, *Egypt's Destiny*, p. 172; Lambeth Palace Archives LEC 87: Crisis in the Coptic Patriarchate, September 1952.

[25] *Proche Orient Chretien*, July–September 1952; *Misr*, 1st September 1953.

[26] *Al-Yaqazah*, November 1947.

[27] *Al-Yaqazah*, November 1947.

[28] Lambeth Palace Archives LEC 87: Crisis in the Coptic Patriarchate, September 1952; *Proche Orient Chretien,* July–September 1952.

[29] *Misr,* 31st August 1952.

[30] A similar committee though planned was not implemented in the Coptic Church until late 1954; *Misr,* 5th September 1952.

[31] *Misr,* 20th and 21st August 1952.

[32] *Ruz al-Yusuf,* 8th September 1952 and *Al-Jamahir al-Misri,* 8th September 1952.

[33] *Misr,* 5th September 1952.

[34] For re-print of excommunication decree see *Misr,* 30th September 1952.

[35] Lambeth Palace Archives LEC 87: Crisis in the Coptic Patriarchate, September 1952.

[36] Although, following Sergius' death on the 5th September 1964, thousands of mourners went out into the streets. Nasser's government issued a statement which acknowledged and praised Sergius' national unity role played in 1919. On the fortieth day traditional commemoration, a large gathering was convened at the Mar Girgis (St. George) Monastery which included prominent nationalist mourners and as well as the JUQ leader Ibrahim Fahmi Hilal. For more details see: Luqa, *Al-Aqbat, al-Nashaah wa-al-sira'a,* p. 715.

[37] *Misr,* 20th August 1952.

[38] See Chapter 3 for details; Yusuf, *Al-Aqbat wa-al-Qawmiyah,* p. 144.

[39] Yusuf, *Al-Aqbat wa-al-Qawmiyah,* p. 144.

[40] *Misr,* 18th August 1952.

[41] *Misr,* 18th August 1952.

[42] Erlich, *Students and University,* p. 170.

[43] Fu'ad I University became Cairo University following the revolution.

[44] *Al-Manarah al-Misriyyah,* December 1951.

[45] *Misr,* 1st September 1954.

[46] There is considerable controversy over the figures given by Hilal, See Anthony Gorman, *Historians, State and Politics in Twentieth Century Egypt: Contesting the Nation,* (London: Routledge, 2003) p. 169; Carter, *Copts in Egyptian Politics,* p. 289.

[47] Antuni, *Wataniyat al-Kanisah,* p. 13 ; 'The Long revolution' in *Al-Ahram Weekly,* 18–24 July 2002.

[48] Samira Bahr, *Al-Aqbat fi al-hayah al-Siyasiyah al-Misriyah,* (Cairo: Maktabat al-Anjlu al-Misriyah, 1979).

[49] Bahr, *Al-Aqbat fi al-hayah,* p. 143.

[50] Yusuf, *Al-Aqbat wa-al-Qawmiyah,* pp. 142–44.

[51] Rafiq Habib, *Al-Masihiyah al-siyasiyah fi Misr: madkhal ila al-tayyarat al-siyasiyah lada al-Aqbat,* Cairo: Yafa lil-Dirasat wa-al-Nashr, 1990.

[52] Published posthumously, Hassan Al-Banna, *Al-Wasayah al-'ashirah*, (Cairo:Dar al-Sharuq, Second Edition, 1979).

[53] For example, the second command in al-Banna's covenant addresses the attachment of Muslims to the Quran, its text and its spirituality. *Al-Wasayah al-'ashira*, p. 44; Reprint of JUQ manifesto, 11th September 1953 in Antuni, *Wataniyat al-Kanisah*, Vol. II. pp. 12–13.

[54] *Misr*, 10th May 1946.

[55] See Chapter 4 for details of *Misr al-Fatat;* Open Letter published by *Jama'at al-Ummah al-Qibtiyyah*, 1st September 1953.

[56] Open Letter published by *Jama'at al-Ummah al-Qibtiyyah*, 1st September 1953: Text reprinted in full in Antuni, *Wataniyat al-Kanisah*, Vol. II. pp. 242–250.

[57] Open Letter published by *Jama'at al-Ummah al-Qibtiyyah*, 1st September 1953.

[58] Open Letter published by *Jama'at al-Ummah al-Qibtiyyah*, 1st September 1953.

[59] Quoted in Bahr, *Al-Aqbat fi al-hayah*, p. 354; Yusuf, *Al-Aqbat wa-al-Qawmiyah*, p. 142; Open Letter published by *Jama'at al-Ummah al-Qibtiyyah*, 1st September 1953.

[60] Open Letter published by *Jama'at al-Ummah al-Qibtiyyah*, 1st September 1953.

[61] For copy of letter see Antuni, *Wataniyat al-Kanisah*, Vol. II. p. 14.

[62] Enid Hill, 'Al-Sanhuri and Islamic Law: The Place and Significance of Islamic Law in the Life and Work of 'Abd al-Razzaq Ahmad al-Sanhuri, Egyptian Jurist and Scholar, 1875–1971' in *Arab Law Quarterly*, Vol. 3, No. 1 (1988), pp. 22–64; Erlich, *Students and University*, pp. 103–4.

[63] Antuni, *Wataniyat al-Kanisah*, Vol. II. p. 13.

[64] Malak returned to Cairo on 31st December 1952; *Misr*, 3rd January 1953.

[65] Similarities can perhaps be drawn between the way in which Nahhas viewed Obeid's role in the Cabinet, and the role played by al-Malek during the RCC; Babawi, Nabil Luca., *Mashakil al-Aqbat fi Misr wa hululha* , (Cairo: Al-Ahram Publishing, 2001) p. 119; TNA: PRO, FO 371/80589, British Embassy Alexandria, 14th July 1950.

[66] *Misr*, 26th July 1954, 29th July 1954.

[67] *Misr*, 22nd September 1954.

[68] *Al-Ahram*, 27th July 1952.

[69] *Misr*, 12th August 1954.

[70] *Misr*, 31st July 1954.

[71] Interview with Luqa, *Al-Aqbat, al-Nashaah wa-al-Sira'a*, pp. 589–90.

[72] Interview with Luqa, *Al-Aqbat, al-Nashaah wa-al-Sira'a*, pp. 589–90.

[73] *Misr*, 31st July 1954.

[74] Yusab died in 1956 whilst Nasser died in September 1970.

75 *Al-Ahram,* 26th July 1954.

76 *Al-Manarah al-Misriyyah* was suspended along with political parties in 1953.

77 *Misr,* 31st July 1954.

78 *Misr,* 29th July 1954.

79 Naguib was removed from his position as President of Egypt on 14th November 1954, See *Al-Akhbar,* 15th November 1954.

80 Erlich, *Students and Universities,* p. 171.

81 Ghali Shukri, *Egypt: Portrait of a President,* (London: Zed Press, 1981) pp. 271–3.

82 *Misr,* 31st July 1954.

83 Luqa, *Al-Aqbat, al-Nashaah wa-al-Sira'a,* p. 590; See also TNA: PRO, FO 371/113775, Memorandum from the British Embassy Cairo, 7th November 1955.

84 Shukri, *Egypt: Portrait of a President,* p. 272.

85 *Misr,* 27th July 1954.

86 Statement released by *Majlis al-Milli* concerning abduction of Yusab, republished in *Misr.* 13th August 1954.

87 Statement released by *Majlis al-Milli* concerning abduction of Yusab, republished in *Misr.* 13th August 1954.

88 Report of Holy Synod Meeting, *Misr,* 1st October 1954.

89 Speech by Bishop Michael of Asyut; Report of Holy Synod Meeting, *Misr,* 1st October 1954.

90 *Misr,* 1st October 1954.

91 Personal request by Bishop Yu'annis of Giza with the backing of 16 bishops; Report of Holy Synod Meeting, *Misr,* 1st October 1954.

92 'The Coptic Association supports the Holy Synod', *Misr,* 1st October 1954.

93 *Misr,* 1st October 1954.

94 *Misr,* 31st July 1954.

95 *Misr,* 12th October 1954.

96 Papal letter sent to Public prosecutor, *Misr,* 30th September 1954.

97 *Misr,* 26th October 1954.

98 TNA: PRO, FO 371/113775, British Embassy Cairo to London, 7th November 1955.

99 TNA: PRO, FO 371/113775, British Embassy Cairo to London, 7th November 1955.

100 TNA: PRO, FO 371/113775, British Embassy Cairo to London, 7th November 1955.

101 Shoucri, 'Yusab II', in *Coptic Encyclopaedia,* pp. 2363–4; Erlich, *Students and Universities.*

## Epilogue

[1] TNA: PRO, FCO 51/32: Summary of the Presidential Decree of 2 November 1957 regulating the election of the Coptic Orthodox Patriarch.

[2] Ibrahim, *The Copts*, p.17.

[3] TNA: PRO, FCO 51/32: Memorandum: The Copts, 15 March 1967.

[4] Upon Kyrillos' death in 1971, Bishop Shenouda was elected Pope of the See of St Mark.

[5] Hasan, *Christians versus Muslims*, p.88.

[6] Hasan, *Christians versus Muslims*, p.87.

[7] Ibrahim, *The Copts*, p. 17.

[8] *Al-Ahram*, 21 April 1967.

[9] The *Majlis* remained closed until Pope Shenouda reconvened it in 1971.

[10] For more see Haggai Erlich, *The Cross and the River: Ethiopia, Egypt and the Nile*, (London: 2002).

[11] See *The Virgin of Zeitoun*, Worldview Magazine, Volume 16 No. 9 September 1973 http://worldview.cceia.org/archive/worldview/1973/09/2208.html

[12] Thomas Philipp, 'Copts and Other Minorities in the Development of the Egyptian Nation-State' in *Egypt: From Monarchy to Republic, A Reassessment of Revolution and Change*, Shamir, Shimon., (ed.) (Boulder: Westview Press, 1995). p. 139.

[13] For further details see, Babawi, *Mashakil*, pp.13–38.

## Notes on Church Structure

[1] Archbishop Basilios, 'Consecration of Patriarch' in *Coptic Encyclopaedia*, pp. 1909–1911.

[2] Edward Lane, *An Account of the Manners and Customs of Modern Egyptians*, (London : Charles Knight and Co., 1836) p. 538.

[3] Otto Meinardus, *Two Thousand Years of Coptic Christianity*, (Cairo: American University Press, 1999) p. 9.

[4] In the larger diocese, the bishop is also referred to as a Metropolitan or *Matran*, although for our purposes both *Usquf* and *Matran*, will be termed Bishop.

[5] Lane, *An Account of the Manners and Customs*, p. 539.

[6] Archbishop Basilios, 'Deacon' in *Coptic Encyclopaedia*, pp. 885–888.

# BIBLIOGRAPHY

## A. PRIMARY SOURCES

### Archival Material

**Lambeth Palace Archives, London**

Church of England Council for Foreign Relations relating to the Coptic Church:

Minutes of Ancient Oriental Churches Committee (1946-1960).

General Correspondence (1882-1949).

Correspondences in Papers of Archbishop Fisher (1936-1961).

**The National Archives: Public Record Office, Kew**

| | | |
|---|---|---|
| War Office | Series 157 | Intelligence Summaries, First World War, 1914-1923. |
| Foreign Office | Series 141 | Embassy and Consulates, Egypt: General Correspondence, 1815-1973. |
| | Series 371 | Political Departments: General Correspondence, 1906-1966. |
| | Series 372 | Treaty Department and Successors: General Correspondence from 1906. |
| | Series 369 | Consular Department: General Correspondence from 1906. |
| | Series 395 | News Department: General Correspondence from 1906. |
| Foreign and Commonwealth Office | Series 51 | Research Department: Registered Files (LR and RR Series), 1967-1976. |

## Newspapers and Magazines
*Dar al-Kutub wal-Watha'iq al-Qawmi* (Egyptian National Books and Archives), Cairo - *In Arabic*

*Al-Ahram* (Cairo), 1944-1946, 1952-1954.
*Al-Ahli* (Alexandria), 1911.
*Al-'Ailah al-Qibtiyyah* (Alexandria), 1909-1910.
*Al-Akhbar* (Cairo), 1953-1954.
*Akhir Sa'a* (Cairo), 1944.
*Al-'Alam,* (Cairo), 1911.
*Al-Aqaleem* (Asyut), 1937.
*Al-Fida* (Cairo), 1952-53.
*Al-Firu'an* (Alexandria), 1910-11, 1913.
*Al-Fata al-Qibti* (Cairo), 1905-1910.
*Al-Hilal* (Alexandria), 1892.
*Al-Iman* (Cairo), 1905-1908, 1941-1942.
*Al-Ittihad al-Misri* (Cairo), 1910.
*Al-Jamahir al-Misri* (Cairo), 1952.
*Kulliyyat al-Aqbat* (Cairo), 1918.
*Al-Liwa* (Cairo), 1900, 1910-1911.
*Madaris al-Ahad* (Cairo), 1947-1953.
*Al-Majallah al-Jadida* (Cairo), 1929-1938.
*Al-Majallah al-Qibtiyyah* (Cairo), 1907-1930.
*Al-Manar* (Cairo).
*Al-Manarah al-Misriyyah* (Cairo), 1935-1953.
*Al-Manarah al-Murqusiyyah* (Cairo), 1928-1935.
*Al-Mansurah* (Cairo), 1969.
*Misr* (Cairo), 1944-1954.
*Al-Misri* (Cairo), 1944; 1953-54.
*Al-Mu'ayyad* (Cairo), 1911.
*Al-Musawwar* (Cairo), 1954.
*Al-Muqattam* (Cairo), 1944.
*Al-Mustaqbal* (Cairo), 1914-1916.
*Al-Rabta al-Masihiyyah* (Cairo), 1909.
*Risalat al-Hayah* (Cairo), 1947; 1950-51.
*Risalat al-Mahaba* (Cairo), 1941.
*Ruz al-Yusuf* (Cairo), 1926, 1945.
*Al-Sibaq* (Cairo), 1924.
*Al-Sha'ab* (Cairo), 1910.
*Al-Shu'lah* (Cairo), 1938-40.
*Al-Tawfiq* (Cairo), 1898, 1903, 1907-1908.
*Al-Watan* (Cairo), 1908-1911.
*Al-Wafd* (Cairo), 1986.

*Al-Watani* (Cairo), 1964.
*Al-Wataniyyah*, (Cairo), 1911-1953.
*Al-Yaqazah* (Cairo), 1927-1928; 1943-1948.

**British Library, Colindale - *In English and French***
*Al-Ahram Weekly*, (Cairo), 2002-2008.
*La Bourse Egyptienne*, (Cairo), 1944-1956.
*The Daily Telegraph* (London), 1908.
*The Egyptian Gazette*, (Cairo), 1910; 1944; 1947-1948; 1954.
*The Egyptian Mail*, (Cairo), 1943-45; 1952.
*The Glastonbury Bulletin*, (Glastonbury), 1996.
*La Journal d'Egypte* (Cairo), 1945 ; 1947.
*El-Keraza Magazine* (Cairo), 2004-2008.
*New York Times*, (New York), 1945.
*Le Progrès Égyptien* (Cairo), 1944.
*Time Magazine*, (US), 1945.
*The Times* (London), 1911.
*Yes Magazine*, (Great Britain), 1999.

## Unpublished Materials
Abdel-Sayid, Ranya, *Church Politics: A Modernist Approach to the Role of the Coptic Orthodox Church of the See of Alexandria in Constructing Group Identity among Egyptian Copts*, Thesis (M.A.)–American University Cairo, 2003.

Abdel-Wahab, Youssef, *Egypt: A Historical Analysis of Public Personnel Policies in Relation to the Social System, 1883-1967*, Thesis (PhD.)–American University, 1972.

Al-Antuni, Father Bishoy., *Enhancing Leadership in the Christian Community: A Case Study of Shubra al-Khema, Egypt*, Thesis (PhD.)–Northwest Graduate School, Seattle, 2003.

Amin, Juzif Ramiz., *Dawr Al-Kanisah Al-Qibtiyah fi Ifriqya*, Thesis (M.A.)–Cairo University, 2000.

Carter, B. L., *Communalism in Egyptian Politics : The Experience of the Copts, 1918-1952*, Thesis (Ph.D.)–University of London, School of Oriental and African Studies, 1982.

Al-Feki, Mustafa, *Makram Ebeid, a Coptic Leader in the Egyptian National Movement : A Case Study in the Role of the Copts in Egyptian Politics, 1919-1952*, Thesis (Ph.D.)–University of London, School of Oriental and African Studies, 1977.

Khoury, Nabeel Abdo, *Islam and Modernization in the Middle East: Muhammad Abduh, an Ideology of Development*, Thesis (Ph.D.)–State University of New York at Albany, 1976.

234THECOPTSOFEGYPT

Kirollos, Miriam Aziz., *A Social and Semantic History of the Concept of Minority with Particular Reference to the Coptic Question,* Thesis (M.A.)–American University Cairo, 1997.

Merriam, Kathleen Howard., *The Role of Leadership in Nation-Building: Egypt, 1922,* Thesis (PhD.)–Indiana University, 1971.

El-Mountacer, Maghraoui., *The Dilemma of Liberalism in the Middle East: A Reading of the Liberal Experiment in Egypt, 1920s-30s,* Thesis (Ph.D.)–Princeton University, 1991.

Sedra, Paul., *Ecclesiastical Warfare: Patriarch, Presbyterian and Peasant in Nineteenth Century Egypt,* Working Paper: Yale Centre for International and Area Studies, 2005. www.128.36.236.77/workpaper/pdfs/MESV5-10.pdf

Scott, Rachel Marion, *Egyptian Islamist thought on the Copts and Christians,* Thesis (Ph.D.)–University of London, School of Oriental and African Studies, 2004.

Whidden, James., *The Egyptian Revolution: Politics and the Egyptian Nation 1919-1926,* Thesis (Ph.D.)– University of London, School of Oriental and African Studies, 1998.

Zaki, Leila Moukhtar., *The Coptic Orthodox Church: The Religious Revival,* Thesis (M.A.)–American University Cairo, 1986.

## Official Publications
### Colonial Rule, Egypt, 1882-1922
*Essai de statistique générale de l'Egypte: Annnes 1873-1877,* Cairo 1879.
*Statistique Scolaire d'Egypte 1912-1912* Cairo, 1913.
### United Arab Republic (UAR), 1958-1971
*Khutab Al-Ra'is Jamal 'Abd al-Nasir fi Ihtifalat Al-'id Al-Sabi' lil-Thawrah,* Cairo: Ministry of Information, 1959.
*Khutab wa-tasrihat al-Ra'is Jamal 'Abd al-Nasir, 1952-1959,* Cairo: Ministry of Information, 1959 Vol. I-VII.
*President Gamal Abdel-Nasser's Speeches and Press Interviews,* United Arab Republic Information Department, Cairo, 1958.
*Rasa'il Tarikhiyah min Mustafa Kamil,* Cairo: Dar al-Nahdat al-'Arabiyah, 1969 .
*Safahat Matwiyah min Tarikh al-Za'im Mustafa Kamil: Rasa'il Jadidah li-Mustafa Kamil min 8 Yuniyu 1895 ila 19 February 1896,* Cairo: Maktabat al-Anjlu al-Misriyah, 1962 .
### Arab Republic of Egypt
*Central Agency for Public Mobilisation and Statistics: The General Population and Housing Census, 1976,* Cairo: 1977.
*Majmu'ah Khutab wa ahadith Al-Ra'is Muhammad Anwar al-Sadat,* Cairo: Ministry of Information,197_ , Vol. I-V.

*Yawmiyat Al-Thawrah wa-waqa'i'uha: kashshaf lil-Suhuf lil Fatrah min 1952-1956,* Cairo: Matba'at Dar al-Kutub wa-al-Watha'iq al-Qawmiyah bi-al-Qahirah, 2002.

## Collections of Archival Documents

*British Documents on Foreign Affairs: Reports and Papers from the Foreign Office Confidential Print,* Woodward, P., (ed.)

-Part II: *From the First to the Second World War. Series G, Africa, 1914-1939* University Publications of America, 1994-c1997.

*British Documents on Foreign Affairs : Reports and Papers from the Foreign Office Confidential Print: Near and Middle East,* Bourne, K., Watt, D. C., Gillard, D., Partridge, M., Bidwell, R., Preston, P., Yapp, M., and Gökay, B., (ed.)

-Part I: *From the Mid-Nineteenth Century to the First World War. Series B The Near and Middle East, 1856-1914,* University Publications of America, 1984-1985.
-Part II: *From the First to the Second World War. Series B. Turkey, Iran, and the Middle East, 1918-1939,* University Publications of America, 1985-1997.
-Part III: *From 1940 through 1945. Series B. Near and Middle East,* University Publications of America, 1997.

*Confidential U.S. State Department Central Files: Egypt Internal Affairs and Foreign Affairs 1945-1949,* Davis, Michael., (ed.), University Publications of America, 1985.

## Collections of Missionary Documents

Church Missionary Society, *Register of Missionaries (Clerical, Lay & Female) and Native Clergy from 1804 to 1904. In Two Parts,* No publisher, 19–?

*Treaties, Acts and Regulations Relating to Missionary freedom,* International Missionary Council, London: International Missionary Council, 1923.

## Memoirs, Dairies, Chronicles and Pamphlets
### In Arabic
'Abdel-Nasser, Gamal., *Falsafat al-thawrah,* Cairo: Dar al-Maarif , 1959.
Bulus, Basili., (Qommus) *Dhikrayati fi nisf qarn,* No Publisher, 1991.
Haykal, Muhammad Husayn., *Mudhakkirat fi al-siyasah al-Misriyah,* Cairo: Dar al-Ma'arif, 1951-1978.

Al-Jabarti, 'Abd al-Rahman., *'Adja'ib Al-Athar: Fil-taradjim wal-akhbar*, Cairo: Dar al-Kutab, 1998, Vol. I-IV.

_____ *Mazhar al-taqdis bi-dhahab dawlat al-Faransis*, Cairo: Al-'Arabi lil-Nashr wa-al-Tawzi', 1998.

_____ *Tarikh Muddat al-Faransis bi Misr: Napoleon in Egypt : Al-Jabarti's chronicle of the French occupation, 1798*, New Jersey: Markus Wiener Publishers, 2004.

Al-Misri, Iris Habib., *Qissat al-Kanisah al-Qibtiyyah*, Cairo, 1982, Vol. I-VI.

Musa, Salama., *Tarbiyat Salama Musa*, Cairo: Al-kitab al-Misri publishers, 1947.

_____ *Mukhtarat Salama Musa*, Beirut: Maktabat al-Ma'arif, 1963.

Sadat, Anwar., *Al-Qa'idah al-Sha'biyah*, Cairo, 1959.

_____ *Qissat al-thawrah kamilah*, No date, No publisher.

Tahtawi, Rifa'ah Rafi', *Manahij Al-Albab Al-Misriyah*, Cairo: Bulaq Press, 1869.

_____ *Takhlis al-ibriz ila talkhis bariz*, Cairo: Bulaq Press, 1849.

'Urabi, Ahmad., *Mudhakkirat al-Za'im Ahmad 'Urabi : Kashf al-sitar 'an sirr al-asrar fi al-nahdah al-Misriyah al-mashhurah bi-l-Thawrah al-'Urabiyah*, Cairo: Matba'at Dar al-Kutub wa-al-Watha'iq al-Qawmiyah bi-al-Qahirah, 2005, Vol. I-III.

Zaghlul, Sa'd., *Mudhakkirat Sa'd Zaghlul*, Cairo: al-Hay'ah al-Misriyah al-'Ammah lil-Kitab, 1990-1998, Vol. I- IX.

*Muhadarat Ma'ali al-Ustath Makram Obeid Pasha fi-al-Jami'a al-Misriyyah*, Cairo: 1936.

## In English

Blunt, Wilfred., *Secret History of the English Occupation of Egypt : Being a Personal Narrative of Events*, London : T. Fisher Unwin, 1907.

Butcher, Edith Louisa., *The Story of the Church of Egypt: Being an Outline of the History of the Egyptians under their Successive Masters from the Roman Conquest until now*, 1897.

Cromer, Evelyn Baring, *Modern Egypt*, London: Macmillan, 1908.

Farid, Muhammad., *The Memoirs and Diaries of Muhammad Farid, an Egyptian Nationalist Leader (1868-1919)*, San Francisco: Mellen University Research Press, 1992.

Fowler, Montague., *Christian Egypt: Past, Present and Future*, London: Church Newspaper Company, 1901.

Gollock, G. A., *A Winter's Mail from Ceylon, India and Egypt: Being Journal Letters Written Home*, London: Church Missionary Society, 1895.

Gollock, M. C., *River, Sand and Sun: Being Sketches of the C.M.S. Egypt Mission*, London: Church Missionary House, 1906.

Lane, Edward., *An Account of the Manners and Customs of the Modern Egyptians*, London: Charles Knight and Co., 1836.

Leeder, S. H., *Modern Sons of Pharoahs: A Study in the Manners and Customs of the Copts in Egypt*, London, 1918.

George, David Lloyd., *War Memoirs of David Lloyd George*. London: Odhams Press, 1938. Vol. I-II.

Milner, Alfred (Viscount)., *England in Egypt*, London: Edward Arnold, 1892.

Naguib, Muhammad., *Egypt's Destiny: A Personal Statement*, Westport: Greenwood Press, 1984.

Al-Sadat, Anwar., *Revolt on the Nile*, London: Allen Wingate, 1957.

____*Those Who I have known*, London: Cape, 1985.

Stotts, Ronald., *The Memoirs of Sir Ronald Storrs*, New York: G.P. Putnam's Sons, 1937.

Watson, Charles., *In the Valley of the Nile: A Survey of the Missionary Movement in Egypt*, New York: Fleming Revell Company, 1908.

Sir Ronald Wingate, *Wingate of the Sudan: The Life and Times of General Sir Reginald Wingate, Maker of the Anglo-Egyptian Sudan*, London: J. Murray, 1955.

No Author, *The Coptic Congress, held in Assiout on March 6, 7 and 8, 1911: The Speeches*, Pamphlet, 1911 .

## B. SECONDARY SOURCES

### Reference Works

*The Coptic Encyclopedia*, Atiya, Aziz Suryal, (ed.), New York: Macmillan, 1991, Vol. I-VIII

*Encyclopedia of Islam*, Bearman, Bianquis, Bosworth, van Donzel and Heinrichs (ed.), Brill Online, 2007

*Dictionary of Church Terms*, http://www.copticchurch.net/topics/thecopticchurch/dictionr.pdf

*Qammus al-tarajim al-Qibtiyyah*, Alexandria: St Mina Educational Services, 1995

### Books and Articles

**In Arabic**

'Abd Allah, Ismail Sabri., *Al-Harakat al-Islamiyah al-mu'asirah fi al-watan al-'arabi*, Cairo: Markaz Dirasat al-Wahdah al-'Arabiyah, 1987.

'Abd al-Sami, 'Amr., *Al-Aqbat wa-al-raqm al-sa'b: Hiwarat Hawla al-Mustaqbal* Cairo: al-Dar al-Misriyah al-Lubnaniyah, 2001.

'Abd al-Sayyid., *Hafl al-dhikra al-mi'awiyya al-'ula li-abi al-islah*, Cairo, 1960.

'Abd al-Sayyid, Ibrahim., *Amwal al-Kanisah al-Qibtiyah: man Yadfa'u!? wa-man yaqbidu!?* Giza: Dar Diwan, 1997.

'Abd al-Zahir, Mahmoud Said., *Yahud Misr: Dirasah fi al-Mawqif al-Siyasi, 1897–1949,* Giza: Markaz al-Dirasat al-Sharqiyah, 2000.

Abu 'Arjah, Taysir., *Al-Muqattam: Jaridat al-Ihtilal al-Baritani fi al-Misr,* Cairo: Al-Hay'ah al-Misriyah al-'Ammah lil-Kitab, 1997.

'Afifi, Muhammad., *Al-Aqbat fi Misr fi al-'asr al-'Uthmani,* Cairo: Al-Hayah al-Misriyyah, 1992.

____*Al-Din wa-l Siyassah fi Misr al-Mu'asar: Qommus Sergius,* Cairo: Dar al-Shuruq, 2001.

Al-Antuni, Antuniyus., *Wataniyat al-Kanisah al-Qibtiyah wa-tarikhuha,* Cairo: Dar al-Tiba'ah al-Qawmiyah, 1995.

'Aryan, Ayman., *Rajul al-Islah wa al-salah: Min wa'qa Muthaqirat al-Baba Macarius al-Thani,* Cairo: Al-Horriya Publishers, 2006.

'Awad, Girgis Filuthawus., *Tarikh al-Ighumanus Filitha'us,* Cairo, 1905.

'Awad, Luwis., *Al-Huriyya wa Naqd al-Huriyyah,* Cairo, 1971.

Babawi, Nabil Luca., *Mashakil Al-aqbat fi Misr wa Hululha,* Cairo: Al-Ahram Publishing, 2001.

Badawi, Jamal and al-Muti'i, Lami., *Tarikh al-Wafd,* Cairo: Dar al-Shuruq, 2003.

Bahr, Samira, *al-Aqbat fi al-hayah al-siyasiyah al-Misriyah,* Cairo: Maktabat al-Anjlu Misriyah, 1979.

Al-Banna, Hasan., *Fiqh al-waqi': Maqalat tunshiru li-awwal marrah,* Cairo: Dar al-Kalimah, 1999.

____*Nahw al-Nur,* Cairo: Jam'iyyat al-Ikhwan al-Muslimin, 1936.

____*Al-Wasayah al-'ashira,* Cairo: Dar al-Shuruq, Second Edition, 1979.

Basili, B., *Hal rahab al-Aqbat bi-fath al-'Arab?* No Publisher, no date.

Bayyumi, Zakariya Sulayman., *Al-Ikhwan al-Muslimun wa-al-Jama'at al-Islamiyyah fi al-hayat al-siyasiyah al-Misriyah, 1928–1948,* Cairo: Maktabat Wahbah, 1979.

Al-Bishri, Tariq., *Al-Muslimun wa-al-Aqbat fi itar al-Jama'ah al-Wataniyah,* Beirut: Dar al-Wahdah, 1982.

____*Bayna al-Jami'ah al-Diniyah wa-al-jami'ah al-wataniyah fi al-fikr al-siyasi,* Cairo: Dar al-Shuruq, 1998.

Fawzi, Mahmud., *Al-Baba Shenouda wa-tarikh al-Kanisah al-Qibtiyah,* Cairo: Dar al-Nashr Hatyih, 1991.

____*Al-Baba Shenouda wa-al-Mu'aradah fi al-Kanisah,* Cairo: Dar al-Nashr Hatiyah, 1992.

____*Al-Baba Kyrilloss wa-al-Baba Shenouda,* Cairo: Dar al-Nashr Hatiyah, 1996.

Ghali, Mirrit Boutros., *Al-Aqbat fi Misr,* Cairo, 1979.

Habib, Rafiq., *Al-Masihiyah al-siyasiyah fi Misr: Madkhal ila al-Tayyarat al-siyasiyah lada al-Aqbat*, Cairo: Yafa lil-dirasast wa-al-nashr, 1990 .

_____ *Al-Ummah wa-al-dawlah: Bayan tahrir al-ummah*, Cairo: Dar al-Shuruq, 2001.

Al-Hakim, Tawfiq., *'Awdat al-ruh*, Cairo, 1933.

Hamza, 'Abd al-Latif., *Adab al-Maqalah al-Suhufiyah fi Misr*, Cairo: Dar al-Fikr al-'Arabi, 1950.

Hamrush, Ahmad., *Qissat al-Sihafah fi Misr*, Cairo: Dar al-Mustaqbal al-'Arabi, 1989.

Hanna, Milad, *Na'am...Aqbat, Lakin...Misriyun*, Cairo: Maktabat Madbuli, 1980.

Harb, Muhammad Tal'at., *'Ilaj Misr al-iqtisadi wa-mashru' Bank al-Misriyin wa Bank al-Ummah*, Cairo: Dar al-Kutub wa-al-Watha'iq al-Qawmiyah, 2002.

Al-Harmasi, 'Abd al-Baqi., *al-Din fi al-Mujtama' al-'arabi*, Beirut: Markaz Dirasat al-Wahdah al-'Arabiyah, 1990.

Heikal, Muhammad Hassanein., *Bayna al-sihafah wa-al-siyasah*, Cairo: 1984

Haykal, Muhammad Husayn., *Hayat Muhammad*, Cairo: Misr Publications, 1933.

Husayn, Taha., *Mustaqbal al-thaqafa fi-Misr*, Cairo: Matba'at al-Ma'arif, 1938.

Iskarus, Tawfiq., *Nawabigh al-Aqbat wa-mashahiruhum fi al-qarn al-tasi' 'ashar*, Egypt: Matba'at al-Tawfiq, 1910-1913.

Labib, Hani., *Azmat al-Himayah al-Diniyah: Al-Din wa-al-dawlah fi Misr*, Cairo: Dar al-Shuruq, 2000.

_____*Al-Muwatanah wa-al-'awlamah: Al-Aqbat fi mujtama' Mutaghayir*, Cairo: Dar al-Shuruq, 2004.

Luqa, Malak., *Al-Aqbat, al-Nashaah wa-al-sira'a: Min al-qarn al-awwal ila al-qarn al-'ishrin*, Cairo: Maktabat Anjilus, 2001.

Mattewos, Anba., *Tarikh Babawat al-qursi al-Askandiriyyah*, Cairo: Harmony, Second Edition, 2002 .

Al-Misri, Iris Habib., *Qissat al-Kanisah al-Qibtiyah*, Cairo : Al-Mahaba, 1981, Vol. I-VI.

Murqus, Samir., *Al-Himayah wa-al-'iqab: al-Gharb wa-al-mas'alah al-diniyah fi al-Sharq al-Awsat*, Cairo: Mirit lil-Nashr wa-al-Ma'lumat, 2000.

Musa, Salama., *Misr asl al-haddara*, Cairo: Al-'Asriyyah Publishers, 1935.

_____ *Al-Balagha al-asriyyah wa-l-lugha al-'arabiyyah*, Cairo: Al-'Asriyyah Publishers, 1945.

Al-Muti'i, Lami., *Mawsu'at hadha al-rajul min Misr*, Cairo: Dar al-Shuruq, 1997.

Al-Rafi'i, 'Abd al-Rahman., *'Asr Isma'il*, Cairo 1932, Vol. I-II.

_____ *Fi a'qab al-Thawrah al-Misriyah*, Cairo, 1950, Vol. I-III.

_____ *Mustafa Kamil ba'ith al-harakah al-wataniyah,* Cairo: Matba'at al-Sharq, 1939.

_____ *Al-Thawrah al-'urabiyah wa-al-ihtilal al-injilizi,* Cairo, 1937.

_____ *Thawrat sanat 1919: Tarikh Misr al-qawmi min sanat 1914 ila sanat 1921* Cairo: Maktabat al-Nahdah, 1946.

Negm, Ahmad Fouad., *Bayan hamm: shi'r,* Beirut: Dar al-Farabi, 1976.

Ben-Nefissa, Sarah., *Al-Intikhabat wa-zaba'iniyah al-siyasiyah fi Misr: tajdid al-wusta wa-'awdat al-nakhib,* Cairo: Markaz al-Qahirah li-dirasat huquq al-Insan, 2005.

Al-Qaradawi, Yusuf., *Al-Ikhwan al-muslimun : 70 'aman fi al-da'wah wa-al-tarbiyah wa-al-jihad,* Cairo: Maktabat Wahbah, 1999.

Ramadan, 'Abd al-'Azm., *al-Dawr al-watani lil-kanisah al-Misriyah 'abra al-'usur : a'mal Nadwat Lajnat al-Tarikh wa-al-Athar bi-al-Majlis al-A'la lil-Thaqafah* Cairo: al-Hay'ah al-Misriyah al-'Ammah lil-Kitab, 2002.

Rizq, Yunan Labib., *Al-Ahzab al-Misriyah 1922-1953* Cairo: al-Ahram, Markaz al-Dirasat al-Siyasiyah wa-al-Istratijiyah, 1995.

Rufila, Yacoub Nakhla., *Tarikh al-ummah al-Qibtiyyah,* Cairo, 1898.

Salama, Girguis., *Athar al-Ihtalal al-Britani fi al-Ta'lim al-Qawmi fi Misr 1882-1922* Cairo, 1966.

Salim, Latifah Muhammad., *Al-Sihafah wa-al-harakah al-Wataniyah al-Misriyah 1945-1952: Min Milaffat al-kharijiyah al-Baritaniyah.* Cairo: Al-Hay'ah al-Misriyah al-'Amah lil-kitab, 1987.

Sami, Riyad., *Shahid 'ala 'asr al-ra'is Muhammad Najib,* Cairo: al-Maktab al-Misri al-Hadith, 2002.

Severus ibn-al-Muqaffa', Anba, *Tarikh Misr: min Bidayat al-qarn al-awwal al-Miladi .hatta nihayat al-qarn al-'ishrin: min khilal makhtutat Tarikh al-batarikah,* Cairo: Maktabat al-Madbuli, 2006.

Shalabi, Ahmad Hilmi., *Al-Aqbat wa-al-islah al-ijtimai fi Misr : Dawr Jam'iyyat al-Tawfiq, 1891-1952,* Cairo: Maktabat al-Anjlu al-Misriyah, 1992?

_____*Fusul min tarikh harakat al-islah al-ijtimai fi Misr,* Cairo: al-Hay'ah al-Misriyah al-'Ammah lil-Kitab, 1988.

Sharqawi, Mahmud., *Salama Musa al-mufakkir wa-al-insan.* Beirut: Dar al-'Ilm lil-Malayin, 1965.

Shukri, Ghali., *Salama Musa wa-azmat al-damir al-'Arabi.* Beirut: Manshurat al-Maktabah al-'Asriyah, 1965.

_____*Al-Aqbat fi watan mutaghayyir* Cairo: Dar Sharqiyat, 1996.

Souror, Maqari Armanious., & Kyrillos, Magdi Garnet., *Tarikh Hafl al-Baba Yusab al-Thani,* Cairo: Dar Alfa, 2006.

Stadiem, William., *Mamlaka fi-sabeel Imra'a,* Cairo: Dar al-Huda, 1993.

Sulayman, Nasim., *Tarikh al-Tarbiyah al-Qibtiyah,* Cairo: Dar al-Karnak, 1963.

Tadrous, Ramzi., *Al-Aqbat fi al-qarn al-'ishrin ,* Cairo, 1911.

Tajer, Jacques., *Aqbat wa Muslimun munthu al-fath al-Arabi ila 'Aam 1922*, Cairo, 1951.

Al-Tukhi, Rushdi Amin., *Misr wa-al-Aqbat fi Mi'at 'am: Dirasah tarikhiyah muwaththaqah li-munasabat yubiliha al-mi'awi 1891-1991*, Cairo: Dar al-'Alam al-'Arabi lil-Tiba'ah, 1991-5.

Yasin, al-Sayyid., *Al-Muwatanah fi zaman al-'awlamah*, Cairo: Al-Markaz al-Qibti lil-dirasat al-ijtima'iyah, 2002.

Yusuf, Abu Sayf., *Al-Aqbat wa-al-qawmiyah al-'arabiyah: Dirasah istitla'iyah*, Beirut: Markaz Dirasat al-Wahdah al-'Arabiyah, 1987.

Zakariya, Fuad., *'Abd al-Nasir wa-al-yasar al-Misri*, Cairo: Ruz al-Yusuf, 1977.

## In Western Languages

Abdel-Malek, Anouar., *Egypt, Military Society: The Army Regime, the Left, and Social change under Nasser*, New York: Randon House, 1968.

Abdel-Nasser, Huda Gamal., *Britain and the Egyptian Nationalist Movement 1936-1952*, Reading: Ithaca Press, 1994.

Abrahamian, E., 'Oriental Despotism: the Case of Qajar Iran', in *International Journal of Middle East Studies*, Vol. 5, 1974.

Abouseif, Doris., 'The Political situation of the Copts, 1799-1923', in Braude, and Lewis,. (ed.) *Christians and Jews in the Ottoman Empire: The Functioning of a Plural Society, Volume II: The Arab Speaking Lands*, Holmes and Meier, 1987.

Ahmed, Jamal Mohammad., *The Intellectual Origins of Egyptian Nationalism*, Oxford: Oxford University Press, 1960.

Ambrosius, Lloyd E., *Wilsonian Statecraft: Theory and Practice of Liberal Internationalism during World War I*, Wilmington: SR Books, 1991.

Anderson, M. S., (ed.) *The Great Powers and the Near East, 1774-1923*, London: Edward Arnold, 1970.

Anderson, Rufus., *History of the Missions of the American Board of Commissioners for Foreign Missions to the Oriental Churches*, Boston: Congressional Publishing Society, 1972.

Antonious, George., *The Arab Awakening*, London: Hamish Hamilton, 1938.

Arberry, A. J., (ed.) *Religion in the Middle East*, Cambridge: Cambridge . University Press, 1969

Atiya, Aziz Suryal., *A History of Eastern Christianity*, New York: Kraus Reprint, 1980.

Ayalon, Ami., Ayalon, Ami., 'From Fitna to Thawra', in *Studia Islamica*, No. 66, 1987.

_____*The Press in the Arab Middle East: A History*, New York: Oxford University Press, 1995.

Badrawi, Malak., *Isma'il Sidqi (1875-1950): Pragmatism and Vision in Twentieth century Egypt*, Richmond: Curzon Press, 1996.

\_\_\_\_*Political Violence in Egypt, 1910-1925: Secret Societies, Plots and Assassinations*, Richmond, Surrey: Curzon, 2000.

\_\_\_\_'Financial Cerberus? The Egyptian Parliament 1924-1952', in Goldschmidt, A., Johnson, A., & Salmoni, B., (ed.), *Re-envisioning Egypt 1919-1952*, Cairo: American University Press, c.2005.

Baer, G., *A History of Landownership in Modern Egypt, 1800-1950*, London: Oxford University Press, 1962.

\_\_\_\_*Studies in the Social History of Modern Egypt*, Chicago: University of Chicago Press, 1969.

Ballard, Brigadier General Colin Robert., *Kitchener*, London: Faber and Faber, 1930.

Baron, Beth., 'Islam Philanthropy and Political Culture in inter-war Egypt: The Activism of Labiba Ahmad', in *Poverty and Charity in Middle Eastern Contexts*, Bonner, et al., (ed.) Albany: State University of New York Press, 2003.

\_\_\_\_*Egypt as a Woman: Nationalism, Gender and Politics*, University of California Press, 2005.

Bayly, C. A., 'Representing Copts and Muhammadans: Empire, Nation and Community in Egypt and India, 1880-1914', in Fawaz, Leila., & Bayly, C. A., (ed.) *Modernity and Culture: From the Mediterranean to the Indian Ocean*, Columbia University Press, 2002.

Be'eri, Eliezer., *Army Officers in Arab Politics and Society*, Prager, 1970.

Beinin, Joel., *The Dispersion of Egyptian Jewry: Culture, Politics and the Formation of a Modern Diaspora*, Berkeley: University of California Press, 1998.

Beinin, Joel., and Lockman, Zachary., *Workers on the Nile: Nationalism, Communism, Islam and the Egyptian Working Class, 1882-1954*, London: Tauris, 1988.

\_\_\_\_ Beinin, and Lockman., '1919: Labour Upsurge and National Revolution', in *The Modern Middle East: A Reader*, Hourani, Khoury and Wilson., (ed.) London: I. B. Tauris, 1993.

Bentley, M., *Modern Historiography*, London: Routledge, 1999.

Berger, M., *Bureaucracy and Society in Modern Egypt: A Study of Higher Civil Service*, Princeton: Princeton University Press, 1957.

Beshai, Adel A., 'The Place and the Present Role of the Copts in the Egyptian Economy: Traditions and Specializations', in Pacini, Andrea., (ed.) *Christian Communities in the Arab Middle East*, Oxford: Oxford University Press, 1998.

Bhambra, Gurminder., *Rethinking Modernity*, New York: Palgrave, 2007.

Black, Jeremy., and MacRaild, Donald D., *Studying History*, New York: Palgrave, 2000.

Bonner, M., Ener, M., and Singer, A., (ed.) *Poverty and Charity in Middle Eastern Contexts,* Albany: State University of New York Press, 2003.

Botman, Selma., *Egypt from Independence to Revolution, 1919-1952,* Syracuse: Syracuse University Press, 1991.

Braude, Benjamin., 'Foundation Myths of the *Millat* System', in Braude, and Lewis,. (ed.) *Christians and Jews in the Ottoman Empire: The functioning of a plural society, Volume I: The Central lands,* Holmes and Meier, 1987.

Brinton, Jasper, Y., 'The Mixed Courts of Egypt', in *The American Journal of International Law,* Vol. 20, No. 4, 1926.

Butler, Alfred., *The Arab Conquest of Egypt and the last Thirty years of Roman Domination,* Oxford: Oxford University Press, 1978 , http://www.copticchurch.net/topics/thecopticchurch/arab_conquest_of _egypt.pdf

Carter, Barbara., *The Copts in Egyptian Politics,* London: Croom Helm, 1986.

Chitham, E.J., *The Coptic Community in Egypt: Spatial and Social Change,* Durham: University of Durham, Centre for Middle Eastern and Islamic Studies, c1986.

Choueiri, Youssef M., *Modern Arab Historiography: Historical Discourse and the Nation-state* London : RoutledgeCurzon, 2003.

Clark, Janine A., *Islam, Charity, and Activism: Middle-class Networks and Social Welfare in Egypt, Jordan, and Yemen,* Bloomington: Indiana University Press, 2004.

Cleveland, W.L., *A History of the Modern Middle East,* Oxford: Westview Press, 2000.

Cohen, Mark 'The Foreign Jewish Poor in Egypt', in *Poverty and Charity in Middle Eastern Contexts,* Bonner, et al., (ed.) Albany: State University of New York Press, 2003.

Cole, Juan R. I., *Colonialism and Revolution in the Middle East: Social and Cultural origins of Egypt's 'Urabi movement,* Cairo: American University in Cairo Press, 1999.

Cooper, Frederick., *Colonialism in Question: Theory, Knowledge, History,* Berkeley: University of California Press, 2005.

Crabbs, Jack., *The Writing of History in Nineteenth Century Egypt: A study in National Transformation,* Cairo: American University Press, 1984.

Cragg, Kenneth., 'Being Made Disciples: The Middle East', in Ward, K. & Stanley, B., *The Church Mission Society and World Christianity 1799-1999,* UK: Curzon Press, 2000.

Cuno, Kenneth., *The Pasha's Peasants: Land, Society, and Economy in Lower Egypt, 1740-1858,* Cambridge: Cambridge University Press, 1992.

Daly, M. W., *The Sirdar: Sir Reginald Wingate and the British Empire in the Middle East,* Philadelphia: American Philosophical Society, 1997.

_____(ed.) *The Cambridge History of Egypt*, Cambridge: Cambridge University Press, 1998, Vol. I-II.

Davison, R. H., 'The Millets as Agents of Change in the Nineteenth-Century Ottoman Empire', in Braude, and Lewis., (ed.) *Christians and Jews in the Ottoman Empire: The Functioning of a Plural Society, Volume I: The Central Lands,* Holmes and Meier 1987.

_____'Turkish Attitudes concerning Christian-Muslim Equality in the Nineteenth Century', in Hourani, Khoury and Wilson, (ed.) *The Modern Middle East: A Reader,* London: I. B. Tauris, 2004.

Deeb, Marius., *Party Politics in Egypt: The Wafd and its Rivals, 1919-1952,* London: Ithaca Press, 1979.

Egger, Vernon., *A Fabian in Egypt: Salama Musa and the Rise of the Professional Classes in Egypt, 1909-1939,* London: University Press of America, 1986.

Eibner, John., *Christians in Egypt: Church under Seige,* Washington: Institute for Religious Minorities in the Islamic World, 1993.

Ener, Mine., *Managing Egypt's Poor and the Politics of Benevolence 1800-1952,* New Jersey: Princeton University Press, 2003.

_____'The Charity of the Khedive' in *Poverty and Charity in Middle Eastern Contexts,* Bonner, et al., (ed.) Albany: State University of New York Press, 2003.

Erlich, Haggai., *Students and University in 20th Century Egyptian Politics,* London: Cass, 1989.

Erlich, H., and Gershoni, I., (ed.) *The Nile: Histories, Cultures, Myths,* London: L. Rienner, 2002.

Fahmy, Khaled., *All the Pasha's Men: Mehmed Ali, His Army and the Making of Modern Egypt,* Cambridge: Cambridge University Press, 1997.

Fargues, Philippe., 'The Arab Christians of the Middle East: A Demographic Perspective', in Pacini, Andrea., (ed.) *Christian Communities in the Arab Middle East,* Oxford: Oxford University Press, 1998.

Al-Feki, Mustafa., *Copts in Egyptian Politics,* Egypt: General Egyptian Book Organization, 1991.

_____*Les Coptes en Politique Egyptienne : Le Rôle de Makram Ebeid dans le Mouvement National,* Paris: Harmattan, 2007.

Findley, C. V., *Bureaucratic Reform in the Ottoman Empire,* Princeton: Princeton University Press, 1980.

Gabra, Gawdat., *Cairo, the Coptic Museum & Old Churches,* Cairo: Egyptian International Publishing, 1993.

Garle, H. E., 'Judicial Reform and the Egyptian Settlement', in *International affairs (Royal Institute of International Affairs 1931-1939),* Vol. 11, No. 2, 1932.

Galbraith, John & al-Sayyid-Marsot, Afaf Lutfi., 'The British Occupation of Egypt: Another View', in *International Journal of Middle Eastern Studies*, Vol. 9, No. 4, 1978.

Al-Gawhary, Karim., 'Copts in the 'Egyptian Fabric', in *Middle East Report*, No. 200, 1996.

Gershoni, Israel., *The Emergence of Pan-Arabism in Egypt*, Tel-Aviv: Shiloah Centre for Middle Eastern and African Studies, 1981.

Gershoni, Israel & Jankowski, James., *Egypt, Islam, and the Arabs: The Search for Egyptian Nationhood, 1900-1930*, Oxford: Oxford University Press in Co-operation with the Dayan Centre and the Shiloah Institute for Middle Eastern and African Studies, Tel Aviv University, 1986.

____'The Reader-'Another Production': The reception of Haykal's Biography of Muhammad and the shift of Egyptian intellectuals to Islamic subjects in the 1930s', in *Poetics Today*, Vol. 15, No.2, 1994.

____*Redefining the Egyptian Nation, 1930-1945*, Cambridge: Cambridge University Press, 1995.

____*Rethinking Nationalism in the Arab Middle East*, New York: Columbia University Press, 1997.

Gesnick, Indira, Falk., 'Nationalist imagery in Egypt's Tabloid Presses: A Drawing from the Egyptian Papagallo', in Fortna, B., et. al (ed.) *The Modern Middle East: A Source Book for History*, Oxford: Oxford University Press, 1997.

El-Ghobashy, Mona., 'Unsettling the Authorities: Constitutional Reform in Egypt', in *Middle East Report*, No.226, Spring, 2003.

Goddard, Hugh., *Muslim Perceptions of Christianity*, London: Grey Seal, 1996.

Goldschmidt, A., Johnson, A., & Salmoni, B., (ed.), *Re-envisioning Egypt 1919-1952*, Cairo: American University Press, c.2005.

Goldsmith, A. Jr., *Modern Egypt: The Formation of a Nation-state*, London: Hutchinson, 1988.

Gorman, Anthony., *Historians, State and Politics in Twentieth Century Egypt :Contesting the Nation*, London: RoutledgeCurzon, 2003.

Haim, S., (ed.) *Arab Nationalism: An Anthology*, Berkeley: University of California Press, 1976.

Al-Hakim, Tawfiq., *The Return of the Spirit*, Hutchinson, William., (Trans.), London: Three Continents Press, London, 1990.

Hanna, Milad., *The Seven Pillars of Egyptian Identity*, Cairo: General Egyptian Book Organisation, 1994.

Harlow, Barbara., 'Cairo Curiosities: E. W. Lane's Account and Ahmad Amin's Dictionary', in *Journal of the History of Ideas*, Vol. 46, No. 3, 1985.

Hartmann, Martin., *The Arabic Press of Egypt*, London: Luzac, 1899.

Hassan, Sana., *Christians versus Muslims in Modern Egypt: The Century-Long Struggle for Coptic Equality*, Oxford: Oxford University Press, 2003.

Heikal, Muhammad Hassanein., *Les Documents du Caire*, Paris: Flammarion, 1972.

_____ *Autumn of Fury: The Assassination of Sadat*, London: Deutsch, 1983.

Hewitt, Gordon., *The Problems of Success: A History of the CMS 1910-1942, Vol I: In Tropical Africa, the Middle East, at home*, London: SCM Press, 1971.

Heyworth-Dunn., J., *An Introduction to the History of Education in Modern Egypt*, London, 1938.

_____*Religious and Political Trends in Modern Egypt*, Washington: The author, 1950.

Hill, Enid., 'Al-Sanhuri and Islamic Law: The Place and Significance of Islamic Law in the Life and Work of 'Abd al-Razzaq Ahmad al-Sanhuri, Egyptian Jurist and Scholar, 1875-1971' in *Arab Law Quarterly*, Vol. 3, No. 1, 1988.

Hoexter, Miriam., *Endowments, Rulers, and Community: Waqf al-Haramayn in Ottoman Algiers*, Leiden: Brill, 1998.

_____'Charity, the Poor and Distribution of Alms in Ottoman Algiers', in *Poverty and Charity in Middle Eastern Contexts*, Bonner, et al., (ed.) Albany: State University of New York Press, 2003.

Holt, P. M., *Egypt and the Fertile Crescent 1516-1922: A Political History*, London: Longmans, 1966.

Hopkins, A. G., 'The Victorians and Africa: A reconsideration of the occupation of Egypt 1882', in *The Journal of African History*, Vol. 27, 1986.

Hourani, Albert., *Minorities in the Arab World*, Oxford: Oxford University Press, 1947.

_____ *Arabic Thought in the Liberal Age 1798-1939*, Cambridge: Cambridge University Press, 1983.

Hourani, A., Khoury, P., and Wilson, M., (ed.) *The Modern Middle East: A Reader*, London: I. B. Tauris, 1993.

Horowitz, Donald., *Ethnic Groups in Conflict*, Berkeley: University of California Press, 1985.

Hugh, Matthews., *Allenby and British Strategy in the Middle East 1917-1919*, London: Frank Cass, 1999.

Hunter, Robert., *Egypt under the Khedives 1805-1879: From Household Government to Modern Bureaucracy*, Pittsburgh: University of Pittsburgh Press, 1984.

Husri, Khaldoun., S. *Three Reformers: A Study in Modern Arab Political Thought*, Beirut, 1966.

_____*Origins of Modern Arab Political Thought*, New York: Caravan Books, 1980.

Hyde, Georgie D. M., *Education in Modern Egypt: Ideals and Realities*, London: Routledge and Kegan Paul, 1978.

Ibrahim, Saad Eddin., *The Copts of Egypt*, London: Minority Rights Group, 1996.

Ismael, Tareq Y., & El-Sa'id, Rifa'at., *The Communist Movement in Egypt, 1920-1988*, New York: Syracuse University Press, 1990.

Issawi, Charles., *Egypt: An Economic and Social Analysis*, London: Oxford University Press, 1947.

_____ 'The transformation of the economic positions of the Millets in the Nineteenth century', in Braude, and Lewis., (ed.) *Christians and Jews in the Ottoman Empire: The Functioning of a Plural Society, Volume I: The Central lands*, Holmes and Meier, 1987.

Jankowski, James., *Egypt's Young Rebels: 'Young Egypt', 1933-1952*, Stanford: Hoover Institution Press, 1975.

Karas, Shawky., *Copts Strangers in their Own Land*, Jersey City: American, Canadian and Australian C. Coptic Associations, 1986.

Karpat, Kepal., 'Millets and Nationality: The roots of the incongruity of Nation and State in the Post-Ottoman Era', in Braude, and Lewis., (ed.) *Christians and Jews in the Ottoman Empire: The functioning of a plural society, Volume I: The Central lands*, Holmes and Meier, 1987.

_____ 'The Ottoman and Ethnic Confessional Legacy in the Middle East', in Esman and Rabinovich,. (ed.) *Ethnicity, Pluralism and the state in the Middle East*, London: Cornell University, 1988.

Keddie, Nikki., *Sayyid Jamal al-Din al-Afghani: A Political Biography*, Berkeley: University of California Press, 1972.

_____ *The Chatham House Version and Other Middle-Eastern Studies*, Hanover: University Press of New England, 1984.

Kedourie, Elie., 'Ethnicity, Majority, and Minority in the Middle East', in Esman and Rabinovich,. (ed.) *Ethnicity, Pluralism and the state in the Middle East*, London: Cornell University, 1988.

Kerboeuf, Anne-Claire., 'The Cairo Fire of 26th January 1952 and the Interpretations of History', in Goldschmidt, A., Johnson, A., & Salmoni, B., (ed.) *Re-envisioning Egypt 1919-1952*, Cairo: American University Press, c.2005.

Khan, Nyla Ali., *The Fiction of Nationality in an Era of Transnationalism*, London: Routledge, 2005.

El-Khawaga, Dina., 'The Political dynamics of the Copts: Giving the Community an Active Role', in Pacini, Andrea., (ed.) *Christian Communities in the Arab Middle East*, Oxford: Oxford University Press, 1998.

Khoury, Philip S., *Urban Notables and Arab Nationalism*, Cambridge: Cambridge University Press, 1983.

Kramer, Gudrun., *The Jews in Modern Egypt, 1914-1952*, London: Tauris, 1989.

Labib, Pahor., *The Coptic Museum and the Fortress of Babylon at Old Cairo*, Cairo: General Organisation for Government Print Offices, Fifth edition, 1962.

Lapidus, Ira., *A History of Islamic Societies*, Cambridge: Cambridge University Press, Second Edition, 2002.

Landen, Robert., 'The Rise of Mass Doctrinal Parties: The Program of Hasan al-Banna and the Muslim Brotherhood, 1936', in Fortna, B., et. al (ed.) *The Modern Middle East: A Source Book for History*, Oxford: Oxford University Press, 2007.

Lane-Poole, Stanely., *A History of Egypt in the Middle Ages*, London, 1901.

Lawson, F. H., *The Social Origins of Egyptian Expansion during the Muhammad Ali Period*, New York, Columbia University Press, 1992.

Lia, Brynjar., *The Society of the Muslim Brothers in Egypt: The Rise of an Islamic Mass Movement 1928-1942*, Reading: Garnet, 1998.

McCarthy, Justin., *The Ottoman Turks: An Introductory History in 1923*, Longman, 1997.

McIntyre, John D., *The Boycott of the Milner Mission: A Study in Egyptian Nationalism*, New York: P. Lang, 1985.

Mahajan, Gupreet., & Sheth, D. L., (ed.), *Minority Identities and the Nation State* Oxford: Oxford University Press, 1999.

Maila, Joseph., 'The Arab Christians: From the Eastern Question to the Recent Political Situation of the Minorities', in Pacini, Andrea., (ed.) *Christian Communities in the Arab Middle East*, Oxford: Oxford University Press, 1998.

Malaty, Tadrous Y., *Tradition and Orthodoxy*, Alexandria: St. George Coptic Church, 1979.

_____*Introduction to the Coptic Orthodox Church*, Ottowa: St. Mary Coptic Church, 1997 .

Mardin, Serif., 'Religion and Secularism in Turkey', in Hourani, A., Khoury, P., & ilson, M., (ed.) *The Modern Middle East: A Reader*, London: I. B. Tauris, 1993.

Maspero, M., *Histoire Ancienne des Peuples de l'Orient.*

Mattson, Ingrid., 'Status Based Definitions of Need in Early Islamic Zakat and Maintenance Laws' in Bonner, et al., (ed.) *Poverty and Charity in Middle Eastern contexts*, Albany: State University of New York Press, 2003.

Meinardus, Otto., *The Copts in Jerusalem*, Cairo: Commission on Ecumenical Affairs of the See of Alexandria, Cairo, 1960.

_____*Monks and Monasteries of the Egyptian Deserts*, 1961.

_____ *Christian Egypt: Faith and Life*, Cairo: American University in Cairo Press, 1970.

_____*Two Thousand Years of Coptic Christianity*, Cairo: American University Press, 1999.

_____ *Coptic Saints and Pilgrims*, Cairo: American University in Cairo Press, 2002.

_____*Christians in Egypt: Orthodox, Catholic and Protestant Communities, Past and Present*, Cairo: American University in Cairo Press, 2006.

Al-Messiri, Sawsan., *Ibn al-Balad- A Concept of Egyptian Identity*, Leiden: Brill, 1978.

Mikhail, Kyriakos., *Copts and Moslems under British Control: A Collection of Facts and a Résumé of Authoritative Opinions on the Coptic Question*, London: Smith, Elder, 1911.

_____ *The Freedom of the Press in Egypt: An Appeal to the Friends of Liberty by Kyriakos Mikhail*, 3rd Edition, London 1914.

Mitchell, R. P., *The Society of the Muslim Brothers*, Oxford: Oxford University Press, 1993.

Mitchell, Timothy., *Colonising Egypt*, Cambridge: Cambridge University Press, 1988.

_____(ed.), *Questions of Modernity*, Minneapolis: University of Minnesota Press, 2000.

Meijer, Roel., *The Quest for Modernity: Secular Liberal and Left Wing Political thought in Egypt 1945-1958*, Richmond, Surrey: RoutledgeCurzon, 2002.

Moore, Peter., *Bishops, but what Kind? : Reflections on Episcopacy*, London: SPCK, 1982.

Morsy, Soheir., 'Beyond the Honorary 'white' classification of Egyptians: Societal Identity in Historical Context', in Gregory, Steven., & Sanjek, Roger., (ed.) *Race* New Brunswick: Rutgers University Press, 1994.

Moscovici, Serge., *Perspectives on Minority Influence*, Cambridge: Cambridge University Press, 1985.

Muhammad, Ali Fahmi, *The Future of Egypt*, Cairo: Hilal Publishers, 1911 .

Munoz, Gema Martin., *Política y Elecciones en el Egipto Contemporáneo (1922-1990)*, Madrid: Agencia Española de Cooperación Internacional, Instituto de Cooperación con el Mundo Árabe, 1992.

O'Mahony, Anthony., (ed.) *The Christian Communities of Jerusalem and the Holy Land*, Cardiff: University of Wales Press, 2003.

Naguib, Saphinaz Amal., 'The Era of Martyrs: Texts and Contexts of Religious Memory', in Nelly van Doorn-Harder & Kari Vogt (ed.), *Between Desert and City: The Coptic Orthodox Church Today*, Oslo: Novis Forlag, 1997.

Newman, Saul., 'Does Modernisation Breed Ethnic conflict?', in *World Politics*, Vol. 43, No. 2, April 1991.

Pacini, Andrea., (ed.) *Christian Communities in the Arab Middle East*, Oxford: Oxford University Press, 1998.

Padwick, C. E., *Temple Gairdner of Cairo*, London: SPCK, 1929.

Philipp, Thomas., 'Copts and Other Minorities in the Development of the Egyptian Nation-State' in Shamir, Shimon., (ed.) *Egypt: From Monarchy to Republic, A Reassessment of Revolution and Change*, Boulder: Westview Press, 1995.

_____ 'Image and Self-Image of the Syrians in Egypt: From the Early Eighteenth Cntury to the Reign of Muhammad 'Ali', in Braude, and Lewis (ed.) *Christians and Jews in the Ottoman Empire: The Functioning of a Plural Society, Volume I: The Central lands*, Holmes and Meier, 1987.

Reid, Donald Malcolm., 'Educational and Career Choices of Egyptian Students, 1882-1922', in *International Journal of Middle East Studies*, Vol. 8, No. 3, 1977.

_____ 'Political Assassination in Egypt 1910-1954', in *International Journal of African Studies*, Vol. 15, 1982.

_____ 'Nationalising the Pharaonic Past: Egyptology, Imperialism and Egyptian nationalism, 1922-1952' in Gershoni, Israel., and Jankowski, James., (ed.), *Rethinking Nationalism in the Arab Middle East*, New York: Columbia University Press, 1997.

_____*Whose Pharaohs?: Archaeology, Museums and Egyptian National Identity from Napoleon to World War I*, Berkeley: University of California Press, 2002.

Richter, J., *A History of the Protestant Missions in the Near East*, Edinburgh: Oliphant, Anderson and Ferrier, 1910

Robinson, Ronald., & Gallagher, John., *Africa and the Victorians: The Climax of Imperialism in the Dark Continent*, New York, 1961.

Ryzova, Lucie., 'Egyptianizing Modernity through the 'New Effendiya': Social and Cultural Constructions of the Middle Class in Egypt under the Monarchy', in Goldschmidt, A., Johnson, A., and Salmoni, B., (ed.), *Re-envisioning Egypt 1919-1952*, Cairo: American University Press, c.2005.

Safran, Nadav., *Egypt in Search of Political Community: An Analysis of the Intellectual and Political Evolution of Egypt, 1804-1952*, London: Harvard University Press, 1961.

Samir, Khalid Samir., 'The Christian Communities, Active members of Arab Society throughout History', in Pacini, Andrea., (ed.) *Christian Communities in the Arab Middle East*, Oxford: Oxford University Press, 1998.

Al-Sayyid-Marsot, Afaf Lutfi., *Egypt's Liberal Experiment, 1922-1936*, Berkley: University of California Press, 1977.

_____*Egypt in the Reign of Muhammad Ali*, Cambridge: Cambridge University Press, 1984.

_____'Religion or Opposition? Urban Protest Movements in Egypt', in *International Journal of Middle East Studies*, Vol. 16, No.4, 1984.

_____'The British Occupation of Egypt from 1882' in Porter, Andrew., (ed.) *The Oxford History of the British Empire: The Nineteenth Century*, Oxford University Press, 2001.

Schulze, Kirsten., Stokes, Martin., & Campbell, Colm., (ed.), *Nationalism, Minorities and Diasporas: Identities and Rights in the Middle East*, London: Tauris Academic Studies, 1996.

Sedra, Paul., 'Class Cleavages and Ethnic Conflict: Coptic Christian Communities in Modern Egyptian Politics', in *Islam and Muslim Christian Relations*, Vol. 10. No. 2, 1999.

Seikaly, Samir., 'Coptic Communal Reform: 1860-1914', in *Middle Eastern Studies* Vol. 6, No. 1, 1970.

Shaham, Ron., 'Christian and Jewish Waqf in Palestine during the late Ottoman Period', in *Bulletin of the School of Oriental and African Studies, University of London*, Vol. 54, No. 3, 1991.

Shakry, Omnia., 'Schooled Mothers and Structured Play: Child rearing in Turn of the Century Egypt', in Abu-Lughod, Lila., (ed.) *Remaking Women: Feminism and Modernity in the Middle East*, Princeton University Press, 1998.

Shalabi, Ahmad., *A History of Muslim Education*, Beirut: Dar al-Kahshaf, 1954.

Shukri, Ghali., *Egypt: Portrait of a President, 1971-1981: The Counter-Revolution in Egypt, Sadat's road to Jerusalem*, London: Zed Press, 1981.

Shedd, Clarence., *History of the World's Alliance of Young Men's Christian Associations*, London: SPCK, 1955.

Simaika, Marcus H., *A Brief Guide to the Coptic Museum and to the Principle Ancient Coptic Churches of Cairo*, Cairo: Government Press, 1938.

Smith, Charles., *Islam and the Search for the Social Order in Modern Egypt: A Biography of Muhammad Husayn Haykal*, Albany: State University of New York, 1983.

Smith, I., *To Islam I Go: Temple Gairdner of Cairo*, London: Edinburgh House Press, Fifth edition, 1955.

Sonbol, Amira el-Azhary., *The New Mamluks: Egyptian Society and Modern Feudalism*, New York: Syracuse University Press, 2000.

Stock, Eugene., *The History of the Church Missionary Society*, London: Church Missionary Society, 1899-1916.

Suleiman, Yasir., *The Arabic Language and National Identity: A Study in Ideology*, Edinburgh: Edinburgh University Press, 2003.

Szyliowicz, Joeseph., 'Education and Political Development in Turkey, Egypt and Iran', in *Comparative Education Review*, Vol. 13, 1969.

Terry, Janice., *The Wafd 1919-1952: Cornerstone of Egyptian Political Power*, London: Third World Centre for Research and Publishing, 1982.

Tignor, Robert., 'The 'Indianization' of the Egyptian Administration under British Rule', in *The American Historical Review*, Vol. 68, No.3, 1963.

____'Bank Misr and Foreign Capitalism', in *International Journal in Middle Eastern Studies*, Vol 8, No. 2, April 1977.

____*Modernisation and British Colonial Rule in Egypt, 1882-1914*, New Jersey: Princeton University Press, 1996.

Toledano, Ehud., 'Social and Economic Change in the Long nineteenth century', in *The Cambridge History of Egypt*, Vol. II, in Daly, M. W., (ed.) *The Cambridge History of Egypt*, Cambridge: Cambridge University Press, 1998 .

Vatikiotis, P. J., *The History of Modern Egypt: From Muhammad Ali to Mubarak*, London: Fourth Edition, 1991 .

Vogt, Kari., & van Doorn-Harder, Nelly., *Between Desert and City: The Coptic Orthodox Church Today*, Oslo: Novis Forlag, 1997.

Von Nieuwkerk, Karin., *A Trade Like Any Other: Female Singers and Dancers in Egypt*, Austin; University of Texas Press, 1995.

Wakin, Edward., *A Lonely Minority: The Modern Story of Egypt's Copts*, New York: William Morrow & Company, 1963.

Ward, K., & Stanley, B., *The Church Mission Society and World Christianity 1799-1999*, UK: Curzon Press, 2000.

Waterbury, John., 'The 'Soft State' and the Open Door; Egypt's Experience with Economic Liberalisation, 1974-1984', in *Comparative Politics*, Vol. 18, No. 1, 1985.

Waterfield, Gordon., *Professional Diplomat: Sir Percy Loraine of Kirkland, 1880-1961*, London: J Murray, 1973.

Watson, John H., *Among the Copts*, Brighton: Sussex Academic Press, 2002.

Yapp, Malcolm., *The Making of the Modern Near East 1792-1923*, London: Longman, Eighth Edition, 1996.

Zaki, Magdi Sami., *Histoire des Coptes d'Egypte*, Paris, 2005.

Zeidan, David., 'The Copts-Equal, Protected or Persecuted? The impact of Islamization on Muslim-Christian Relations in Modern Egypt', in *Islam and Christian-Muslim Relations*, Vol. 10, No. 1, 1999.

# INDEX

## C

Catholic, 25, 29, 34
Civil Service, 41–2, 71, 76–77, 138, 168
Constitution, 5, 35, 69, 73, 79, 88, 92, 131,166–7, 170, 172–3
Coptic Brethren, 91
Coptic Congress, 54–59
*Coptic Question*, 9, 42, 46–48, 58, 116
Coptic Reform Association, 52–3, 173
Coptic Youth Association, 125, 160
Cromer, Lord Evelyn Baring, 39– 41, 44, 76–7, 120–1, 123

## D

*Daily Mail*, 46
Dinshawi Trial, 55
Diocletian, Emperor, 4
*Divide and Rule*, 9, 42, 57, 166
Doss, Tawfiq, 56, 74, 139–40

## E

Education, 10, 17–20, 22–33, 36, 40–2, 44–45, 50–1, 53, 58–9, 61–70, 76–7, 79–80, 101–3, 105–7, 109, 111–114, 116, 118, 124, 127, 133, 136, 138–9, 144–6, 148, 175–6
*Effendiyya*, 96-8
Egyptian Conference, 57
*Egyptian Gazette*, 46
*Egyptian Question*, 48
Egyptian Uprising 2011, xii-xiv, 178
Employment, 9, 16, 41, 44, 71–3, 75–77, 85, 129
Era of Martyrs, 4–7, 91
Ethiopia, 135, 168, 178
*Evening Times*, 46

## F

Fahim, Galal, 78
Fahmi, Murqus, 56
Fahmi, Mustafa, 119
Fanous, Akhnoukh, 9, 53–4, 57–8
Farag, Ibrahim, 142, 159
Farouk I, King, 90, 93, 156–7, 160, 168–9, 171
Feminist Congress, 60
Feki (al-), Mustafa, 60
*Firu'an (al-)* newspaper, 53, 124, 126
Fowler, Arthur, 31
Free Officers, 10, 129, 155–6, 158, 165–6
Friends of the Holy Bible Society, *see Asdiqa' al-kitab al- Muqaddas*
Fu'ad I, King, 65–6, 78, 131
Fu'ad II, Prince Regent, 156

## G

Gabra, Sami, 135, 176
Gabrawi, Ramsis, 163
Gabriel, Thabet, Girgis, 168
Gairdner, Canon Temple, 107
Ghali, Boutros, 27, 35, 42, 50, 54–6, 62, 85, 104, 113, 118–9, 138
Ghali, *Mu'allim* Basilious, 19
Ghali, Wasif Boutros, 70
Girgis, Barsum, 34
Girgis, Malak, 160–2, 164, 168, 169, 172–4
Great Coptic Benevolent Society, 104–5, 106, 112–4, 118–120, 124, 160, 168
Great Coptic Schools, 25–6, 27, 32, 34, 50, 136, 148
Greek, 14–16, 18, 22, 29, 135
Gobat, Bishop, 29